NOLO *Your Legal Companion*

"*In Nolo you can trust.*" —THE NEW YORK TIMES

OUR MISSION
Make the law as simple as possible, saving you time, money and headaches.

Whether you have a simple question or a complex problem, turn to us at:

NOLO.COM

Your all-in-one legal resource

Need quick information about wills, patents, adoptions, starting a business—or anything else that's affected by the law? **Nolo.com** is packed with free articles, legal updates, resources and a complete catalog of our books and software.

NOLO NOW

Make your legal documents online

Creating a legal document has never been easier or more cost-effective! Featuring Nolo's Online Will, as well as online forms for LLC formation, incor... ...change—and m... **http://nolonow**...

NOLO'S LA...

Meet your new...

If you want adv... turn to Nolo's ... directory that ... in-depth attorn... the one that's r... **lawyers.nolo.c...**

ALWAYS UP TO DATE

Sign up for NOLO'S LEGAL UPDATER

Old law is bad law. We'll email you when we publish an updated edition of this book—sign up for this free service at nolo.com/legalupdater.

Find the latest updates at NOLO.COM

Recognizing that the law ... ...n before you ... e post legal ... :he life of this ... :om/updates.

...west?

...this is ...ition ...us a call

Please note

We believe accurate, plain-English legal information should help you solve many of your own legal problems. But this text is not a substitute for personalized advice from a knowledgeable lawyer. If you want the help of a trained professional—and we'll always point out situations in which we think that's a good idea—consult an attorney licensed to practice in your state.

5th edition

The Inventor's Notebook

A "Patent It Yourself" Companion

By Fred Grissom & Attorney David Pressman

Fifth Edition	MAY 2008
Editor	RICHARD STIM
Cover Design	SUSAN PUTNEY
Proofreading	EMILY K. WOLMAN
Printing	CONSOLIDATED PRINTERS, INC.

Grissom, Fred E.
    Inventor's notebook : a "patent it yourself" companion / By Fred Grissom &
David Pressman. -- 5th ed.
        p. cm.
    ISBN-13: 978-1-4133-0644-6 (pbk.)
    ISBN-10: 1-4133-0644-6 (pbk.)
    1. Patent practice--United States--Popular works. I. Pressman, David, 1937– II.
Title.
KF3120.Z9G75 2008
346.7304'86--dc22

                        2007051646

Quantity Sales: For information on bulk purchases or corporate premium sales, please contact the Special
Sales Department. For academic sales or textbook adoptions, ask for Academic Sales. Call 800-955-4775 or
write to Nolo at 950 Parker Street, Berkeley, CA 94710.

Dedication

To our wives—Shelley, for her faith and sense of humor, and Roberta, for her perseverance and style.

Acknowledgments

The authors wish to express their thanks and appreciation to the crew at Nolo, especially Jake Warner, Richard Stim, and Steve Elias of Nolo for their invaluable advice and sustaining enthusiasm. We also thank Paul Guyton and David Joyner for stoking the creative fires with their critical insights, and Andromache Warner for her valuable advice on doing market research. And thanks to Terri Hearsh for her thoughtful design of the 3rd edition.

Table of Contents

Appendixes

Your Legal Companion

I f you're an inventor, you're probably aware of the four main activities that all successful inventors must normally undertake:

- conceiving, building, and testing the invention
- legally protecting the invention
- marketing the invention, and
- financing the first three tasks.

The Inventor's Notebook is designed to help you organize the records you need to successfully complete each of these activities. Specifically, *The Inventor's Notebook* will show you how to document the details of your invention in order to:

- Maintain good records of your inventing process. By doing this you will always know exactly where you are in the invention process and what remains to be done. This will help you avoid dead ends and the repetition of mistakes.
- Create a legal record that you are the first and true inventor. If your invention is ever challenged, your completed notebook will be the foundation of the legal protection for your idea.
- Convince others of the worth of your invention.
- Proceed realistically in terms of your invention's commercial potential.
- Organize all the information pertaining to your invention in one location.

The Inventor's Notebook is designed for a single invention. You should use a separate book for each invention. The purpose of *The Inventor's Notebook* is to provide you with an organized means for documenting your inventive efforts. We do not explain here the details of patent law or the intricacies of how to create and run a business based on your invention. Before devoting your time, energy, and economic resources to an invention, it is appropriate to figure out the relationship between what you might put into the invention and what you expect to get out of it. In this sense, launching an invention is the same as starting a business—in both situations you should carefully calculate your profit potential before you get in too deeply. It is this activity that we refer to when we later speak of creating a business plan for your invention.

Nolo also publishes *Patent It Yourself*, an excellent source of detailed information on obtaining and using a patent. For a full understanding of the legal principles associated with the information you will be entering in *The Inventor's Notebook*, we recommend that you obtain a copy of this comprehensive and clearly written resource. It is widely available in libraries and bookstores, and can also be obtained by ordering directly from Nolo. See the Nolo catalog and ordering information at the back of this book. In *Patent It Yourself*, author David Pressman has formulated numerous statements or instructions (termed "Inventor's Commandments") that focus the reader's attention on the crucial steps necessary to the successful development of his or her invention. Throughout *The Inventor's Notebook* we provide cross-references to the relevant portions of *Patent It Yourself* and feature some of its "Inventor's Commandments" where appropriate.

Proposed Legislation That May Affect Your Patent

As this edition goes to press, important changes have been proposed in the patent rules and laws. If implemented, these changes will likely reduce the strength of patents. Some powerful entities—mainly computer, software, and financial service companies—are in favor of these changes. Other powerful entities—mainly drug companies, independent inventors, Nobel laureates, and some legislators—want to keep patents strong and thus are opposed to these changes. The winner will be determined to a large extent by the influence of each side over our legislators. Here is a status report as of January 2008.

New Rule Changes Halted: The Patent and Trademark Office (PTO) issued new rules regarding (a) the number of applications that may be permitted in a chain of continuing applications, and (b) the number of claims that may be filed. However a number of organizations have sued the PTO, contending that these changes go beyond the PTO's powers. A court tentatively agreed and has issued a temporary injunction, ordering the PTO not to implement the new rules until the issues are resolved after a full trial.

New Patent Revision Bill Stalled: A complete revision of the patent statutes is pending (H.R. 1908 and S. 1145 in the 110th Congress, 2007), but has been derailed because of protests by inventors, concerned legislators, drug and biotech companies, labor unions, manufacturing and chemical companies, and research universities. Complete information about the bill and the arguments against its provisions can be found on the Professional Inventors' Alliance site, www.piausa.org.

While this revision has some provisions that would help independent inventors, I believe that its overall effect would be harmful. I urge you to call and write to your federal representatives and senators to urge them to oppose this bill in order to keep our patent system strong, since I believe that this is one of the main factors that has made the U.S. a technological leader.

I will post the resolution of these issues on the update site for *Patent It Yourself* at www.patentityourselfupdates.blogspot.com and at Nolo's site at www.nolo.com.

—David Pressman

Introduction

A. How The Inventor's Notebook Is Organized

The Inventor's Notebook is designed to focus your attention on all major activities associated with successful inventing, and on the documentation that is appropriate and necessary to each. As our organizing tool we use the Inventor's Decision Chart, below, which presents a concise overview of the basic steps of the inventive process.

In the real world, of course, an invention can go from idea to marketplace in a great variety of ways. However, the paths outlined in the Inventor's Decision Chart serve as logical guidelines to the way in which a large percentage of inventing efforts will tend to develop, primarily because the fundamental questions addressed by the chart—legal protection, financial feasibility, marketing potential, and perfecting the final design of the product—must be addressed in most instances.

At the end of this introduction, we offer a brief description of the different paths represented in the Inventor's Decision Chart. A more extensive discussion can be found in *Patent It Yourself*.

B. How to Use The Inventor's Notebook

The boxes on the Inventor's Decision Chart are numbered 10, 12, 14, and so on up to 40, then A–F and X. Each box contains a brief description of its step and provides a cross-reference to the chapters in *Patent It Yourself* that discuss the step. Each step is discussed in one or more chapters of *Patent It Yourself* and one or more sections of *The Inventor's Notebook*. The Table of Cross-References, below, shows the links between boxes on the chart and the text in the two books.

To see how this cross-reference table works, assume you have conceived an invention (Box 10) and now are at Box 12 of the inventive process (record conception, build and test it as soon as practicable, and make a proper record, or consider filing a Provisional Patent Application). The Table of Cross-References tells you that you should read Chapter 1, Section B, "Record Your Conception"; Chapter 1,

Table of Cross-References		
Inventor's Decision Chart	*Inventor's Notebook* (Chapter & Section)	*Patent It Yourself* (Chapter)
#10	1B, 1E, 2H	1, 2
#12	1B, 1C, 1D, 1E, 2H, 3A, 4A	1, 3
#14	1B, 1C, 2B, 2E, 3C, 3E	4
#16	2A, 2B	5, 6
#18	2D, 2E, 2H, 2I, 4A	1, 8
#20	3E, 3F, 4A, 4C	11
#22	2A, 2B, 2D, 2E, 2H, 2I	6, 8, 9, 10, 12, 13, 14, 15
#24	2A, 2B, 3A, 3B, 3C	4
#26	1F, 1G, 2F	1
#28	1G, 2E, 2F	10
#30	3E, 3F, 4A, 4C	11
#32	2H, 2I	1
#34	2H, 2I	1
#36	2D, 2E, 2H, 2I	6, 8, 9, 10, 12, 13, 14, 15
#38	2H, 2I, 3E, 4A	7
#40	—	7
A	2H, 2I, 3F, 4B	11, 15, 16
B	2A, 2B, 2H, 2I, 3F, 4B	1, 11
C	—	1, 11
D	2H	1, 11
E	2H	1, 11, 15
F	2C	6, 8, 9, 10, 12, 13, 14, 15
X	Begin a new Inventor's Notebook	2

Inventor's Decision Chart

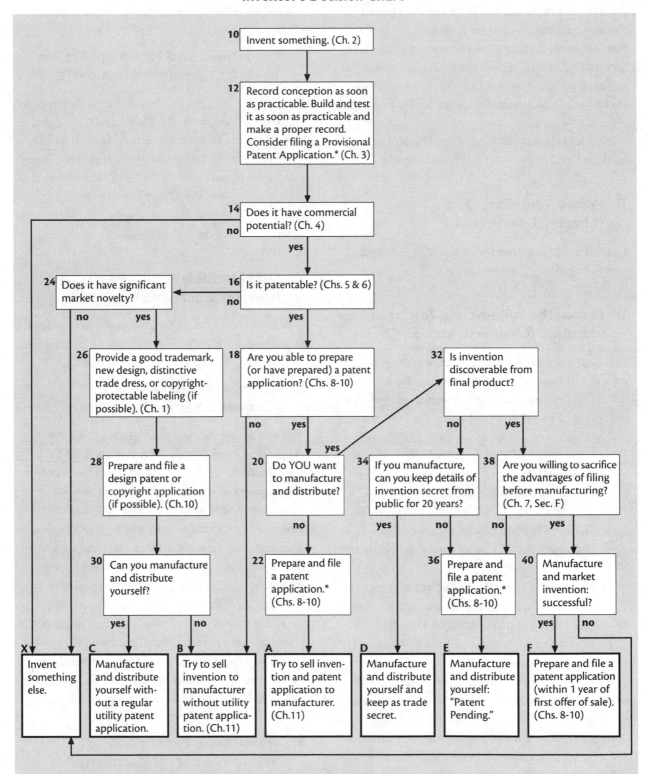

* If you filed a Provisional Patent Application, you must file a regular patent application and any desired foreign convention applications within one year—see Chapter 3. (File non-convention applications before invention is made public or any patent issues on it.)

Section C, "Record the Building and Testing of Your Invention" or Section D, "File a Provisional Patent Application"; Chapter 1, Section E, "Other Possible Applications of Your Invention"; Chapter 2, Section H, "Record of Contacts"; Chapter 3, Section A, "Evaluation of Positive and Negative Factors of Invention"; and Chapter 4, Section A, "Determination of Funds Needed".

Now let's take a brief look at what each of the sections listed in the chart for this example calls for.

1. Record Your Conception (Chapter 1, Section B)

Chapter 1, Section B, provides specific guidelines as to how to record your conception.

2. Record the Building and Testing of Your Invention (Chapter 1, Section C)

This section explains the importance of recording your efforts to build and test your invention. The better this documentation, the easier it will be for you to apply for a patent and the better your legal position will be if:

- you ever get into an inventorship dispute (one person claims that another person stole the invention from the first person);
- an interference is declared (a contest initiated in the PTO when two patent applications from different inventors claim the same invention); or
- you need to swear behind a cited reference (in other words, show that you conceived or built and tested the invention before the date of a reference that would otherwise be "prior art" to your invention).

When determining whether your invention is sufficiently innovative under the Patent Act (that it's novel and nonobvious), the PTO and your adversaries in any court case will examine all known references that bear on your claims. It is very important to show that your earliest effective date of invention (patent application filing date, building and testing date, or date when you first began to diligently work towards building and testing) occurred prior to all such references; otherwise, your claims can be rejected.

3. File a Provisional Patent Application (Chapter 1, Section D) (optional)

An inventor can file a Provisional Patent Application (PPA) as an alternative to building and testing the invention. The PPA will serve as an alternative only if the inventor files a regular patent application that claims the same invention disclosed in the PPA within one year of the PPA's filing date. If the regular patent application is filed within one year, the regular application may claim the PPA's filing date.

4. Other Possible Applications (Chapter 1, Section E)

This section asks you to focus on possible applications of your work that differ from those you have imagined.

5. Record of Contacts (Chapter 2, Section H)

This section permits you to keep track of all the people who know of your invention and who have signed confidentiality agreements. This information will be essential if a dispute arises later over inventorship or if you wish to take action against others under the trade secret laws for violation of a confidentiality agreement. (Many inventors maintain their invention as a trade secret until such time as the patent application is published—see sidebar, "Publication of Patent Applications", below—or, if the application is not published, a patent issues or the invention is manufactured and placed on the market. This allows the inventor to take action against anyone who discloses the details of the invention to others in violation of a confidentiality agreement.)

6. Evaluation of Positive and Negative Factors of Invention (Chapter 3, Section A)

This section guides you in evaluating the positive and negative factors of your invention so that you can make refinements while building and testing it.

7. Determination of Funds Needed (Chapter 4, Section A)

Finally, this section lets you document any special financial needs for the building and testing phase.

To sum up this example, Box 12 of the Table of Cross-References directs you to the sections of this book you should use for recording your conception and either documenting the building and testing of your invention or filing a Provisional Patent Application. As you proceed through the chart, other boxes will similarly direct you to other appropriate sections of this book. Careful documentation of your invention process will save time in the long run. Your organized approach will make it easy to retrieve essential information when you need it, and you will be able to prove your inventorship if called on to do so.

SKIP AHEAD

Direct access. You can directly access *The Inventor's Notebook* without going through the Inventor's Decision Chart if you already understand what documentation is needed. Simply turn to the relevant form and enter the appropriate information. For guidance on the type of documentation needed to protect your invention, read the relevant portions of *Patent It Yourself* (or other resources recommended by us) that are referenced at the beginning of each section of Chapter 1.

CAUTION

You are responsible for understanding the legal requirements for documentation and what steps have to be taken to obtain a patent and protect your invention from theft or unauthorized use. While we preface each section with a very brief overview of what should be entered there, and why it should be entered, this is not a substitute for reading the meticulous discussion of these issues provided by *Patent It Yourself.*

C. Explanation of Inventor's Decision Chart

As we mentioned, different inventions take different paths through the Inventor's Decision Chart. Here we outline the various paths. If you are not using the Inventor's Decision Chart as an organizational guide to this book, you may skip this discussion.

1. Drop It If You Don't See Commercial Potential (Chart Route 10-12-14-X)

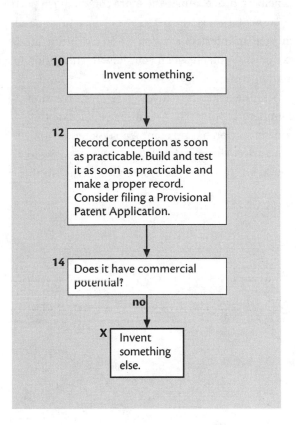

If you've invented something and recorded it properly, you should then proceed to build and test your invention as soon as practicable and/or optionally file a Provisional Patent Application (PPA) and then file a regular patent application within one year that claims the PPA filing date. If you choose to build and test the invention and this presents appreciable difficulty, you should wait until after you evaluate your invention's commercial potential or patentability. But always keep the building and testing as a goal; it will help you to evaluate commercial potential and may be vital in the event an "interference" occurs (unless you file a valid PPA; see Chapter 1, Section D, for a discussion on what makes a PPA valid). An interference is a proceeding in the PTO which is instituted when two or more applications by separate inventors claim the same invention. It usually occurs when a patent examiner in the PTO discovers two pending applications that claim the same invention. It can also occur when the PTO publishes a newly granted patent in the *Official Gazette* and another inventor claims to have invented it first. Since interferences are long and expensive proceedings, the more convincing a party's documentation is, the better the chance to win and shorten an interference. You'll find a working model extremely valuable when you show the invention to a manufacturer.

Your next step is to investigate your invention's commercial potential. Assuming you decide that your invention has no commercial potential and you answer the question "no," follow an arrow to Box X, which says "Invent something else." In this instance, this sort of structured analysis may seem simplistic. It's not. In our direct experience we have seen hundreds of inventors waste thousands of hours because they would not confront the issue of "commercial potential" or lack thereof at an early stage of the invention process.

Publication of Patent Applications

Every pending patent application will be published for the public to view 18 months after its earliest effective filing date (or earlier if requested by the applicant), unless, at the time of filing, the applicant files a Nonpublication Request (NPR). This publication will terminate any trade secrecy rights in the claimed invention. An applicant whose application is published and later issues as a patent may obtain royalties from an infringer from the date of publication if the infringer had actual notice of the published application.

Adjustable Sleeping Bag with Drawcords

2. Try to Sell Invention to Manufacturer Without "Regular" Patent Application (Chart Route 12-14-16-18-B)

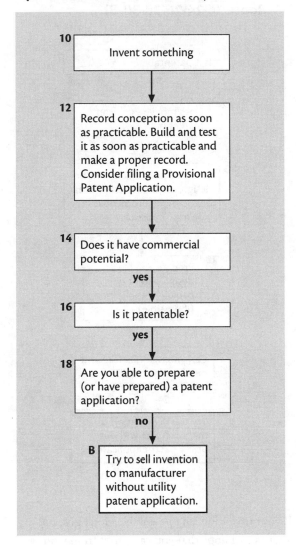

PPA is properly prepared or that you've properly documented conception, building, and testing. We recommend this route only if you can't prepare or can't afford to have prepared a regular patent application because:

- if you've built and tested the invention without properly recording your activities, you run the risk of an unscrupulous manufacturer stealing your invention by filing a patent application on your invention before you do so, and

- if you've filed a PPA, you'll have all of the disadvantages of the PPA (see Chapter 1, Section D, for more discussion of the advantages and disadvantages of filing a PPA).

3. File a Patent Application and Sell or License It to a Manufacturer (Chart Route 14-16-18-20-22-A)

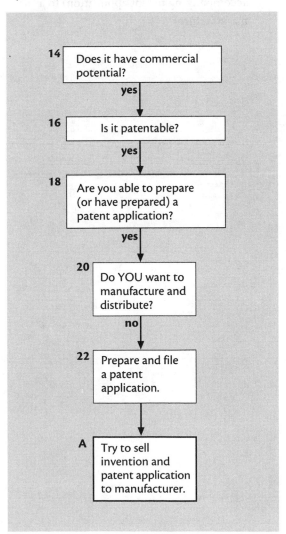

This route is especially useful if you've filed a PPA on the invention, but can also be used if you've built and tested the invention and properly recorded your building and testing activities. After filing a PPA and/or building and testing and recording your efforts, see if the invention has commercial potential and if it's patentable. If so, whether or not you're able to prepare—or have prepared—a regular patent application, try to sell your invention to a manufacturer in the hope that the manufacturer will have the application prepared for you, either on the basis of your PPA or without the PPA. If you take this route, you should be sure either that your

Filing a patent application and selling rights to the invention to someone else is the usual way most inventors profit from their work. This is because inventors seldom have the capability (and often don't have the desire) to establish their own manufacturing and distribution facilities. If you are in this situation, the chart works like this:

- Box 14—your invention has good commercial potential
- Box 16—your decision on patentability is favorable
- Box 18—you're able to prepare a regular patent application (or have one prepared for you)
- Box 20—you don't wish to manufacture and distribute your product or process yourself
- Box 22—you prepare a regular patent application, and
- Box A—you try to sell your invention (and accompanying patent application) to a manufacturer.

4. Sell or License Your Invention to a Manufacturer Without Filing a Patent Application (Chart Route 16-24-26-28-30-B)

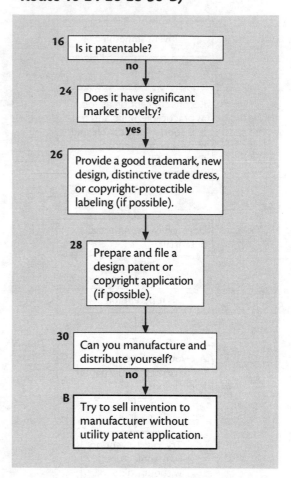

If your invention isn't patentable, don't give up. There's still hope that you can profit from your work. If your invention nevertheless possesses "significant market novelty," it may in fact be quite profitable if introduced to the market. Put differently, if your patentability search produces close "prior art" (but not a dead ringer), this may indicate that no one has tried to market your specific idea before.

Prior art is the sum of all developments prior to your conception that are used to determine whether your efforts were really inventive and "unobvious." Examples of prior art (relevant to your invention) are (1) prior patents showing your invention or any part or feature of it, (2) prior and related technological developments that are known to the public, (3) previous descriptions of your invention (or any part or feature of it) in periodicals or textbooks, and (4) previous indications of any kind that others considered some or all of your invention's elements. For example, the prior art that precludes you from getting a patent may have been used only to make computer screens, while your invention is designed for lampshades.

Assuming that your invention does have significant market novelty but does not qualify for protection under a utility patent, you may consider protecting it under trademark law; with a design patent; through distinctive "trade dress," such as a uniform color (as Kodak does with its yellow film packages); or with a symbol (such as the McDonald's golden arches).

5. Make and Sell Your Invention Yourself Without a Utility Patent Application (Chart Route 16-30-C)

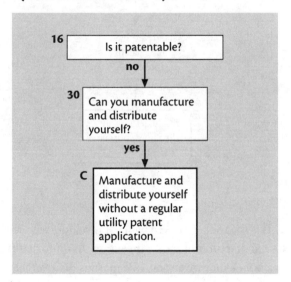

Here we assume again that you have an unpatentable invention that is unique and serves a useful purpose (there isn't anything on the market just like it and people will buy it). If you can make and distribute it yourself, it may be better to do so than to try to sell it to a manufacturer outright. Even if you have a good trademark, a design patent application, distinctive trade dress, and/or a unique label, you cannot offer a manufacturer a truly privileged market position on your invention unless it's covered by a utility patent application that looks like it will lead to a

patent being granted. This means it will probably be hard to sell your invention to a third party, and if you do, the amount you receive for it will be modest. However, if you decide to manufacture the invention yourself, and you reach the market first, you'll have a significant marketing advantage despite the lack of a utility patent.

6. Manufacture and Distribute Your Invention Yourself, Keeping It As a Trade Secret (Chart Route 20-32-34-D)

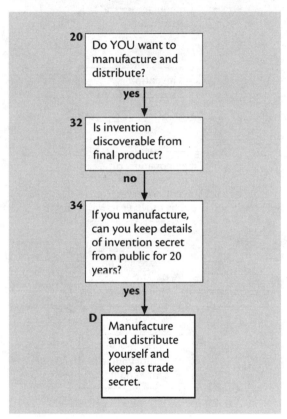

Even though your invention may be commercially valuable and patentable, it isn't always in your best interest to patent it. Instead you may profit more by keeping the invention secret and using it in your business to obtain a competitive advantage. For instance, suppose you invent a formula that truly makes hair grow. Instead of seeking a patent, which would require public disclosure of your formula and invite others to figure out why your formula works and perhaps invent alternatives, you might be better off keeping your formula locked in your safe and disclose it only to a few trusted associates who would be sworn to secrecy. For more on trade secret protection for inventions, see Chapter 1 of *Patent It Yourself.*

7. File Patent Application and Manufacture and Distribute Your Invention Yourself (Trade-Secretable Invention) (Chart Route 20-32-34-36-E)

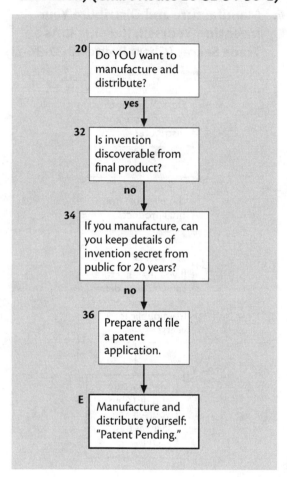

8. File Patent Application and Manufacture and Distribute Invention Yourself (Non–Trade-Secretable Invention) (Chart Route 20-32-38-36-E)

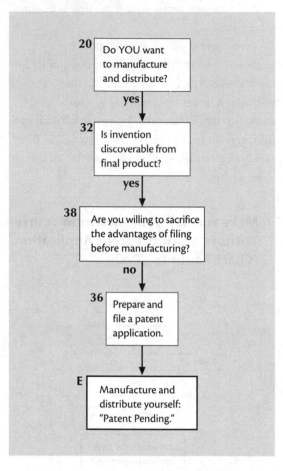

Suppose the essence of your invention is not easily discoverable from your final product so that you could keep it secret for a while, but probably not for the life of a patent. Or, suppose, after evaluating the advantages and disadvantages of maintaining your invention as a trade secret (Section 6, above), you decide against the trade secret protection route, preferring instead to patent your invention. Either way, you should prepare and file a patent application, and then manufacture and distribute the invention yourself with the notice "patent pending" affixed to the invention.

This is the route followed by most inventors who wish to manufacture their own invention. Assume that the essence of your invention, like most, is discoverable from the final product. In this case you won't be able to protect it as a trade secret. Also assume that you don't want to sacrifice the advantages of filing before manufacturing (Section 9 below). You should prepare and file a patent application, and then manufacture and distribute the invention yourself with a patent-pending notice.

9. Test-Market Before Filing (Chart Route 20-32-38-40-F)

Although you might like to manufacture and test-market your invention before filing a patent application on it, we generally don't recommend this for patentable inventions. This is because, under the "one-year rule," you have less than one year to do the test-marketing before your patent application must be filed. This very important rule is based upon a statute that states that, with certain exceptions, you must file your patent application within one year after the invention was exposed to the public. Since one year is a relatively short time, you may get discouraged unjustifiably if you try to market your invention and you aren't successful. Also, you'll lose your foreign rights, since most foreign countries or jurisdictions, including the European Patent Office, have an "absolute novelty" requirement (which means no patent will be issued if the invention was made public anywhere before its first filing date). Lastly, there is a possibility of theft, since anyone who sees it can copy it (assuming it's not trade secretable) and file a (fraudulent) patent application on it. There are also other significant disadvantages to test-marketing an invention.

Nevertheless, you may still choose to manufacture and market your invention before filing your patent application. If you discover, within about nine months of the date you first introduce your product, that it is a successful invention and likely to have good commercial success, begin immediately to prepare your patent application, so that you'll be able to get it on file within one year from the date you first offered your invention for sale or used it to make a commercial product.

If your manufacturing and market tests are not successful, you should consider dropping the invention and inventing something else, even though you still have the right to get a patent on your invention. On the other hand, as stated above, a nine-month testing period may not have been adequate. In other words, be realistic but don't get discouraged unnecessarily from filing a patent application.

Using the Notebook

A well-maintained notebook will be of crucial importance should your inventorship or your eligibility for a patent ever be called into question by the Patent and Trademark Office (PTO), other inventors, or companies that you have sued for infringement.

A. How to Make Entries

When using Appendix I: Notebook, it is important to remember that the more secure your notebook appears to be from the possibility of after-the-fact modifications by you, the better evidence it is. The first step in achieving this credibility is to use a bound notebook like this one. Your textual entries, sketches, and diagrams should be clearly written in ink to preclude erasure and the making of later entries. No large blank spaces should be left on a page. If you do need to leave space between separate entries, or at the bottom of a page, draw a large cross over the blank space to preclude the possibility of any subsequent entries. If you make a mistake in an entry, don't attempt to erase it; merely line it out neatly and make a dated note of why it was incorrect. Your entries should be worded carefully and accurately to be complete and clear in themselves so that a disinterested person could verify that you had the ideas or did the work stated on the dates in question.

Where we indicate, your entries in Appendix I should be signed, dated, and witnessed. This should be done frequently. You should date each entry the same day you (and any co-inventors) make the entries and sign your name(s). If it is impossible to have a witness sign the same day you do, add a brief candid comment to this effect when the witness does sign. Similarly, if you made and/or built the invention some time ago, but haven't made any records until now, again state the full and truthful facts, and date the entry as of the date you write and sign it. Remember, though, that entries made contemporaneously with your work or ideas will carry much more weight than after-the-fact entries, should you ever have to prove prior inventorship.

If possible, items that by their nature can't be entered directly in the notebook by hand should be made on separate sheets. These, too, should be signed, dated, and witnessed and then pasted or affixed in the notebook in proper chronological order. The inserted sheet should be referred to by entries made directly in the notebook, thus tying them in to the other material. Photos or other entries which cannot be signed or written should be pasted in the notebook and referenced by legends (descriptive words, such as "photo taken of machine in operation") made directly in the notebook, preferably with lead lines which extend from the notebook page over onto the photo, so as to preclude a charge of substituting subsequently made photos. The page the photo is pasted on should be signed, dated, and witnessed in the usual manner.

If an item covers an entire page, it can be referred to on an adjacent page. It's important to affix the items to the notebook page with a permanent adhesive, such as white glue or non-yellowing transparent tape.

If you have to draw a sketch in pencil and want to make a permanent record of it (to put in your notebook) without redrawing the sketch in ink, simply make a photocopy of the penciled sketch. Voilà—a permanent copy!

Finally, if there are more than two inventors, make a new space for each additional inventor to sign.

Choose witnesses who are as impartial and competent as possible, which means that ideally they should not be close relatives or people who have been working so closely with you as to be possible co-inventors. Witnesses should also be people who are likely to be available to testify later, should a dispute over your inventorship arise.

B. Record Your Conception

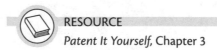

RESOURCE
Patent It Yourself, Chapter 3

There are many reasons to accurately record the date and surrounding circumstances of your original conception of your invention. The most important of these is to have proof that you are the true inventor in case another inventor claims prior inventorship. Recording your conception in the manner we suggest here is like giving your invention a pedigree. With proper records, your invention will be recognized as yours; without this documentary evidence, your invention's special identity and origins are subject to challenge.

There are a number of elements involved in recording the conception of your invention. These are:

- your invention's title
- the circumstances of its conception
- its purpose or the problem solved
- a brief functional and structural description of the invention as you have conceived it
- an informal sketch
- all possible applications of your invention (ramifications)
- your invention's novel features, insofar as you know them now
- a brief description of the closest known prior art, and
- the advantages of the invention over previous developments and/or knowledge in the relevant field.

We can't overemphasize the importance of accurately documenting the conception of your invention, which is summed up in the following Inventor's Commandment from *Patent It Yourself.*

Inventor's Commandment

After conceiving of your invention, you should not proceed to develop, build, or test it, or reveal it to outsiders until you first:

1. make a clear description of your conception
2. sign and date the same, and
3. have this document signed and dated by two people you trust to the effect that they have "witnessed and understood" your creation.

Following this commandment will help you:

- prove prior conception in case of an interference or theft of your idea
- establish your inventorship in case someone else claims inventorship, and
- antedate any prior art that may be cited by the PTO that may cast doubt on the originality of your invention. (A prior art reference is any previous patent, article, or other document or actual public knowledge or use that is relevant to the PTO's decision on whether your invention deserves a patent.)

 NOTEBOOK

Record of Conception pages are located in Appendix I: Notebook.

If you use no other part of this book, we urge you to provide the documentation we suggest here. When filling out the Record of Conception of Invention, remember our instructions for making entries set out in the introduction to this chapter.

TIP

You should use this form only when you have arrived at a relatively firm idea of what your invention consists of. Then, if you change your approach or think of additional complications after you have recorded your conception but prior to your building and testing activity, put these new ideas on the blank pages provided for this specific purpose at the end of the Record of Conception pages.

A sample record of the conception of an invention is provided on the following pages.

Record of Conception of Invention

Title of invention:

"Orange Peeling Knife" or "knife that can score oranges through skin without cutting pulp."

Circumstances of conception:

On March 2 or 3 of this year, when visiting my sister Shirley Goldberger in Lancaster, PA, I decided to eat an orange just before we all went shopping. When I tried to score through the orange's skin to peel it, I cut too deeply, and the juice dripped onto my lap. It stained my new pants and embarrassed me in front of Shirley, my wife, and my mother. I had to change my pants, delaying everyone in the process.

   After we eventually got in the car, I remarked that there must be a better way to score and peel oranges. The problem preoccupied me so much that I didn't go shopping; instead, I came up with a solution while waiting in my car for my family. I remember telling them, on the way back, "Why not make a knife with an adjustable blade stop so that the depth of the cut could be controlled? That way you wouldn't cut into the orange's pulp, it would be easier to peel and it wouldn't drip."

   I didn't make any record of the invention at that time since I didn't know I should until I read this book yesterday.

Purpose or problem solved:

To peel oranges (or grapefruits or pomelos), it is desirable to score them first, preferably with two encircling cuts that cross at the blossom and stem ends so that the skin can be neatly peeled off in quarters. However, this is difficult with an ordinary knife because one inevitably cuts past the skin into the pulp, making the orange drip and the peel difficult to remove without removing some of the pulp with it. The problem is compounded because the thickness of orange peels varies among varieties. A tool that could neatly score oranges with peels of various thicknesses without cutting into the pulp would solve the problem.

Invented by: _Edward R. Furman_   Date: _July 23, 20xx_

Invented by: _____   Date: _____

The above confidential information is witnessed and understood by:

Ruben Santiago   Date: _July 23, 20xx_

    Date: _____

Record of Conception of Invention

Description and operation:

My knife will have a handle and blade similar to those on a conventional paring knife. Attached to each side of the blade, however, will be a strip of plastic or wood that will serve as a stop or fence to control the depth of cuts that can be made with the knife. These fences will be moveable, allowing the depth of the cut to be varied by adjustments made to a thumbscrew that will be attached to the two fences. For thin-skinned oranges, the fences will be adjusted to permit a shallow cut, and for thick-skinned oranges, the fences will be adjusted to allow a deeper cut. In either case, the knife will be used to score easily through the skin completely around the orange without cutting deeper than the distance from the edge of the blade to the fences, and thus without cutting its pulp.

Invented by: _Edward R. Furman_   Date: _July 23, 20xx_

Invented by: _____   Date: _____

The above confidential information is witnessed and understood by:

Ruben Santiago   Date: _July 23, 20xx_

_____   Date: _____

Record of Conception of Invention

Drawing:

Invented by: _Edward R. Furman_   Date: _July 23, 20xx_

Invented by: _____   Date: _____

The above confidential information is witnessed and understood by:

Ruben Santiago   Date: _July 23, 20xx_

_____   Date: _____

Record of Conception of Invention

Ramifications:

Instead of adjustable stop strips on both sides of the blade, a fixed stop strip, on one or both sides, can be used. This fixed stop strip can be mounted parallel to the edge, or it can even be included on the edge so that the depth of cut can be controlled by changing the longitudinal part of the blade that contacts the orange.

Novel features:

I have never seen or heard of any knife with a depth-of-cut controlling stop strip, much less an adjustable one.

Closest known prior art:

I have seen orange peelers comprising a curved knife and a curved metal rod that is inserted under the peel to move it around and free the peel from the pulp; and, of course, conventional paring knives.

Advantages of my invention:

My knife is the only one that can cut through an orange's peel to any desired depth. It makes peeling an orange neater, safer, and faster. All one has to do is score around the skin with two encircling cuts and then peel off the four quarter peels, leaving a peeled orange that is ready to segment and eat. The messy and difficult-to-use prior-art methods, which involve cutting the orange in quarters and peeling off the pulp, are tools that require skill to use and are not nearly as fast, neat, and easy to use as mine.

Invented by: _Edward R. Furman_   Date: _July 23, 20xx_

Invented by: _____   Date: _____

The above confidential information is witnessed and understood by:

Ruben Santiago   Date: _July 23, 20xx_

_____   Date: _____

C. Record the Building and Testing of Your Invention

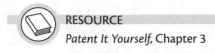

RESOURCE
Patent It Yourself, Chapter 3

NOTEBOOK
Record of Building and Testing of Invention pages are located in Appendix I: Notebook.

Inventor's Commandment

1. Try to build and test your invention (if at all possible) as soon as you can.
2. Keep full and true written, signed, and dated records of all the efforts, correspondence, and receipts concerning your invention, especially if you build and test it.
3. Have two others sign and date that they have "witnessed and understood" your building and testing. (As an alternative—or in addition—to documenting, building, and testing in this manner, you can use the PTO's Provisional Patent Application program.

When documenting the building and testing of your invention, you should record as much factual data about the process as possible. Provide conclusions only if they are supported by factual data. Items that by their nature can't be entered directly in the notebook by hand—such as formal sketches or photos—should be signed, dated, and witnessed, and then pasted or affixed in the notebook in proper chronological order. You should also save all of your "other paperwork" involved with the conception, building, and testing of your invention, such as loose notes, bedside notes, receipts, letters, memos, etc. These items can be very convincing as supporting evidence to a judge if you ever need to prove any of the pertinent dates related to your invention. Because of the potential importance of this documentation,

do yourself a favor and provide a place to save these papers. We suggest that you paste a 6" × 9" manila envelope inside the back cover of this book or use an expansion pocket file if the papers become too voluminous.

If you build and test your invention immediately after you conceive of it, fill out the Record of Conception of Invention and add a brief note indicating that you also built and tested it at the same time. Make a reference to and then complete the Record of Building and Testing of Invention, which is also in Appendix I: Notebook.

If you can't build and test your invention yourself, many model makers, engineers, technicians, teachers, etc., are available who will be delighted to do the job for you for a fee, or for a percentage of the action. If you do use a model maker (consultant), you should take precautions to protect the confidentiality and proprietary status of your invention. There's no substitute for checking out your consultant carefully by asking for references (assuming you don't already know the consultant by reputation or referral).

In addition, have your consultant sign a copy of the Consultant's Work Agreement included in Appendix V: Tear-Out Forms. See Chapter 4, Section F, of *Patent It Yourself* for instructions on completing this form.

TIP
When providing this documentation, remember to follow the instructions given at the beginning of this chapter.

D. File a Provisional Patent Application

Suppose you don't have the facilities, skill, or time to build and test your invention, and you can't file a patent application right away. In 1994 the government enacted the GATT (General Agreement on Tariffs and Trade) implementation law, which, for the first time in the U.S., enables an inventor to file a Provisional Patent Application (PPA) as a legal alternative to building and testing the invention. Let's explore the PPA and its advantages and disadvantages.

What it is

A PPA is a short version of a patent application that an applicant can use to establish an early filing date for a later-filed Regular Patent Application (RPA). A PPA consists of the following:

- a detailed description of the invention telling how to make and use it
- drawing(s), if necessary to understand how to make and use the invention
- a cover sheet
- a fee, and
- a return receipt postcard.

What it is not

For those readers already familiar with the regular patent application process (see Chapter 2, Section E), unlike an RPA, a PPA does not require:

- a Patent Application Declaration (PAD)
- an Information Disclosure Statement (IDS)
- claims
- an abstract and summary
- a description of the invention's background, or
- a statement of the invention's objects and advantages.

Your PPA cannot by itself result in a patent. If you don't file an RPA within a year of your PPA's filing date, your PPA will go abandoned and will be forever useless. Also, your PPA cannot provide a filing date for subject matter that is not disclosed in it.

What type of detailed description is necessary for a valid PPA?

Your PPA must disclose clearly and fully how to make and use the invention. That is, it must have the same level of detail that is required in the part of the Specification section of a regular patent application where you describe the invention's main embodiment and operation.

When to file a PPA

We recommend that you file a PPA only if:

- you have a good invention on which you wish to file an RPA, but are not currently able to do so due to lack of funds or resources
- you wish to lock in an early date, since you feel your invention is potentially valuable and

might be independently developed by others or stolen from you

- a paper or other public disclosure of your invention is going to be made and you don't have evidence sufficient to show that your "date of invention" antedates the public disclosure, or
- a paper or other public disclosure of your invention was already made, for example 11.5 months ago, and you don't have time to prepare and file an RPA before the one-year deadline.

Reasons you may not wish to file a PPA:

1. You may tend to forego building and testing and lose the concomitant advantages, such as determining whether the invention is operable, practical, or useful, and having a working prototype to demonstrate to prospective manufacturers.

2. Your PPA may fail to contain a full description of how to make and use of the invention or any embodiment of it. In this case, you won't be able to rely on the PPA's filing date for the invention or any embodiment.

3. You may unintentionally forego foreign protection. This is because you cannot wait one year after filing the RPA, as is usually done, to foreign file. Instead you must make your foreign filing decision, as well as your regular U.S. filing decision, within one year after your PPA is filed. Note that foreign filing is extremely expensive and few foreign filers ever get their outlay back.

4. You may try to license or interest a manufacturer in your invention in the approximately ten-month period between the time you file the PPA and the time you must begin preparation of your RPA. Since ten months is usually too short a period to license an invention, you may get discouraged and fail to file an RPA, and thus give up a potentially valuable invention.

5. If you file an RPA that claims the date of your PPA and you do not file a Nonpublication Request at the time you file the RPA, your RPA will be published 18 months after you file the PPA, or

about six months after you file the RPA. You may not want your application published so early.

6. A PPA's date can be relied upon only if an RPA is filed within one year, while a properly witnessed record of building and testing generally can be relied upon even if the RPA is filed several years later.

7. If you file a PPA and then file an RPA claiming benefit of the PPA, but don't file a Nonpublication Request, your RPA will be published about six months after your RPA's filing date. Such a publication will destroy the trade secret status, if any, of your invention at an early date.

See Chapter 2, Section D, for the steps necessary to prepare a PPA.

E. Other Possible Applications of Your Invention

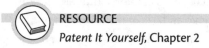

RESOURCE
Patent It Yourself, Chapter 2

As you proceed to build and test your invention, you will probably have flashes of insight as to other possible uses for it. This section of the notebook is designed specifically for you to immediately record these "bolts from the blue" so that later on, when you draft your patent application or formulate marketing plans, you can easily refer to them.

F. Record Your Trademark Conception

RESOURCE
Patent It Yourself, Chapter 1

The brand name or design symbol (or both) that you attach to or associate with your invention for marketing purposes is known as a trademark. Needless to say, if your product is successful in the marketplace, your trademark can become very valuable.

NOTEBOOK
The Trademark Conception and Protection form in Appendix I: Notebook is provided for recording a drawing or description of any trademark you create. We provide space for four trademark conceptions in case a trademark search reveals a conflict.

For each trademark, you should provide the mark itself—a name, graphic design, or a name with a graphic design together with the generic descriptor "goods" or "service" with which the mark is to be used. For example, with Ivory soap, "IVORY" is the mark and "soap" is the goods or generic descriptor.

TIP
Although your proposed trademark will not be subject to protection under federal and state trademark laws until you either use it or apply to register it on the basis of intended use, it can be considered a trade secret until that time. Accordingly, we suggest these pages be signed, dated, and witnessed so you can prove that you came up with the name first in case of a trade secret dispute on this point. In Chapter 2, Section G, you can read how to record details as to the use and registration of your trademark in case of a later dispute over its ownership.

G. Record Your Distinctive Design Conception

RESOURCE
Patent it Yourself, Chapter 1

NOTEBOOK
On the Distinctive Design Conception form in Appendix I: Notebook, you should enter any distinctive product designs you feel might qualify for either copyright or design patent protection.

By product design, we mean the shape of your invention, such as the shape of a computer case, the shape of a bottle, the design of jewelry, etc. We provide four pages for you to do this. You should record the conception and the building and testing of your design, just as you did for a utility invention. If, however, your design is already shown in the Record of Conception of Invention or the Record of Building and Testing of Invention documentation of your utility invention, then of course that will suffice and you don't have to make separate documentation records for the design.

If your invention has a distinctive design that is basically unrelated to its function, you may be able to protect the design from use by others by a design patent or copyright.

Design patents last for 14 years and give you the right to prevent others from using your distinctive design for that period of time, even if they created the design independently of you. (How to get a design patent is discussed in Chapter 10 of *Patent It Yourself.*) Copyright protection is usable for designs of toys and nonutilitarian articles, such as jewelry, or even utilitarian articles where the artwork is separable

from the article, such as fabric design. Copyright protection lasts for your life plus 70 years (or for 95 to 120 years if the design was created as a work made for hire) and gives you the right to exclude others from copying your work. Each form of protection has some advantages and disadvantages. The primary advantage of the design patent is that it offers a broader scope of protection. The copyright, on the other hand, is much easier to create and maintain, and offers protection for a longer period of time. Because of the greater value of its advantages, we recommend that you use copyright protection for all toys, nonutilitarian articles, and objects. If the object is utilitarian and its aesthetic features can't be separated from the article, use design patent protection. We recommend that you not try to obtain both forms of protection for one design. Asserting two "monopolies" over one creation may be construed by the courts as overreaching and, therefore, may result in a loss of protection for your design.

Legal Protection

This chapter describes how to organize and record the information you will need to obtain the fullest possible legal protection for your invention. It explains the following nine worksheets:

- The Prior Art Search worksheet helps you keep track of the prior art that will ultimately determine whether your invention receives a patent (and that you must disclose to the PTO as part of your patent application). This section also alerts you to any public use or exposure of your invention that might trigger the rule requiring filing of a patent application within one year of such public use or exposure.

- The Patentability Checklist helps you assess the patentability of your invention.

- The Provisional Patent Appliction Checklist helps you make sure your Provisional Patent Application is complete.

- The Patent Application Checklist helps you keep track of the many items and steps involved in preparing and filing a complete patent application.

- The Design Patent Application Checklist helps you organize your effort to obtain a design patent.

- The Trademark Use and Registration form documents the results of any trademark search you have conducted regarding your proposed trademark for your invention, the first use (if any) of the trademark, and information about steps you have taken to protect the trademark (registration and renewal with the PTO and state agencies).

- The Record of Contacts keeps track of all contacts you make with outside individuals and companies about your invention, and whether you have obtained confidentiality agreements (we call them Proprietary Materials Agreements) as appropriate. This information will help you maintain your invention as a trade secret pending the issuance of a patent.

- The Legal Protection Summary checklist lets you know whether you have done what you should to legally protect your invention and trademark.

A. Prior Art Search

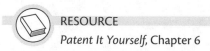

RESOURCE
Patent It Yourself, Chapter 6

Inventor's Commandment

You should make (or have made) a thorough patentability search of your invention before you file a patent application, and you should not file a patent application unless you believe your invention has novel features over the prior art that you feel are unobvious.

NOTEBOOK
Complete the Prior Art Search form in Appendix II: Worksheets to determine whether your invention is patentable (Box 16).

As you probably know, whether your invention is patentable depends in large part upon previous developments in the same field (prior art). Most specialized inventors have a good working grasp of the relevant prior art and are able to come up with something different, at least to some degree. (Of course, many inventors invent first and then check to see whether it qualifies for a patent.) Awareness of prior art usually comes from:

- reviewing previously issued patents
- researching trade journal articles, and
- carefully checking wholesale and retail channels to see whether a similar product has been marketed.

It is important for you to conduct a preliminary search of relevant prior art to determine whether your invention is sufficiently innovative to qualify for a patent. Keep careful track of the prior art references you accumulate in the course of your preliminary search. This is because later, when you file your patent application, you will need to list all prior art known to you. Documenting all prior art you discover as you go along will make your actual patent application process a whole lot easier.

This section also asks you to document the date your invention is first exposed to or used in public in a way that might trigger the one-year rule.

1. Locating Relevant Patents Online

You can locate information about previously issued patents by using online patent databases, such as the one at the PTO website (www.uspto.gov) or the European Patent Office (EPO) website (http://ep.espacenet.com), both of which are free, or by using the facilities at the Patent and Trademark Depository Libraries (PTDLs) located in major cities (a complete listing of PTDLs is provided at the USPTO website, www.uspto.gov).

Online searching is ideal for locating a specific patent and performing preliminary research. Beware, however, most online patent data banks usually go back only to 1971 or 1976, and it is possible that a patent issued before these dates might demonstrate the obviousness or lack of novelty for a new invention. This is not a problem for most high-tech inventions, because the relevant prior art is post-1960s. Despite its limitations, online searching has some obvious advantages such as cost and ease of use.

Free databases:

- **The PTO website.** The PTO provides free keyword combination searches in bibliographic format (name, title, assignee, city, state, date, and so on) back to 1976 and by patent number and current classification back to 1790. To use this service, visit www.uspto.gov/patft/index.html. To view the actual images of patents (as opposed to simple text versions of the patents), go to the link "How to Access Full-Page Images" and download and install the TIFF viewer AlternaTIFF (www.alternatiff.com) that is available for free. Then use the "Quick Search" or "Advanced Search" links to make the search using the instructions to follow. If you simply want to look up a patent by its number, go to the "Patent Number Search" link.

Determining an Invention's Classification

When performing patent searches, you will need to determine your invention's most relevant search classification (called "class" and "subclass"). Every type of invention is categorized in a class. For example, if you invented something that has to do with sewing, you would search in Class 112. If the invention had to do with sewing gloves, it would be in Class 112, Subclass 16. You can find the appropriate classifications in any of the following references, all of which are available at the USPTO website. These consist of:

- *Index to the U.S. Patent Classification*—lists all possible subject areas of invention alphabetically, from "abacus" to "zwieback," together with the appropriate class and subclass for each. The *Index* also lists the classes alphabetically.
- *Manual of Classification*—lists all classes numerically and subclasses under each class. After locating the class and subclass numbers, the *Manual of Classification* is used as an adjunct to the *Index*, to check the selected classes, and to find other, closely related ones.
- *Classification Definitions*—contains a definition for every class and subclass in the *Manual of Classification*. At the end of each subclass definition is a cross-reference of additional places to look that correspond to the subclass. Search classifications can also be obtained at a PTDL by using the CD-ROM CASSIS (Classification and Search Support Information System).

The *Index to the U.S. Patent Classification, Manual of Classification,* and *Classification Definitions* can be searched online by accessing the PTO website (www.uspto.gov). Click "Patents," then click "Guidance, Tools and Manuals" under "Patenting Guides." All three publications can be found under "Tools and Manuals."

- Google Patents (www.google.com/patents) is an excellent free resource that includes US patents back to the beginning. We recommend this site.
- Patent Monkey (www.PatentMonkey.com) is another good free search site that goes back to 1976 and includes the maintenance-fee status (expired or in-force) and claims, abstract or description on the front page.
- Clearly Understood (www.clearlyunderstood. com) is a comprehensive patent services site that requires registration but also provides an additional searching capability.
- The EPO (http://ep.espacenet.com) provides Quick and Advanced search capabilities in three languages (English, Deutsch, and Français), but for patentability searches only the Quick search in English is necessary. Searches can be made in four databases: Worldwide (covers the European country, EPO, and U.S. patents), Japanese, EP (EPO patents), or WIPO (World Intellectual Patent Organization, which administers the PCT)

Sandbag Shovel

databases. To search all databases, you need to search just the Worldwide and Japanese databases. To make a search, simply type the appropriate keyword combinations in the keyword box with a suitable connector, for example "bicycle AND plastic OR wood". The dates of the databases vary; see the site for more information.

Fee-based databases:

- **Delphion** (www.delphion.com) offers bibliographic and patentability search services for a fee. The system has several advantages over the PTO. Delphion's database goes back to 1971 for U.S. patents and contains the front pages of Europatents and PCT published patent applications. However, Delphion requires a signup and charges for use and downloading patent images.
- **MicroPatent** (www.micropatent.com) is a commercial database of U.S. patents searchable from 1836 to the present. It also includes Japanese and International PCT patent applications from 1983, European patents from 1988, and the Official Gazette (Patents). The U.S. patents before 1971 have been entered into the database by optical character recognition, so expect some errors.
- **LexPat** (www.lexis-nexis.com) is a commercial database of U.S. patents searchable from 1971 to the present. In addition, the LEXPAT library offers extensive prior-art searching capability of technical journals and magazines.
- **QPAT** (www.qpat.com) and **Questel/Orbit** (www.questel.orbit.com) are commercial services access the QPAT database that includes U.S. patents searchable from 1974 to the present and full-text European A (1987–present) and B (1991–present) patents.
- **PatentMax** (www.patentmax.com) enables you to search U.S. and foreign patent databases and perform batch loading, a process that automates patent downloads.
- **PatentCafé** (www.patentcafe.com) is a service that uses "concept" searching that is more

complete than traditional Boolean searching and covers many databases.

- **PatBase** (www.patbase.com) is a new database that can search back to the 1800s through many nations' patents, and permits batch downloading.

Several of the fee-based databases provide foreign patent information.

2. Obtaining Copies of Patents

Although portions of patents are available and can be printed directly from the PTO's website free of charge, they must be downloaded and printed one page at a time. To view and print actual patent pages or images (as opposed to an ASCII file of the patent) from the PTO's site, you must first download and install an "AlternaTIFF" viewer from a link on the main search page. This viewer provides a bitmapped image with one page per file. If you want to get numerous patents, this will be a time consuming process, especially if you have a dial-up Internet service. Instead, you may order copies of the patents and have them delivered to you, but at a cost. To order patents, click the title or number of the patent; this will produce a full-text view page. Then, click "Add To Shopping Cart." Have your credit card ready.

You can also obtain a copy of a patent as follows:

- Download a text copy or image copy of the patent from the free patents online site (http://freepatentsonline.com) or the free patent fetcher site (http://free.patentfetcher.com). These sites provide an Adobe Acrobat PDF copy of the entire patent. The PTO's site (www.uspto.gov/patft/index.html) supplies the patents one page at a time in a special TIFF format. These three services are cheapest, fastest, and easiest.
- Order the patent from the PTO by phone (703-305-8716), fax (703-305-8759), or letter (Mail Stop Document Services, Commissioner for Patents, P.O. Box 1450, Alexandria, VA 22213-1450) with a list of the patents you want by number and the payment for the price per patent (see the fee schedule at the PTO website) times the total number of patents you've

ordered. The PTO will normally furnish the copies by mail, but will also fax or FedEx them for an additional fee. The PTO accepts credit cards.

- Order a copy from a private supply company such as micropatent (www.micropatent.com) or Thompson Derwent (www.thompsonderwent.com).

Inventor's Commandment

One-Year Rule: You should treat the "one-year rule" as holy. You must file your patent application within one year of the date on which you first publish; publicly use; sell; or offer your invention, or any product which embodies same, for sale. Moreover, if you wish to preserve your foreign rights and frustrate pirates of your creation, you should actually file your patent application before you publish or sell your creation.

B. Patentability Checklist

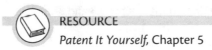

RESOURCE
Patent It Yourself, Chapter 5

NOTEBOOK
Record the reasons why you believe your invention is patentable on the Patentability Checklist in Appendix II: Worksheets.

To be patentable, an invention must:

- fit within one of the statutory classes of patentable inventions
- be useful
- be novel, and
- be unobvious from the standpoint of one skilled in the relevant art.

By completing the checklist you will gain a preliminary understanding of whether your invention is patentable or whether any alternate form of legal protection should be sought. We provide three copies in Appendix II, as it is possible that you will come up with a number of versions of your invention in the course of prosecuting your patent application in the Patent and Trademark Office.

What Happened to the Document Disclosure Program?

Readers of previous editions may wonder why there is no mention of the PTO's Document Disclosure Program (DDP). In 2007, the PTO discontinued the program. The DDP was a method of documenting conception for inventors who did not want to rely on witnesses. Inventors can, of course, still rely on the traditional methods of document conception via a signed and dated record which is also witnessed and dated.

C. Provisional Patent Application Checklist

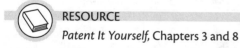

RESOURCE
Patent It Yourself, Chapters 3 and 8

NOTEBOOK
The Provisional Patent Application Checklist in Appendix II: Worksheets keeps track of the basic components that make up a Provisional Patent Application (PPA). Check off each step of the process as it is completed.

Keep in mind, the PPA won't do you any good unless you adequately describe your invention in it and then file a regular patent application within one year. Also remember that your PPA filing date begins the one-year period you have to accomplish most foreign filings. See Chapter 3 of *Patent It Yourself* for specific filing instructions, and Chapter 8 of *Patent It Yourself* for instructions on how to adequately describe the structure and operation of your invention. You will need to:

1. Prepare drawings, if necessary
2. Describe your invention
3. Describe its operation
4. Prepare a cover letter
5. Write a check for the specified fee (see Appendix IV: Fee Schedule)
6. Prepare a stamped receipt postcard, and
7. Mail all papers to Mail Stop DD, Commissioner for Patents, P.O. Box 1450, Alexandria, VA 22313-1450.

D. Patent Application Checklist

RESOURCE
Patent It Yourself, Chapters 8, 13, and 15

Inventor's Commandment

Your patent application must contain a description of your invention in such full, complete, clear, and exact terms, including details of your preferred embodiment at the time you file, so that anyone having ordinary skill in the field will be readily able to make and use it, and preferably so that even a lay judge will be able to understand it.

NOTEBOOK
The Patent Application Checklist in Appendix II: Worksheets records the basic components that make up a patent application.

When you think you are ready to file your patent application, you will want to consult this list and see whether in fact you are ready to fulfill the requirements of each component.

You should check off (in the space provided) each step of the patent process as it is completed. This will help you know exactly where you stand in respect to your application as a whole.

After your patent application has been submitted, there will be additional transactions with the PTO.

We also provide a checklist for the most common of these transactions.

E. Design Patent Application Checklist

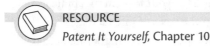

RESOURCE
Patent It Yourself, Chapter 10

NOTEBOOK
The Design Patent Application Checklist in Appendix II: Worksheets keeps track of the components that go into a design patent application.

If you have decided that a separate design patent is appropriate for your invention, you will want to consult this list and see whether you are ready to file. Again, check off each step as you complete it so that you can help keep track of where you are. You need to:

1. Prepare a Design Patent Application
2. Prepare drawings, if necessary
3. Prepare a Patent Application Declaration
4. Write a check for the filing fee (see Appendix IV: Fee Schedule)
5. Prepare a stamped receipt postcard
6. Prepare an Information Disclosure Statement and List of Prior Art Cited, and
7. Mail all papers to Mail Stop Design Patent, Commissioner for Patents, P.O. Box 1450, Alexandria, VA 22313-1450.

F. Trademark Use and Registration

NOTEBOOK
The Trademark Use and Registration form in Appendix II: Worksheets documents the steps you should take to make sure this trademark is valid and cannot be used by competitors.

In Chapter 1, Section F, we ask you to describe the trademark (if any) under which you plan to market your invention. (For more information on all aspects of trademark law and comprehensive instructions on how to register a trademark, see *Trademark: Legal Care for Your Business and Product Name,* by Attorneys Richard Stim and Stephen Elias (Nolo).)

The first step is to determine whether your proposed trademark is sufficiently distinguishable from existing trademarks to avoid later charges of trademark infringement. This effort (termed a "trademark search") usually involves, at a minimum, an examination of:

- the list of trademarks registered (and pending registrations) with the PTO
- the list of trademarks registered in your state
- existing product and service names (trademarks and service marks), and
- trade and product journals covering subjects related to your invention.

It is possible to conduct a preliminary online search to determine if your trademark is distinguishable from other federally registered trademarks. This can be accomplished using the PTO's free trademark databases (at the PTO's website, www.uspto.gov) that provide free access to records of federally registered marks or marks that are pending (applications undergoing examination at the PTO). The PTO database does not include trademark applications filed during the last two to four months, nor does it contain any information on state, foreign, or common law trademarks or inactive applications and registrations (for example, abandoned applications or canceled or expired registrations).

Privately owned fee-based online trademark databases often provide more current PTO trademark information. Below are some private online search companies.

- **Saegis** (www.thomson-thomson.com) is the most comprehensive trademark searching service and provides access to all Trademarkscan databases (state, federal, and international trademark databases), domain name databases, common law sources on the Internet, and newly filed United States federal trademark applications. Saegis also provides access to *Dialog* services.

- **Dialog** (www.dialog.com) provides access to Trademarkscan databases including state and federal registration and some international trademarks, and provides common law searching of news databases.
- **Micropatent** (www.micropatent.com) provides access to federal and state trademarks, through its MarkSearch Pro and MarkSearch Pro State databases.
- **Trademark.com** (www.trademark.com) provides access to current federal and state trademark registration information.
- **LexisNexis** (www.lexis-nexis.com) provides access to federal and state registrations and permits common law searching via Nexis news services. The PTO utilizes Nexis for its evaluations of descriptive and generic terms.

Many companies hire professional trademark searching companies such as Thomson & Thomson (www.thomson-thomson.com) to perform trademark searches. The cost is usually between two and three hundred dollars.

The name of your searcher and the sources searched (either by your searcher or by you if you did the search yourself) should be entered in the space provided.

The criteria for determining the extent to which you can prevent others from using your trademark, and whether it infringes on other existing trademarks, are discussed briefly in Chapter 1 of *Patent It Yourself*. You should consult a trademark attorney if you have any doubts about either or both of these points.

Once you decide on a trademark, you should file an application to register your trademark on the basis of your good faith intent to use it within the following six months. Then, when the trademark is actually used to market your invention across state lines, you can file an Amendment to Allege Use to get the trademark placed on the federal trademark register. If you are already using a trademark across state lines, your registration would be based on actual rather than intended use.

If you see that you won't be able to actually use the mark across state lines within the six-month period, you can obtain a six-month extension upon a showing of good cause. Four additional six-month extensions can also be obtained if you are able to convince the PTO that you still have a good faith intent to use the mark.

Under this system, you initially have several dates to keep track of:

- the date you first use your work within a state
- the date you file your trademark application to register on the basis of intended use
- the date you put the trademark into actual use across state lines, and
- the date you file your Amendment to Allege Use (or alternatively, your Statement of Use, if the PTO has by then issued the Notice of Allowance provisionally registering your mark).

You should also document when you first used the trademark in a foreign country, as this may be important should your trademark go international.

Your PTO registration provides notice throughout the U.S. that you claim ownership of and have the exclusive right to use the mark for the goods indicated in the registration. This notice can often make the difference between stopping other people from using your trademark and having to share use of the trademark with these later users. Also, it is much easier to collect damages for infringement of a registered trademark than an unregistered one. Use the space provided to document your federal registration efforts, including the date of registration, registration number, and registration classification name and number (all trademarks fall into one or more specific classes of goods, each of which is assigned a number).

When your trademark is registered, you should note the date when you will need to file your declarations of continued use and incontestability (within the last year of the six-year period after your initial registration date). Thus, if you register your trademark with the PTO on July 1, 2005, you will want to file these declarations between July 1, 2010, and July 1, 2011. These declarations are statements that your trademark has been in continuous use for the preceding five-year period and that you qualify to have your trademark made incontestable (which immunizes it from attack on certain grounds).

Failure to file the declaration of continued use will result in your trademark being cancelled. Assuming you are working with a trademark attorney, he or she will keep the date these declarations are due on the law firm calendar. You should also note the date you will want to initiate your ten-year renewal (about six months before the end of the ten-year period following your registration).

CAUTION

The protection and proper use of a trademark can be as commercially important as the underlying invention. We strongly recommend that you get a copy of *Trademark: Legal Care for Your Business and Product Name* by Attorneys Richard Stim and Stephen Elias (Nolo), and, if necessary, work with a trademark attorney on the matters covered in this chapter of *The Inventor's Notebook*.

G. Record of Contacts

RESOURCE

Patent It Yourself, Chapter 1

It is extremely important that an inventor be able to identify each and every person and company who has been contacted about, or had access to, the invention. This information can prove to be very useful in the event of a dispute about:

- the inventor's diligence in building and testing the invention
- who should be considered the true inventor, or
- whether a confidentiality agreement has been violated.

NOTEBOOK

The Record of Contacts in Appendix II: Worksheets lets you keep notes of the people you have called, what you discussed the last time you spoke with them, and what their response was. This can be useful if you need to follow up on any calls.

Every pending patent application will be published 18 months after its filing date. The only exception is if, at the time of filing, the applicant files a Nonpublication Request (NPR) indicating that the application will not be filed abroad. In that case, once the patent issues on your invention, it becomes a matter of public record and is published in the *Official Gazette* (Patents). In both of these situations, publication terminates trade secret protection for the claimed invention. Prior to these publications, you are entitled to treat your invention as a trade secret and obtain court relief against those who improperly disclose your invention to others. Generally, a trade secret is any information that is maintained as confidential and that, because it is not generally known to competitors, provides its owner with a competitive edge. The basic method for preserving information as a trade secret is to limit those who have access to it, and require those who do have access to sign a confidentiality agreement. Blank agreement forms (called Proprietary Materials Agreements) are described in Chapter 1 and included in Appendix V: Tear-Out Forms.

By conscientiously entering all contacts in the Record of Contacts in Appendix II: Worksheets, and noting whether the person contacted has signed a confidentiality agreement, you will have all your contacts and trade secret protection information collected in one place for later reference.

H. Legal Protection Summary

RESOURCE

Patent It Yourself, Chapter 7

An analysis of the relative advantages and disadvantages of the legal protection alternatives open to an inventor is provided in Chapter 7 of *Patent It Yourself.*

NOTEBOOK

The Legal Protection Summary in Appendix II: Worksheets lets you keep track of which methods you have chosen to protect your invention.

This form can be very important when you go to market your invention. Most prospective buyers or developers will first want to know exactly what you've done to protect your right to exclusive use of the invention. By conscientiously keeping this list up-to-date, your record of protection will be instantly available to all who are interested.

Marketing

Inventor's Commandment

You should try to market your invention as soon as you can after filing your patent application; don't wait until your patent issues. You should favor companies who are close to you and small in size.

If you want your invention to be successful, pursue commercial exploitation with all the energy that you can devote to it.

Never pay any money to any invention developer unless the developer can prove to you that it has a successful track record—that is, most of its clients have received more income in royalties than they have paid the developer in fees.

Simply put, this chapter is a preliminary guide to help you analyze the commercial potential of your invention and to help you keep track of your efforts to market it.

Once you invent something, you will naturally want to profit from it. This will involve coming up with a plan under which your invention can be produced and distributed to its ultimate users. To effectively get your invention out there you need to have a handle on what its strong and weak points are from both a marketing and manufacturing point of view (Section A). In addition, it's wise to consider how prospective manufacturers and users are likely to view your invention and to use this knowledge creatively as part of a plan to sell the idea of your new product (Section B). It's also important to understand general market trends in the particular area of your invention so that you will be prepared to tell interested marketers and manufacturers why your invention will be profitable given the costs to make it, the competition, and so on (Section C). In addition, you need to proceed in an organized manner to either seek potential manufacturers or distributors, or to accomplish these activities yourself. Sections E and F help you do this. Section G is an introduction to the Internet and how you can use the Internet to develop and promote your invention.

TIP

The subject of marketing your invention to the public once it is manufactured is far beyond the scope of this book. If you plan to run the whole show, including the actual marketing of your invention, we suggest you consult one or more of the resources listed in Chapter 5.

A. Evaluation of Positive and Negative Factors of Invention

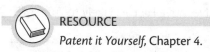

RESOURCE
Patent it Yourself, Chapter 4.

Inventor's Commandment

You should not spend significant time or money on your creation until you have thoroughly evaluated it for commercial potential, including considering all of its advantages and disadvantages.

Before you even prepare a patent application, you will obviously want to give serious consideration to whether your invention has commercial potential. For this reason, *Patent It Yourself* devotes an entire chapter to this question and provides an evaluation sheet to help you answer this key question. This same evaluation sheet has been included in Appendix II: Worksheets (Positive and Negative Factors Evaluation). Instructions from *Patent It Yourself* have been provided for your convenience.

1. The Positive and Negative Factors Test

Every invention, no matter how many positive factors it seems to have at first glance, inevitably has one or more significant negative ones. To evaluate the positive and negative factors objectively, carefully consider each on the list below. Using a Positive and Negative Factors Evaluation worksheet in Appendix II: Worksheets, assign a commercial value or

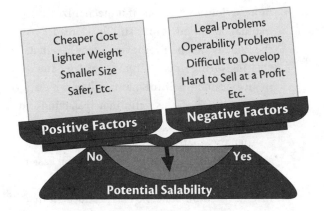

disadvantage weight to each factor on a scale of 1 to 100, according to your best estimate.

For example, if an invention provides overwhelming cost savings in relation to its existing counterparts, assign an 80 or higher to the "Cost" factor (#1) in the positive column. If it requires a moderate capital expenditure to distribute, a 50 would be appropriate for this factor (#43), in the negative column.

The following balance scale analogy will help you understand the positive and negative factors evaluation process. Pretend the positive factors are stacked on one side of a balance scale and the negative factors are stacked on the other side, as indicated above.

If the positive factors strongly outweigh the negative, you can regard this as a "go" indication, that is, the invention is commercially viable. Obviously this balance scale is just an analogy. It can't be used quantitatively because no one has yet come up with a way to assign precise weights to the factors. Nevertheless, you'll find it of great help in evaluating the commercial prospects of your invention.

Before you actually take pen (or word processor) in hand and begin your evaluation, read through the following summary of positive and negative factors.

2. Positive Factors Affecting the Marketability of Your Invention

1. **Cost.** Is your invention cheaper (or more expensive) to build or use than current counterparts? An example where making something more expensive to build would be an advantage is a credit or eligibility card; a more expensive card would be more difficult to counterfeit.

2. **Weight.** Is your invention lighter (or heavier) in weight than what is already known, and is such change in weight a benefit? For example, if you've invented a new automobile or airplane engine, a reduction in weight is a great benefit. But if you've invented a new ballast material, obviously an increase in weight (provided it doesn't come at too great a cost in money or bulk) is a benefit.

3. **Size.** Is your invention smaller (or larger) in size or capacity than what is already known, and is such change in size a benefit?

4. **Safety/Health Factors.** Is your invention safer or healthier to use than what is already known? Clearly there's a strong trend in government and industry to improve the safety and reduce the possible chances for injury, harm, and product liability suits in most products and processes, and this trend has given birth to many new inventions. Often a greater increase in cost and weight will be tolerated if certain safety and health benefits accrue. But beware, some safety devices cause more harm than they prevent: for example, antilock brakes have caused more skids and accidents than conventional brakes, since users tend to pump them, although they are supposed to be pressed continuously.

5. **Speed.** Is your invention able to do a job faster (or slower) than its previous counterpart, and is such change in speed a benefit? This advantage, like #6, is important in software inventions.

6. **Ease of Use.** Is your invention easier (or harder) to use (the current buzzword is "ergonomic") or learn to use than its previously known counterpart? An example of a product where an increase in difficulty of use would be a benefit is the childproof drug container cap. This advantage is especially important if you have a software innovation: If it enables you to use the computer or any other machine more facilely, this counts a great deal.

7. **Ease of Production.** Is your invention easier or cheaper (or harder or more expensive) to manufacture than previously known counterparts? Or can it be mass-produced, whereas previously known counterparts had to be made by hand? An example of something that is more difficult to manufacture yet that is highly desirable is the new credit card with a holographic image: It's far more difficult to forge.

8. **Durability.** Does your invention last longer (or wear out sooner) than previously known counterparts? While built-in obsolescence is nothing to be admired, the stark economic reality is that many products, such as disposable razors, have earned their manufacturers millions by lasting for a shorter time than previously known counterparts.

9. **Repairability.** Is it easier to repair than previously known counterparts?

10. **Novelty.** Is your invention at all different from all previously known counterparts? Merely making an invention different may not appear to be an advantage per se, but it's usually a great advantage: It provides an alternative method or device for doing the job in case the first method or device ever encounters difficulties (such as from government regulation), and in case the first device or method infringes a patent that you want to avoid infringing. It also provides something for ad people to crow about.

11. **Convenience/Social Benefit/Mechanization.** Does your invention make living easier or more convenient? Many inventions with a new function provide this advantage. Although you may question the ultimate wisdom and value of such gadgets as the electric knife, the remote-control TV, and the digital-readout clock, the reality remains that, in our relatively affluent society, millions of dollars have been and are being made from devices that save labor and time (even though the time required to earn the after-tax money to buy the gadget is often greater than the time saved by using it). Even if the invention has one or more serious drawbacks, if it mechanizes a manual operation, it may still fly. Consider the Epilady® leg-hair remover: Even though its rotating spring ripped out m'lady's leg hairs in an extremely painful manner, it became a great success because it eliminated shaving and depilatories.

Then too, many new industries have been started by making an existing invention easier and convenient to use. Henry Ford didn't invent the automobile; he just produced it in volume and made it convenient for the masses to use. Ditto for George Eastman with his camera. And in modern times, the two Steves (Jobs and Wozniak) did much the same for the computer.

In the software field, especially nowadays, people seem willing to buy almost any program that will computerize a manual task, even if the time required to earn the money to buy the program, learn the program, and use it is much greater than the manual route. Many inventors have told me that they would like to use the PTO's Electronic Filing System, even though it requires lots of paperwork to get qualified and a fairly difficult learning curve to be able to use it.

12. **Reliability.** Is your invention apt to fail less or need repair less often than previously known devices?

13. **Ecology.** Does your invention make use of what previously were thought to be waste products? Does it reduce the use of limited natural resources? Does it produce fewer waste products, such as smoke and waste water? If so, you have an advantage that is very important nowadays and that should be emphasized strongly.

14. **Salability.** Is your invention easier to sell or market than existing counterparts?

15. **Appearance.** Does your invention provide a better-appearing design than existing counterparts?

16. **Viewability.** If your invention relates to eye use, does it present a brighter, clearer, or more viewable image? For example, a color TV with

a brighter picture and photochromic eyeglasses that automatically darken in sunlight were valuable inventions.

17. **Precision.** Does your invention operate or provide greater precision or more accuracy than existing counterparts?

18. **Noise.** Does your invention operate more quietly? Does it eliminate or turn unpleasant noise into a more acceptable sound? The noise-canceling headphones fill this bill. Or does it make noise in a desirable situation—for example, a device that produced a warning noise when a VCR cartridge was inserted in the wrong manner would be desirable.

19. **Odor.** Does your invention emanate less (or more) unpleasant fumes or odors? The public would benefit by adding an unpleasant odor to a poisonous or harmful substance. For example, public utilities add mercaptan sulphur to heating and cooking gas to warn users when leaks occur.

20. **Taste.** If your invention is edible or comes into contact with the taste buds (for example, a pill or a pipe stem), does it taste better? Like the foul odor above, a foul taste can also be an advantage, such as for poisons to prevent ingestion by children, and for telephone cables to deter chewing by rodents.

21. **Market Size.** Is there a larger market for your invention than for previously known devices? Because of climatic or legal restrictions, for example, certain inventions are usable only in small geographical areas. And because of economic factors, certain inventions may be limited to the relatively affluent. If your invention can obviate these restrictions, your potential market may be greatly increased, and this can be a significant advantage.

22. **Trend of Demand.** Is the trend of demand for your device increasing? Of course you should distinguish, if possible, between a trend and a fad. The first will provide a market for your invention while the second is likely to leave you high and dry unless you catch it in the beginning stages.

23. **Seasonal Demand.** Is your invention useful no matter what the season of the year? If so, it will usually have greater demand than a seasonal invention, such as a sailboat. But sometimes this will be a negative rather than a positive, if the invention is something like skis or a holiday decoration, which does have a seasonal demand rather than an all-year-around one.

24. **Difficulty of Market Penetration.** Is your device an improvement of a previously accepted device? If so, it will have an easier time penetrating the market and obtaining a good market share than a device that provides a completely new function.

25. **Potential Competition.** Is your invention so simple, popular, or easy to manufacture that many imitators and copiers are likely to attempt to copy it or design around it, or try to break your patent as soon as it's brought out? Or is it a relatively complex, less popular, hard-

Egg Storer

to-manufacture device, that others wouldn't be likely to produce because of such factors as the large capital outlay required for tooling and production? However, don't assume that something that's easy to copy is not worth patenting, since patents on simple devices are upheld and enforced successfully all the time.

26. **Quality.** Does your invention produce or provide a higher quality output or result than existing counterparts? For example, compact disks provide a much better audio quality than do phonorecords or magnetic tape.

27. **Excitement.** (The Neophile and the Conspicuous Consumer/Status Seeker.) Almost all humans need some form of excitement in their lives: Some obtain it by watching or participating in sports, others by the purchase of a new car or travel, and still others by the purchase of new products, such as a 50-inch TV, a DVD player, or a friendly household robot. Such purchasers can be called "neophiles" (lovers of the new); their excitement comes from having and showing off their new "toy." Purchasers of expensive products, like a Mercedes-Benz or a Rolex watch, are commonly motivated by what Thorsten Veblen has called "conspicuous consumption," and what we now call "status seeking." They enjoy showing off an expensive or unique item that they've acquired. Thus, if your invention can provide consumer excitement, either through sheer newness or through evidence of a costly purchase, it has a decided advantage.

28. **Markup.** If your invention is in an excitement category (that is, if it's very different, novel, innovative, or luxurious), it can command a very high markup, a distinct selling advantage.

29. **Inferior Performance.** Yes, I'm serious! If your invention performs worse than comparable things that are already available, this can be a great advantage, if put to the proper use. Consider the 3M Company's fabulously successful Scotch® Post-It® note pads: Their novelty is simply that they have a strip of stickum that is inferior to known adhesives, thus providing removable self-stick notes.

Here the invention may not be so much the discovery of an inferior adhesive as the discovery of a new use for it.

30. **"Sexy" Packaging.** If your invention is or comes in a "sexy" package, or is adaptable to being sold in such a package, this can be a great advantage. Consider the Hanes l'Eggs® stockings where the package (shaped like an egg) made the product!

31. **Miscellaneous/Obviation of Specific Disadvantages of Existing Devices.** This is a catchall to cover anything I may have missed in the previous categories. Often the specific disadvantages that your invention overcomes will be quite obvious; they should be included here, nonetheless.

32. **Long Life Cycle.** If your invention has a potentially long life cycle—that is, it can be made and sold for many years before it becomes obsolete—this is an obvious strong advantage that will justify capital expenditures for tooling and conducting a big ad campaign.

33. **Related Product Addability.** If your invention will usher in a new product line, as did the computer, where many related products, such as disk drives, printers, and software can be added, this will be an important advantage with potentially enhanced profits.

34. **Satisfies Existing Need.** If your invention will satisfy an existing, recognized need, such as preventing drug abuse, avoiding auto collisions, or combating terrorism or crime, your marketing difficulties will be greatly reduced.

3. Negative Factors Likely to Affect the Marketability of Your Invention

Alas, every invention has one or more negative factors, even if the negative factor is merely the need to change—or design and produce—production equipment. We've seen inventions and developments that were better in every way than what already existed, but that were not used solely because the improvement did not justify the cost of replacing existing production equipment, or the cost associated with manufacturing and promoting the device.

The negative factors of your invention are generally more important and require more consideration than the positive factors, since if your invention fails, it will obviously be due to one or more of the negative factors. Since all the positive factors listed above can be disadvantages when viewed in reverse, they should be carefully considered, but will not be reproduced here. For example, consider Factor #23, Seasonal Demand. This will be a negative rather than a positive factor if the invention is something like skis or a holiday decoration, which does have a seasonal demand rather than an all-year-around one.

a. Negatives Are the Reverse of Positive Factors Listed Above

35. **Legality.** Does your invention comply with, or will its use fail to comply with, existing laws, regulations, and product and manufacturing requirements? Or, are administrative approvals required? If your invention carries legal difficulties with it, its acceptance will be problematic no matter how great its positive advantages are. And if ecological or safety approvals are required (for example, for drugs and automobiles), this will be viewed as a distinct disadvantage by prospective buyers. Also, if the legality of a product is questionable, its manufacturer, distributor, or retailer will have difficulty in obtaining product liability insurance.

36. **Operability.** Is it likely to work readily, or will significant additional design or technical development be required to make it practicable and workable? Usually problems of operability will become abundantly clear when you try to build a working model, which you should try to do as soon as possible, even if you've filed a PPA (Chapter 3, Section I). Many great-looking inventions such as the turbine automobile engine turned out to be "techno-fizzle" when built and tested. (Don't forget to fill out another copy of Form 3-2 after you build and test it.)

37. **Development.** Is the product already designed for the market, or will such things as additional engineering, material selection, and appearance work be required?

38. **Profitability.** Because of possible requirements for exotic materials, difficult machining steps, great size, and so on, is your invention likely to be difficult to sell at a profit, or at an acceptable price level?

39. **Obsolescence.** Is the field in which your invention is used likely to be around for a long time or die out soon? If the latter, most manufacturers won't be willing to invest money in production facilities.

40. **Incompatibility.** Is your invention likely to be compatible or incompatible with existing patterns of use, customs, and so on?

41. **Product Liability Risk.** Is your invention in a "safe" area, such as a ruler, or in a problem area, such as safety devices, drugs, firearms, contact sports, and automobiles? In the latter areas, the risks of lawsuits against the manufacturer, due to product malfunction or injury from use, are likely to be greater than average. For example, a client of mine invented an ingenious, economical, and highly useful device for preventing a revolver from being accidentally fired. But, alas, though he tried everywhere, he couldn't get any company to take it on because they were afraid of product liability lawsuits if the device ever failed.

42. **Market Dependence.** Is the sale of your invention dependent on a market for other goods, or is it useful in its own right? For example, an improved television tuner depends on the sale of televisions for its success, so that if the television market goes into a slump, the sales of your tuner certainly will fall also.

43. **Difficulty of Distribution.** Is your invention easy to distribute, or is it so large, fragile, or perishable that it will be difficult or costly to distribute?

44. **Service Requirements.** Is your invention free from service requirements or will it require frequent servicing and adjustment? If the latter, this is a distinct disadvantage. But consider the first commercial color TVs, which, by any

reasonable standard, were a service nightmare, but made millions for their manufacturers.

45. **Production Facilities.** Almost all inventions require new production facilities, a distinct disadvantage. This is because the manufacture of anything new requires new tooling and production techniques. But some inventions require only a modest change or no change, a tremendous advantage.

46. **Inertia Need Not/Must Be Overcome.** An example of a great invention that so far has failed because of user inertia is the Dvorak typewriter keyboard, which, although much faster and easier to use, was unable to overcome the awkward but entrenched Qwerty keyboard. The same goes for the easier-to-use, less confusing, military-European time, or a decimal time system. There's a risk in introducing any new product, and when any invention is radically different, potential manufacturers, users, and sellers will manifest tremendous inertia, regardless of the invention's value.

47. **Minor/Great Technical Advance.** In the '60s, I got a client a very broad patent on a laser pumped by a chemical reaction explosion. We were very pleased with this patent. However, it was so advanced at the time that the technology behind it is just now being implemented in connection with the "Star Wars" defense effort. Unfortunately, the patent expired in the meantime. The same goes for the computer mouse patent, which expired in 1980, just before "mice" became popular; the roller-blade skates, the patent for which expired in 1985, just before the roller-blade craze started and John Hetrick's patent on the automobile air bag, which expired in 1970, before bag use started. An FRB-Dallas survey found that major innovations like the telephone, radio, dishwasher, color TV, microwave oven, VCR, computer, and cell phone took an average of 11.4 years to be owned by 25% of all U.S. households. The moral? Even if you have a great invention, make sure it can be commercially implemented within about 17 years.

48. **Learning Required.** If consumers will have to undergo substantial learning in order to use your invention, this is an obvious negative. An example: the early personal computers. On the other hand, some inventions, such as the automatically talking clock, make a task even easier to do and thus have an obvious strong advantage.

49. **Difficult/Easy to Promote.** If it will be difficult or expensive or will require a long time to promote and market your invention—for example, because it's technically complex, has subtle advantages, or is very expensive, large, or awkward—you've got an obvious disadvantage. But if it solves an omnipresent problem and is cheap and easy to market, this is a clear advantage.

50. **Lack/Presence of Market.** If no market already exists for your invention, you'll have to convince the public that they need it—that is, that you have a "product in search of a market." While not a fatal flaw, and while this type of invention can be most profitable, you (or your licensee) will have to be prepared to expend substantial sums on promotion.

51. **Crowded/Wide Open Field.** If the field is already crowded, you'll have an uphill battle.

52. **Commodities.** If you've invented a new commodity—such as a better plastic, solvent, or grain—you'll face stiff price competition from the established, already streamlined standards.

53. **Combination Products.** If you've invented a "combination product"—that is, a product with two inventions that don't really groove together, like a stapler with a built-in beverage cup holder—people won't be beating a path to your door. On the other hand, the clock-radio was just the ticket.

54. **Entrenched Competition.** Despite its overwhelming advantages, Edison had a terrible time promoting his light bulb because the gas companies fought him bitterly.

55. **Instant Anachronism.** A clever inventor in Oakland, California, invented a wonderful dictionary-indexing device that made it much faster to look up any word. However, he was unable to sell it to any dictionary publisher because the dictionary is being replaced by computerized devices. His clever invention was an "instant anachronism."

56. **Prototype Availability.** Although the presence or absence of a prototype should not affect the marketability or commercial success of your invention, in reality it will! If you have a prototype available, or can make one, you'll find that your invention will be far easier to market, since potential purchasers or licensees will be much more likely to buy something that is real and tangible rather than on paper only.

57. **Broad Patent Coverage Available.** You won't be able to determine whether or not broad patent coverage is likely to be available until you complete Chapters 5 and 6, but keep this factor in mind and come back to it after you evaluate patentability. Obviously, if you can obtain broad patent coverage on your invention, this will affect profitability, because if you're the only source for a device that performs a certain functions you'll be able to charge more than you would in a competitive situation. A legal monopoly is a capitalist's dream!

58. **High Sales Anticipated.** If you can anticipate a high sales volume for your invention—for example, for a device like the Hula-Hoop, which is relatively simple, cheap, and easy to market—this will be a very positive factor.

59. **Visibility of Invention in Final Product.** If your invention is highly visible in or essentially constitutes the entire final product—for example, the sneakers with heels that light up when walking—this will be a distinct marketing advantage to entice buyers who love the new. On the other hand, if the invention is hidden in the final product, such as a stronger frame for an automobile, this factor will not be a plus in marketing.

60. **Ease of Packaging.** If your invention is easy to package—for example, a small gadget that can be put in a cheap blister package—this will be a great aid in marketing. However, if it's difficult and expensive to package, such as a bicycle or hockey stick, this will obviously be a negative factor.

61. **Youth Market.** It's well known that children above about age nine and young adults tend to spend much more than the rest of the population. If your invention is something that will appeal to children or young adults, this will make it command far more sales than something that is not attractive to this age group. In other words, portable digital players will sell much better than arthritis aids.

62. **Part of a Current Fad.** If your invention is part of a current fad—for example, a low-carbohydrate product, a low-fat product, or a spam filter—it will be easier to sell. For example, a few years ago when the lottery was legalized in California, a spate of lottery-number selection products appeared and sold briskly until the public's interest simmered down.

63. **Will a Contingent Fee Litigator Take Your Case?** Before filing, consider whether, if your issued patent is infringed, there will likely be enough sales of the infringing device (or process) by a financially responsible manufacturer to get a litigator to represent you on a contingent-fee arrangement. If there aren't enough sales, or if the infringers are fly-by-night, irresponsible operators, most litigators won't take your infringement case on a contingent fee basis. This is true even if you have a strong patent that is clearly infringed. In other words, the law is far more accessible when substantial amounts are likely to be recovered.

Complete the Positive and Negative Factors Evaluation form by assigning a weight to each listed factor, either in the positive or negative column. Also list and assign weights to any other factors you can think of which I've omitted. Then compute the sum of your positive and negative factors and determine the difference to come up with a rough idea of a net value for your invention. We suggest that you continue to pursue inventions with net values of 50 and up, that you direct your efforts elsewhere if your invention has a net value of less than 0, and that you make further critical evaluation of inventions with net values between 0 and 50.

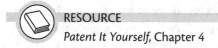

NOTEBOOK

Again, we provide three tear-out copies of the Positive and Negative Factors Evaluation worksheet in Appendix II: Worksheets. The extra copies are in case you find others who can provide you with informed and impartial feedback on the commercial potential of your invention.

B. Potential User Survey

RESOURCE
Patent It Yourself, Chapter 4

As part of your marketing efforts, you will want to show that your invention is likely to be well accepted. One way to do this is a survey among likely users. This involves showing the invention to several such users, collecting their comments, entering them on the Potential User Survey in Appendix II: Worksheets, and (if convenient) having the users sign and date their comments. A good way to conduct this survey is to exhibit at local inventors' or new product fairs and showcases. Try a booth space in a local shopping mall. If your invention is patented, this type of survey can be done without having each person sign a Proprietary Materials Agreement. The important thing is to get as much feedback from the potential customers as possible. A professional marketing firm would charge quite a bit to provide this same information. The Potential User Survey permits this systematic documentation for later disclosure to investors or manufacturers.

TIP

The users should also sign a Proprietary Materials Agreement if you are maintaining your invention as a trade secret (at least until a patent issues). Tear-out copies of this agreement are contained in Appendix V: Tear-Out Forms.

C. Relevant Market Trends

To properly assess your invention's commercial potential, it's wise to carefully consider what existing trends, if any, will affect its acceptance in the marketplace. As mentioned above, a clever inventor in Oakland, California, invented a wonderful dictionary indexing device which made it much faster to look up any word. However, he was unable to sell it to any dictionary publisher because the dictionary was being replaced by computerized devices. His clever invention was an instant anachronism. Obviously, with some inventions, such as a dictionary indexing device, you have little choice but to swim against the commercial stream, unless of course you decide that the current is so swift that you're better off putting the invention aside in favor of something else.

We have designed three forms to document (at least preliminarily) the trends that bear on the marketability of your invention. These forms can be particularly essential if you plan to seek venture capital or a business partner. It also, of course, is the basis of any intelligent marketing strategy. When a potential investor or partner says, "Tell me exactly how this thing will make money," the more persuasive your analysis of market trends, the better your chance of successfully completing the transaction.

Let's say you go back to work and invent a new type of translucent bowling ball that contains holographic images that change as the ball rolls. The images could be attractive patterns, pictures of film or music celebrities, etc. If you want to sell this idea to a large manufacturer of related products, such as AMF or Brunswick, there is probably no point for you to spend time and money on an extensive market survey; they already know more about this area than you could ever hope to. If, on the other hand, you are seeking capital from someone who is not an expert in the field, you are going to have to convince him that the combination of bowling balls and holographic images is likely to be a hot item, at least in some areas of the country or among certain age groups. Simply put, will your bowling ball "play in Peoria"?

To answer this question for your invention, you will want to find data that tells you about:

- previous and forecasted buying patterns for related or competing products in your targeted marketing areas, and
- the projected size and buying power of the population groups of your most likely customers.

Where do you find this type of information? Here are some free resources for U.S. economic forecasts:

- The Survey of Professional Forecasters (www. philadelphiafed.org/econ/spf) provides quarterly macroeconomic forecasts.
- The Institute for Alternative Futures (www. altfutures.com) provides forecasting tools.
- The Congressional Budget Office (CBO) (www. cbo.gov) offers a wide range of statistical information.

Some fee-based services for economic forecasts include the following:

- The Statistical Universe (https://web.lexis-nexis.com/statuniv) is a fee-based service offered through LexisNexis.
- Consensus Economics (www.consensus economics.com) is the world's leading international economic survey organization.
- InfoTech Trends (www.infotechtrends. com) provides market data on computers, peripherals, software, storage, the Internet, and communications equipment.
- TableBase (http://library.dialog.com/ bluesheets/html/bl0093.html) contains tabular information dealing with companies, products, industries, brands, markets, demographics, and countries from around the world.

You can learn about foreign forecasts at the IMF World Economic Outlook International Forecasts (www.imf.org/external/pubs/ft/weo/1999/02/index .htm), published twice a year.

Another alternative is to have someone else search the databases for you. Below is a listing of some information searching companies:

- Research on Demand (www. researchondemand.com)
- Business Research Services (www. marketingresearch.com/contact.htm)
- Infoscope (www.infoscope.com)

These services provide marketing and research reports usually for several hundred dollars or more. While this may seem like a lot of money, the search materials are usually worth the price and the results will enhance your ability to convince others to produce or invest in your invention. You can locate information searching companies on the Internet using search terms such as "business research services."

CAUTION

Before you spend a lot of money for a search conducted by others, ask for and check references. The sources you use should not only be reputable, but should be independently verifiable by anyone from whom you are seeking funds.

Splatter Shield for Paint Roller

D. How to Record Relevant Marketing Trend Data From These Types of Sources

NOTEBOOK

Appendix II: Worksheets contains three forms to record your research on relevant market trends:

- Regional Buying Patterns of Related Products
- Predictions for Targeted Buying Groups
- Conclusions Regarding Market Trends

There are three copies of each form to provide adequate room for more extensive surveys, or for the possibility of subsequent surveys for improved versions of your invention.

On the Regional Buying Patterns of Related Products form, you should enter information you have located for sales of related products by geographical region. Taking our bowling ball example, related products could be (A) bowling balls, (B) holograms, (C) high-tech recreation products, (D) celebrity paraphernalia, and (E) bowling lanes. The relevant geographic regions would most likely begin with your local area and proceed to state or regional comparisons, national surveys, and even, if appropriate, international markets.

The Predictions for Targeted Buying Groups form allows you to enter demographic information gleaned from your research. First, identify the potential purchaser groups that you think will account for the largest number of sales by Age, Sex, and Other. Then, for each group, look at their numbers as a percentage of the overall population in three promising market areas (regions). Also, take a look at the average disposable income of each group by region. For example, Group 1 may be those aged 13–18 of both sexes who bowl, while Group 2 may be identified in the Other category as owners of bowling alleys.

For Group 1, under "% of Population," you would want to record both the present and predicted percentage of the entire population for this group in each region. This category would be irrelevant for Group 2, since the percentage of bowling alley owners is negligible. Under "Disposable Income," you may want to record some data about the relative wealth of teenagers—this would bear on how much they have to spend on recreation. Your Group 2 data in this area might focus on such items as how much owners of bowling alleys spend annually replacing old balls and how much is spent on advertising to get more young people into bowling.

The Conclusions Regarding Marketing Trends form asks you to use the data entered in the first two parts to draw some conclusions about the market trends affecting your product. To see how this is done, let's again return to our example of the holographic bowling ball. You may have found that:

- the numbers of young people in the age groups you hope to sell your invention to are projected to decrease
- the relative buying power of these young people is rapidly rising relative to the population as a whole
- the sales of bowling balls and accessories are fairly steady
- money spent on teen idol "essentials" and futuristic toys is steadily climbing, and
- young people bowl in much larger numbers in the Southeast than the Midwest.

While the first finding is essentially negative from a marketability standpoint, the other findings are essentially positive. Make a written record of both the positive and negative results of your survey and how they may influence your marketing strategy. In your presentation to a venture capital source, you should point out the increase in disposable income and interest in holograms and stars, and that you have decided to introduce your new sensation in the Southeast with the idea of creating a fad that will bring more young people into bowling alleys across the country. If you can back up this marketing approach with some solid information, you have a much better chance of being listened to.

Regional Buying Patterns of Related Products

	Product Name	Source of Information	Sales for Last Year Surveyed	Sales Projected
Region:	_____	_____	_____	_____
Product A	_____	_____	_____	_____
Product B	_____	_____	_____	_____
Product C	_____	_____	_____	_____
Product D	_____	_____	_____	_____
Product E	_____	_____	_____	_____
Region:	_____	_____	_____	_____
Product A	_____	_____	_____	_____
Product B	_____	_____	_____	_____
Product C	_____	_____	_____	_____
Product D	_____	_____	_____	_____
Product E	_____	_____	_____	_____
Region:	_____	_____	_____	_____
Product A	_____	_____	_____	_____
Product B	_____	_____	_____	_____
Product C	_____	_____	_____	_____
Product D	_____	_____	_____	_____
Product E	_____	_____	_____	_____
Region:	_____	_____	_____	_____
Product A	_____	_____	_____	_____
Product B	_____	_____	_____	_____
Product C	_____	_____	_____	_____
Product D	_____	_____	_____	_____
Product E	_____	_____	_____	_____
Region:	_____	_____	_____	_____
Product A	_____	_____	_____	_____
Product B	_____	_____	_____	_____
Product C	_____	_____	_____	_____
Product D	_____	_____	_____	_____
Product E	_____	_____	_____	_____

Predictions for Targeted Buying Groups

Potential Purchasers	Age	Sex	Other	Predicted % of Sales
Group 1 _____	_____	___	_____	_____
Group 2 _____	_____	___	_____	_____
Group 3 _____	_____	___	_____	_____

Source of Information	Last Year Surveyed	Projected

GROUP 1

% of Population

Region 1		
Region 2		
Region 3		

Disposable Income

Region 1		
Region 2		
Region 3		

GROUP 2

% of Population

Region 1		
Region 2		
Region 3		

Disposable Income

Region 1		
Region 2		
Region 3		

GROUP 3

% of Population

Region 1		
Region 2		
Region 3		

Disposable Income

Region 1		
Region 2		
Region 3		

E. Manufacturer/Distributor Evaluation

RESOURCE
Patent It Yourself, Chapter 11

NOTEBOOK
The Inventor's Decision Chart in the introduction asks you to decide whether you want to manufacture your invention yourself, and if so, whether you also plan to handle its distribution. The Manufacturer/Distributor Evaluation forms in Appendix II: Worksheets help you organize the facts on which these decisions should ultimately be based.

F. Choosing the Right Company and Reaching the Decision Maker

If you decide to have someone else manufacture your invention, you need to decide which companies to approach. To do so efficiently:

- Choose companies that operate in your field, or in a related one.
- Consider size—depending on your product, you may want to deal with a small entrepreneurial outfit or a multinational corporation.
- Consider location—companies with headquarters close to you are usually easier to approach.
- Consider company attitudes and products—do you like the company and its products?
- Consider marketing—if your product will require a good deal of consumer education to succeed (for example, a machine that makes a cross between yogurt and peanut butter), will the company commit to a big advertising push or other long-term marketing technique that focuses on consumer education?

Companies can be researched in the same manner as products and services, either through the following written resources or in computer databases.

- *Thomas Register of American Manufacturers*
- *Dun and Bradstreet's Million Dollar Directory*
- *Standard and Poor's Index*
- *MacRae's Verified Directory of Manufacturers' Representatives*
- *Encyclopedia of Associations* (which alerts you to the trade associations and journals that relate your invention)
- *Science Citation Index* (for scientific/technical information), and
- *Business Periodical Index* (for business and finance information).

You can also locate information about companies using online business directories. There are various general business directories on the Internet, and your search engine should be capable of finding them. One website that may be helpful is BigYellow (www.bigyellow.com), the NYNEX business directory. It enables you to search by business category, name, street address, state, or zip code. Most online services have general business directories that perform the same functions. On America Online, consult the American Business Information (ABI) forum to locate companies based on name or industry.

Also helpful are database companies (sometimes known as mailing list or sales leads companies) that compile listings of millions of businesses. For a fee, they will supply you with a listing of all the companies within a particular industry. For example, if you had invented a device that improves air circulation in motor homes, a database company could supply you with a printed mailing list for 128 motor home manufacturers. You can find database companies in your local Yellow Pages, usually listed under "Mailing Lists." For an example of one such company located on the Internet, check out InfoUsa (www.infousa.com).

SIC Codes

Corporations that manufacture products utilize a system known as the Standard Industrial Classification Code (SIC). The SIC is a four-digit number created by the Department of Commerce and is used to classify a business by the type of work it does. For example, if you invented a product to be worn while handling explosives, you might review companies classified as 1795, which is the code for the Wrecking and Demolition Industry. If you invented a timer for video cameras, you would check companies classified as 3651 for Video Equipment and Household Audio. The SIC is helpful when searching, since most corporate directories, whether in print, digital, or online form, include an index of SIC codes.

Information about any given company can also be obtained through a professional search company, as with the marketing information discussed in Section C, above.

You are most likely to do well with smaller companies near enough to you so that you would have no difficulty making a visit to personally demonstrate the advantages of your invention. Choose a company that is in a similar product line and has the marketing, distribution, and advertising appropriate to sell your item. It is important to target companies that are doing well financially; even the simplest of ideas will require a substantial investment to bring to market.

The president of the company is whom you must reach, if at all possible. He or she knows where the company wants to go and if the resources are available to get there. Try phoning before or after normal business hours—presidents are in the office ten or more hours a day, if you are lucky enough to catch them in town. Give a brief listing of the advantages of your product and ask if you can send them your Proprietary Materials Agreement. If you have difficulty getting to the president, obtain an Annual Report and try contacting members of the Board of Directors or past or retired presidents.

The universal key to making a good living as an inventor is perseverance, but it doesn't hurt to work smart. For instance, when seeking out an appropriate company for your invention, you might be wise to attend one or two trade shows. The contacts you can make at these types of gatherings can get more done for you than weeks in a library.

NOTEBOOK
Record the results of your company research on the Choosing the Right Company worksheet in Appendix II: Worksheets.

G. Using the Internet to Develop and Promote Your Invention

As an inventor, you know that creativity is only part of what it takes to be successful. Technical, marketing, and legal knowledge, sources of financing, collaborators, or licensees are also needed to get the most for your efforts. The following websites have been selected specifically as starting points for inventors to explore for purposes of developing and promoting your invention. Remember, the Web is constantly changing, with websites coming and going every minute of every day. Additional sites and resources are provided in Chapter 5.

- **U. S. Patent and Trademark Office** (www.uspto.gov) includes extensive information on profiting from patents in its Independent Inventor Resources.
- **U.S. Small Business Administration** (www.sba.gov) provides thorough online guide for entrepreneurs and small companies.
- **The Institute of Management and Administration** (www.ioma.com) is a super site for business managers.
- **Patent Law Links** (www.patentlawlinks.com) provides links to everything "patent" on the Internet.

Financing

This chapter of *The Inventor's Notebook* helps you organize your search for funds to build and test, manufacture, and distribute your invention. First you need to create a budget so that you can arrive at several estimates of how much capital you are likely to need in the course of getting your invention out of your head and into the marketplace. The Checklist for Selling Invention/Seeking Capital walks you through the steps you should take before trying to sell the invention or before seeking funding to market it yourself. Finally, the Funding Sources and Results helps you to keep track of your funding and/or sales efforts.

A. Determination of Funds Needed

📖 RESOURCE
All I Need Is Money: How to Finance Your Invention, by Jack Lander (Nolo)

Some inventors have the luxury of being able to invent without worrying about who will pick up the tab. Most of us, however, must keep a close eye on our budgets. The Budget worksheet allows you to record cost estimates of your activities before initiating the building, testing, production, and marketing phases of your invention. The Budget contains headings that prompt you to categorize the expenses appropriate to your invention. This means that you may be using some parts of the Budget worksheet and not others. Because there is usually a range of possibilities for costs, we provide space for a high, low, and middle estimate. The documentation called for in this section will help you design an appropriate business plan for your invention to show to persons or organizations you are seeking capital from.

✏️ NOTEBOOK
We include three copies of the budget form in Appendix II: Worksheets. If you modify your invention after making one budget, you can fill out another sheet for the new version.

B. Checklist for Selling Invention/Seeking Capital

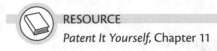

📖 RESOURCE
Patent It Yourself, Chapter 11

✏️ NOTEBOOK
A number of important steps must be taken before you are ready to present your invention to the world. The Checklist for Selling Invention/Seeking Capital in Appendix II: Worksheets provides space for you to keep track of these steps so that you can be equipped to make a thoroughly businesslike presentation when you approach potential buyers. The first page is a checklist of steps necessary to prepare you for the presentation of your invention to potential purchasers or investors. The second page will help you focus on the essential points you want to cover, prepare responses to any possible questions, and reflect on the results of a practice presentation (we recommend that you practice your presentation with an associate or friend prior to the real thing). Your entries here should be brief notes to serve as reminders rather than full-blown essays.

Two Additional Suggestions

One of the most surefire ways to raise money for a new idea is to get a significant number of purchase orders in hand. A good way to do this is to exhibit in one of the major trade shows in your product's industry. If you are going to do this, you should have your homework done—samples that work and have a professional finish, the proper legal protection for your idea, sales literature, attractive packaging, an awareness of who the buyers are for the major accounts you want to land, and the ability to deliver on the orders. If this event goes well, you will not only be able to obtain the financing you need—you may also receive offers from large companies to buy the rights to your invention.

Another way to substantiate the demand for your invention/product, and thereby increase the interest of investors, is from the responses generated by a press release in a national publication. Many magazines print news about new inventions or products. This does not cost you a thing other than the preparation of the materials you submit. Write to the individual publications for their guidelines on the preparation of press releases. Make sure that any photos you submit are of professional quality.

C. Funding Sources and Results

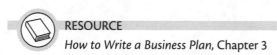

RESOURCE

How to Write a Business Plan, Chapter 3

NOTEBOOK

As you know, funding can come from many different sources (with their attendant pluses and minuses), and it is likely to take more than one try to obtain the money you need. Make a record of those you contact and their response on the Funding Sources and Results in Appendix II: Worksheets. If their reply is positive, note how much money they committed; if negative, why they turned you down. This will give you a current assessment of how much more you need to ask for, and may prompt you to make changes in your method of presentation.

Help Beyond This Book

Throughout this notebook we have suggested specific outside readings for each section. This chapter is designed to help you find additional resources that can extend your understanding of issues addressed in this book, and help you answer questions and address issues not covered by this book.

In Section A, we direct you to sources for more information for inventors. In Section B, we provide additional resources on patents and intellectual property law.

A. Inventor Resources

The following is a list of inventor resources, including organizations, bookstores, and websites with special information on patents and other intellectual property issues:

- **Inventor's Bookstore** (www.inventorhelp.com). The Inventor's Bookstore offers condensed reports and other guidance for inventors.
- **Inventors' Digest** (www.inventorsdigest.com). The *Inventors' Digest* and its accompanying website publish information for independent inventors at a subscription rate of $27/year for six issues. It includes articles on new inventions, licensing and marketing, and advertisements from reputable inventor promotion companies.
- **National Inventor Fraud Center** (www. inventorfraud.com). This organization reports on fraud by invention marketing companies.
- **National Technology Transfer Center (NTTC)** (www.nttc.edu). The NTTC at Wheeling Jesuit University helps entrepreneurs and companies looking to access federally funded research and development activity at American universities. Write to 316 Washington Avenue, Wheeling, WV 26003. Phone: 800-678-6882. Fax: 304-243-4388. Email: technology@nttc.edu.
- **Ronald J. Riley's Inventor Resources** (www. inventored.org). This website provides comprehensive links and advice for inventors.
- **Source Translation and Optimization Patent Website** (www.bustpatents.com). A source of information on questionable patents and

patent practices by one of the PTO's most vocal critics. Also offers a free newsletter.
- **United Inventors Association (UIA)** (www. uiausa.org). A national inventor's organization. Write to P.O. Box 23447, Rochester, NY 14692-3347. Phone: 716-359-9310. Fax: 716-359-1132. Email: UIAUSA@aol.com.

B. Patent and Intellectual Property Resources

Provided below are some additional sources of information on patent and intellectual property law. Many of these sources are accessible through the Internet.

1. Nolo Books on Intellectual Property

There is a world of intellectual property law beyond patents. If you are interested in understanding other principles of intellectual property law that may apply to your invention, Nolo, the publisher of this book, also publishes a number of other titles on intellectual property, including:

- *All I Need Is Money: How to Finance Your Invention,* by Jack Lander
- *How to Make Patent Drawings,* by Jack Lo and David Pressman
- *Nolo's Patents for Beginners,* by David Pressman and Richard Stim
- *Patent Pending in 24 Hours,* by Richard Stim and David Pressman
- *Patent Savvy for Managers,* by Kirk Teska
- *Patent, Copyright & Trademark,* by Richard Stim
- *Profit From Your Idea,* by Richard Stim
- *The Copyright Handbook,* by Stephen Fishman
- *What Every Inventor Needs to Know About Business & Taxes,* by Stephen Fishman
- *The Public Domain,* by Stephen Fishman
- *Trademark: Legal Care for Your Business & Product Name,* by Richard Stim and Stephen Elias
- *Legal Guide to Web & Software Development,* by Stephen Fishman

2. Additional Intellectual Property Resources

- **U.S. Copyright Office** (www.copyright .gov). The Copyright Office has numerous circulars, kits, and other publications that can help you, including one on searching copyright records. These publications and application forms can be obtained by writing to the Copyright Office at Publications Section, LM-455, Copyright Office, Library of Congress, Washington, DC 20559. Most Copyright Office publications can be downloaded at www.loc. gov/copyright. Frequently requested circulars and announcements are also available via the Copyright Office's fax-on-demand telephone line at 202-707-9100.

- **Findlaw** (www.findlaw.com). Findlaw is the highest-trafficked legal website, providing legal resources including cases and codes, legal news, an online career center, and community-oriented tools, such as a secure document management utility, mailing lists, and message boards.

- **Government Printing Office** (www.access.gpo. gov/#info). The Government Printing Office website is a searchable source for U.S. Code of Federal Regulations, *Congressional Record,* and other Government Printing Office products and information.

- **Intellectual Property Mall** (www.ipmall.fplc. edu). Franklin Pierce Law Center's Intellectual Mall provides IP links and information.

- **Internet Patent News Service** (www. bustpatents.com). The Internet Patent News Service is a source for patent news, information about searching, and patent documents.

- **Legal Information Institute** (http://lii.law. cornell.edu). The Legal Information Institute provides intellectual property links and downloadable copies of statutes and cases.

- **U.S. Patent & Trademark Office (PTO): Patent Information** (www.uspto.gov). The PTO website offers a number of informational pamphlets. There is also an alphabetical and geographical listing of patent attorneys and agents registered to practice before the PTO ("Directory of Registered Patent Attorneys and Agents Arranged by States and Countries"). The PTO also has an online searchable database of patent abstracts (short summaries of patents). For purposes of patent searching, this database is an excellent and inexpensive first step in the searching procedure. Most patent forms can be downloaded from the PTO website as well as many important publications, including *General Information About Patents, Manual of Patent Examining Procedures,* and *Guidelines for Computer-Related Inventions.* A PTO products and services catalog is also available. Phone: 800-PTO-9199.

- **Trade Secrets Home Page.** NDAS for Free (www.ndasforfree.com) provides trade secret information and free copies of nondisclosure agreements along with detailed explanations.

- **U.S. Patent & Trademark Office (PTO): Trademark Information.** Trademarks are examined and registered by a division of the PTO. *General Information About Trademarks,* an introductory pamphlet about trademarks, and other information about the operations of the Patent and Trademark Office, is available from the Superintendent of Documents, Government Printing Office, Washington, DC 20402, or from the PTO's website at www. uspto.gov. This site also includes the relevant applications and trademark office forms. You can also write to the Commissioner for Trademarks, 2900 Crystal Drive, Arlington, VA 22202-3515.

- **U.S. Code** (http://uscode.house.gov/search/ criteria.shtml). This website is a source for the United States Code, which includes copyright, trademark, and patent laws.

- **Yahoo Intellectual Property Directory** (www. yahoo.com/Government/Law/Intellectual_ Property). The Yahoo Intellectual Property Directory is a thorough listing of intellectual property resources on the Internet.

- *The PCT Applicant's Guide.* This brochure on how to utilize the PCT is available for free from the PCT Department of the U.S. Patent & Trademark Office. PCT information and software for facilitating completion of the PCT forms is available through the PCT's website (www.wipo.int). It is also available from the World Intellectual Property Organization (WIPO), Post Office Box 18, 1211 Geneva 20, Switzerland.

RESOURCE

Nolo's website (www.nolo.com) also offers an extensive Legal Encyclopedia that includes a section on intellectual property. You'll find answers to frequently asked questions about patents, copyrights, trademarks, and other related topics, as well as sample chapters of Nolo books and a wide range of articles.

Notebook

Record of Conception of Invention

Title of invention:

_____

_____

Circumstances of conception:

_____

_____

_____

_____

_____

_____

_____

_____

_____

_____

_____

_____

Purpose or problem solved:

_____

_____

_____

_____

_____

_____

_____

_____

_____

_____

_____

Invented by: _____ Date: _____

Invented by: _____ Date: _____

The above confidential information is witnessed and understood by:

_____ Date: _____

_____ Date: _____

Record of Conception of Invention

Description and operation:

_____

_____

_____

_____

_____

_____

_____

_____

_____

_____

_____

_____

_____

_____

_____

_____

_____

_____

_____

_____

_____

_____

_____

_____

Invented by: _____ Date: _____

Invented by: _____ Date: _____

The above confidential information is witnessed and understood by:

_____ Date: _____

_____ Date: _____

Record of Conception of Invention

Description and operation:

_____

_____

_____

_____

_____

_____

_____

_____

_____

_____

_____

_____

_____

_____

_____

_____

_____

_____

_____

_____

_____

_____

_____

_____

_____

_____

_____

_____

Invented by: _____ Date: _____

Invented by: _____ Date: _____

The above confidential information is witnessed and understood by:

_____ Date: _____

_____ Date: _____

Record of Conception of Invention

Description and operation:

_____

_____

_____

_____

_____

_____

_____

_____

_____

_____

_____

_____

_____

_____

_____

_____

_____

_____

_____

_____

_____

_____

_____

_____

_____

Invented by: _____ Date: _____

Invented by: _____ Date: _____

The above confidential information is witnessed and understood by:

_____ Date: _____

_____ Date: _____

Record of Conception of Invention

Drawing:

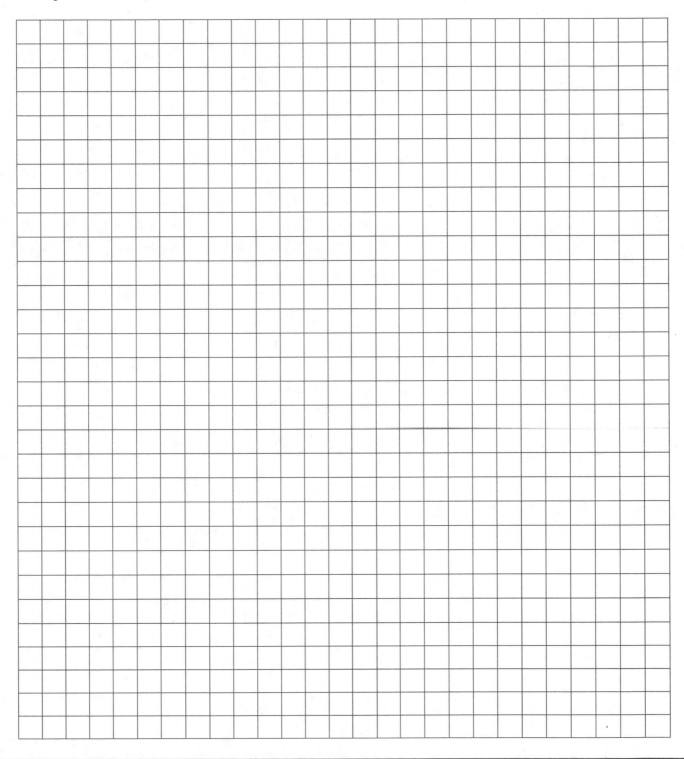

Invented by: _____ Date: _____

Invented by: _____ Date: _____

The above confidential information is witnessed and understood by:

_____ Date: _____

_____ Date: _____

Record of Conception of Invention

Drawing:

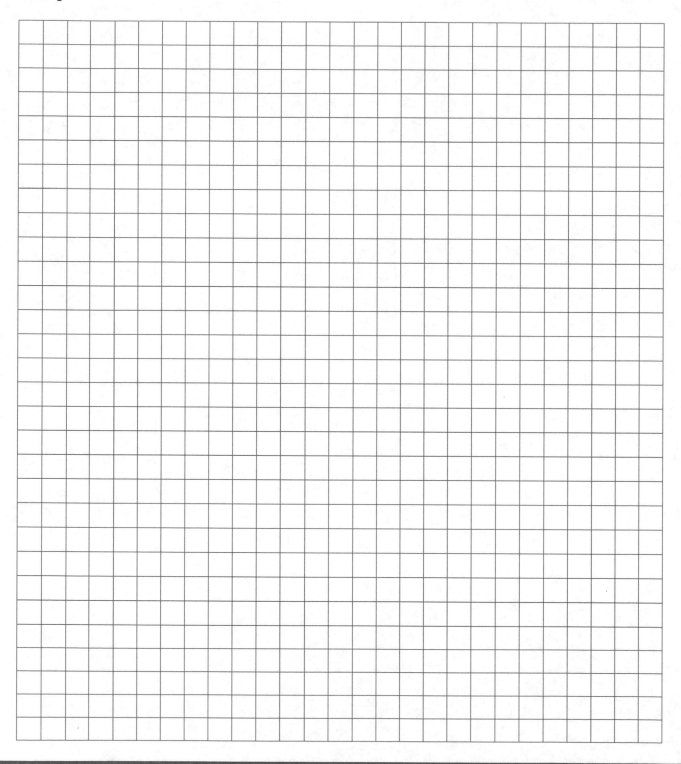

Invented by: _____ Date: _____

Invented by: _____ Date: _____

The above confidential information is witnessed and understood by:

_____ Date: _____

_____ Date: _____

Record of Conception of Invention

Drawing:

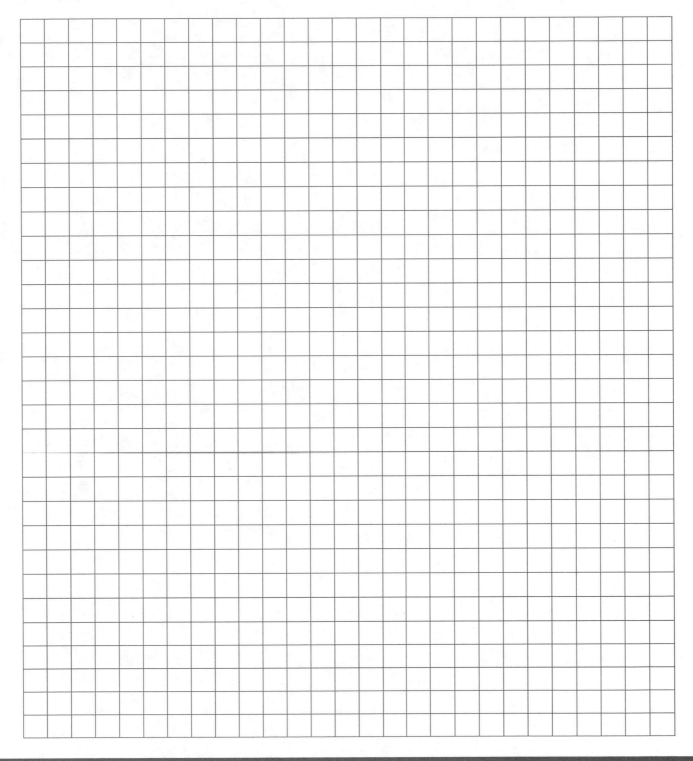

Invented by: _____   Date: _____

Invented by: _____   Date: _____

The above confidential information is witnessed and understood by:

_____   Date: _____

_____   Date: _____

Record of Conception of Invention

Drawing:

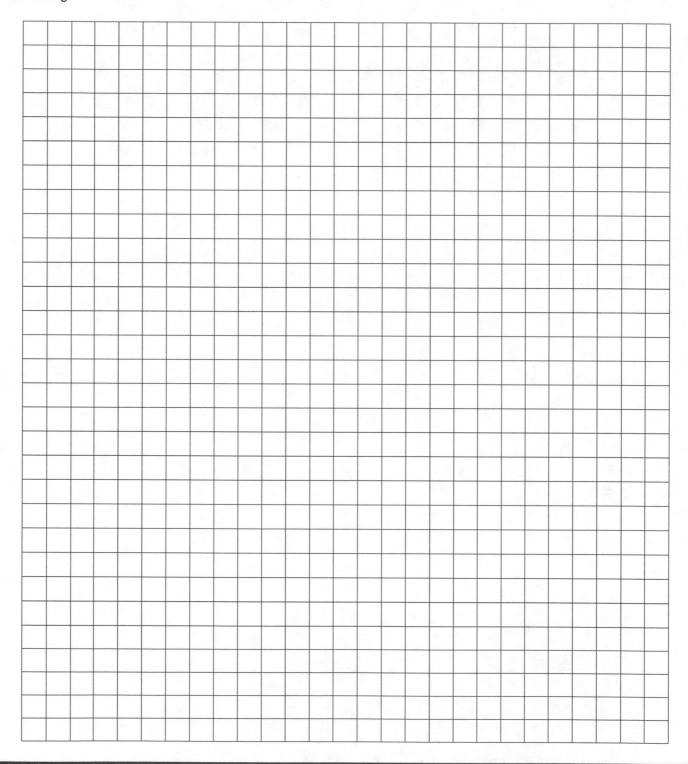

Invented by: _____ Date: _____

Invented by: _____ Date: _____

The above confidential information is witnessed and understood by:

_____ Date: _____

_____ Date: _____

Record of Conception of Invention

Drawing:

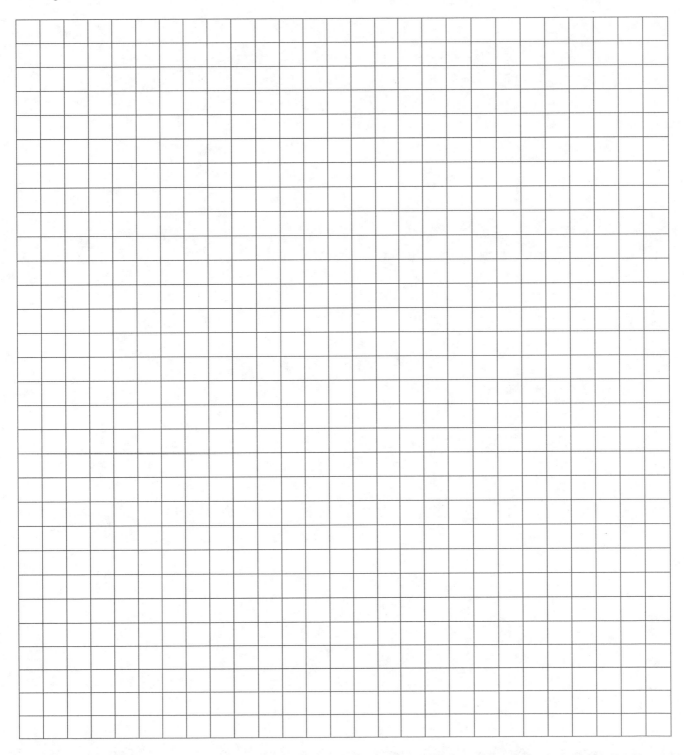

Invented by: _____ Date: _____

Invented by: _____ Date: _____

The above confidential information is witnessed and understood by:

_____ Date: _____

_____ Date: _____

Record of Conception of Invention

Drawing:

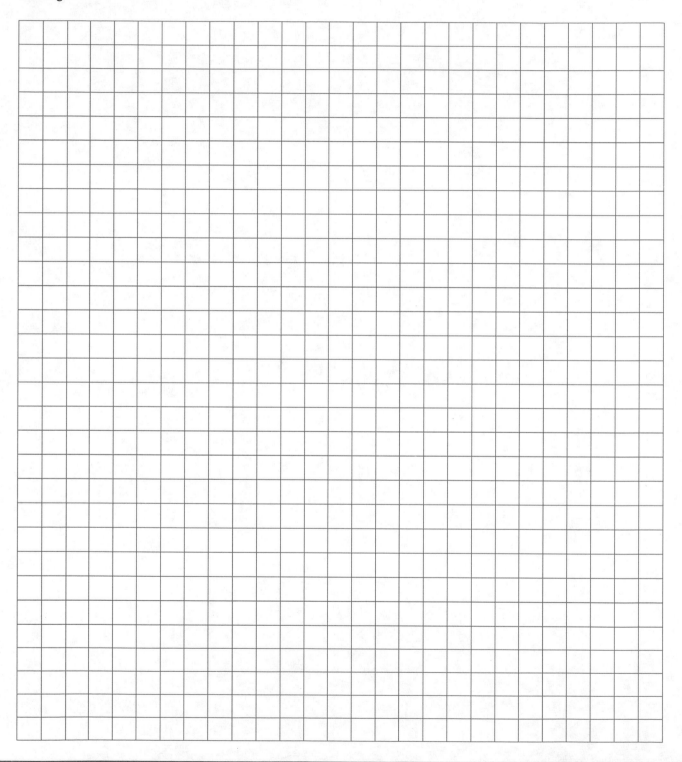

Invented by: _____ Date: _____

Invented by: _____ Date: _____

The above confidential information is witnessed and understood by:

_____ Date: _____

_____ Date: _____

Record of Conception of Invention

Drawing:

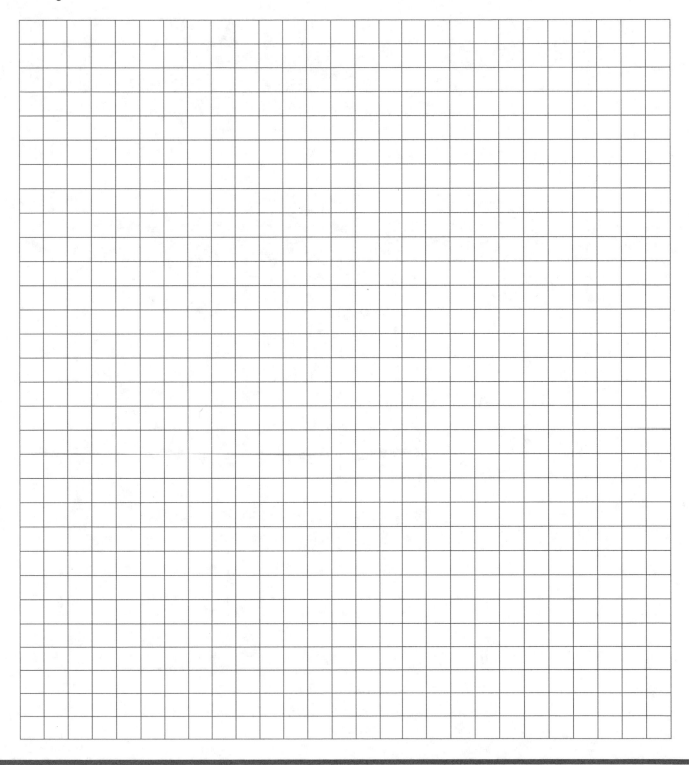

Invented by: _____ Date: _____

Invented by: _____ Date: _____

The above confidential information is witnessed and understood by:

_____ Date: _____

_____ Date: _____

Record of Conception of Invention

Drawing:

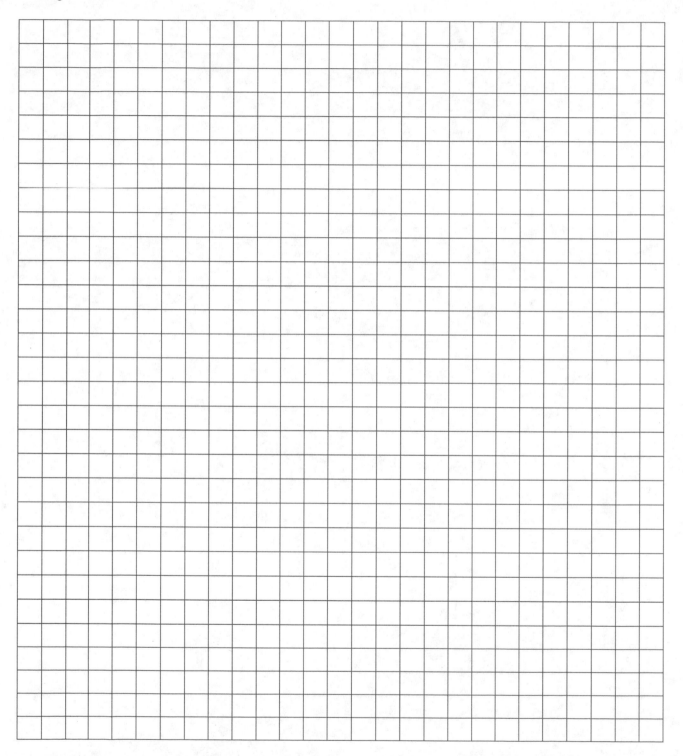

Invented by: _____ Date: _____

Invented by: _____ Date: _____

The above confidential information is witnessed and understood by:

_____ Date: _____

_____ Date: _____

Record of Conception of Invention

Drawing:

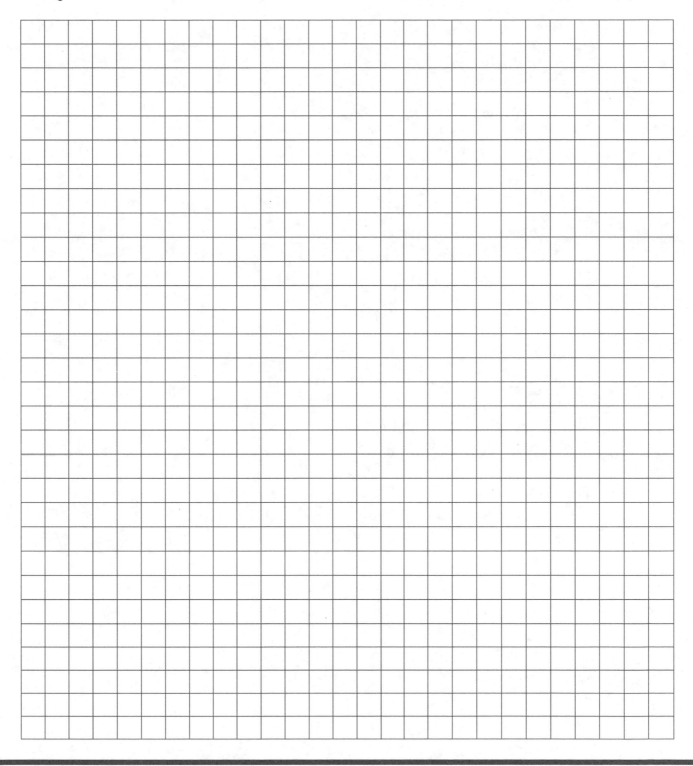

Invented by: _____ Date: _____

Invented by: _____ Date: _____

The above confidential information is witnessed and understood by:

_____ Date: _____

_____ Date: _____

Record of Conception of Invention

Drawing:

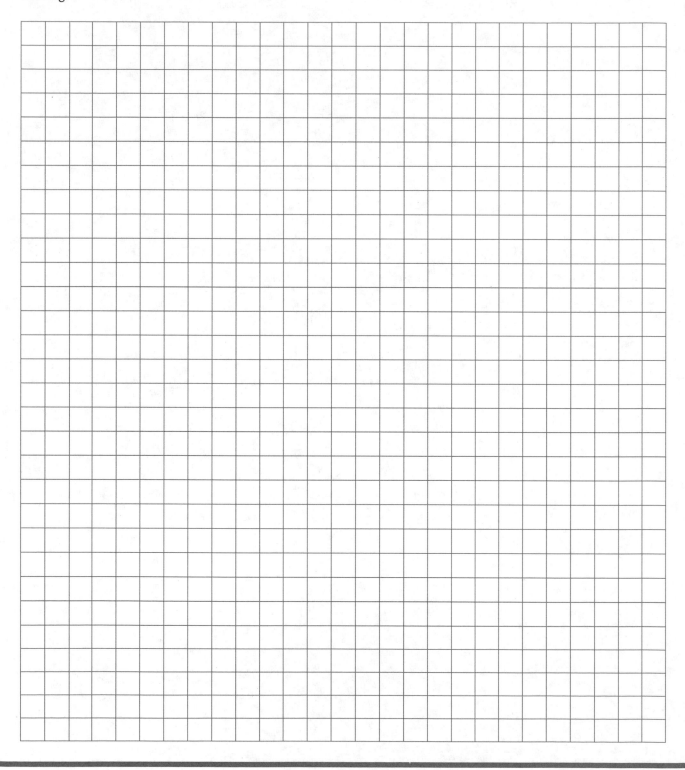

Invented by: _____ Date: _____

Invented by: _____ Date: _____

The above confidential information is witnessed and understood by:

_____ Date: _____

_____ Date: _____

Record of Conception of Invention

Drawing:

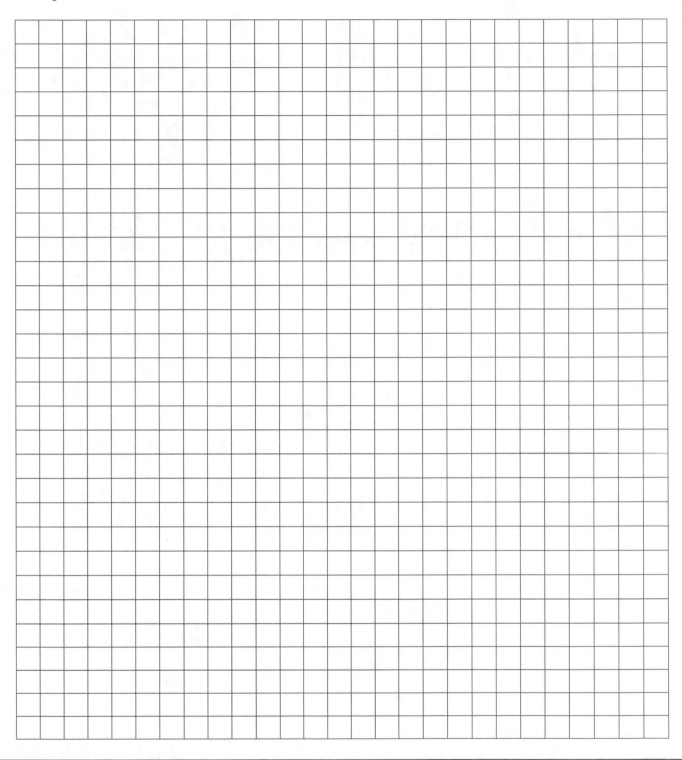

Invented by: _____ Date: _____

Invented by: _____ Date: _____

The above confidential information is witnessed and understood by:

_____ Date: _____

_____ Date: _____

Record of Conception of Invention

Drawing:

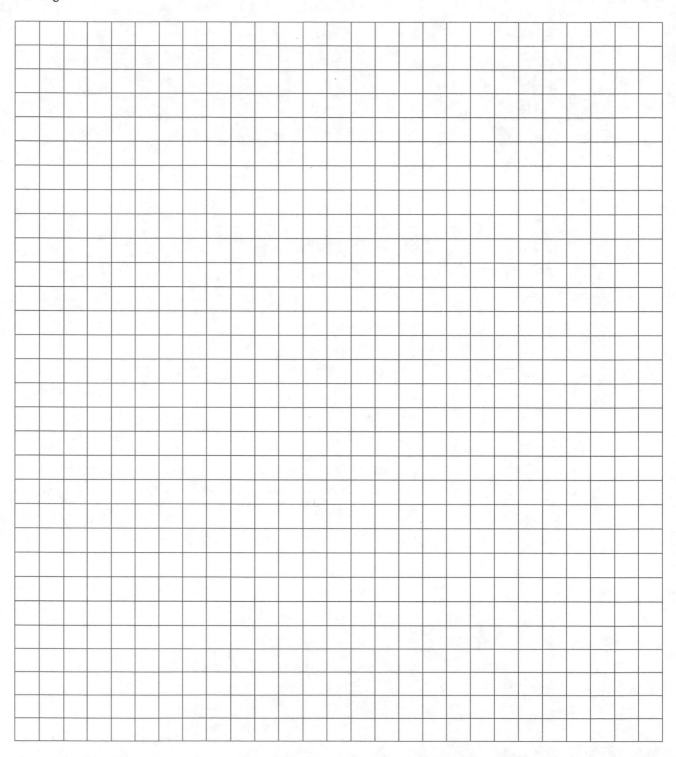

Invented by: _____ Date: _____

Invented by: _____ Date: _____

The above confidential information is witnessed and understood by:

_____ Date: _____

_____ Date: _____

Record of Conception of Invention

Drawing:

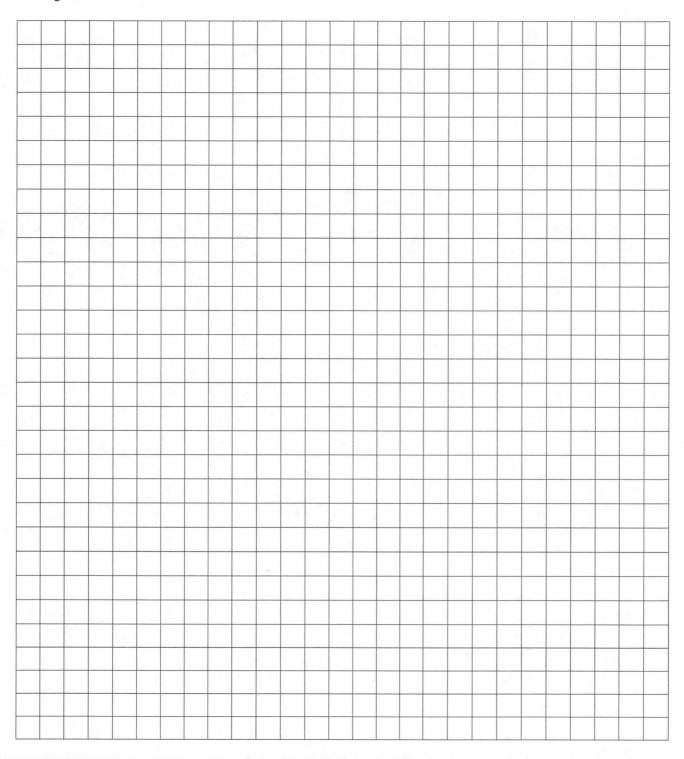

Invented by: _____ Date: _____

Invented by: _____ Date: _____

The above confidential information is witnessed and understood by:

_____ Date: _____

_____ Date: _____

Record of Conception of Invention

Drawing:

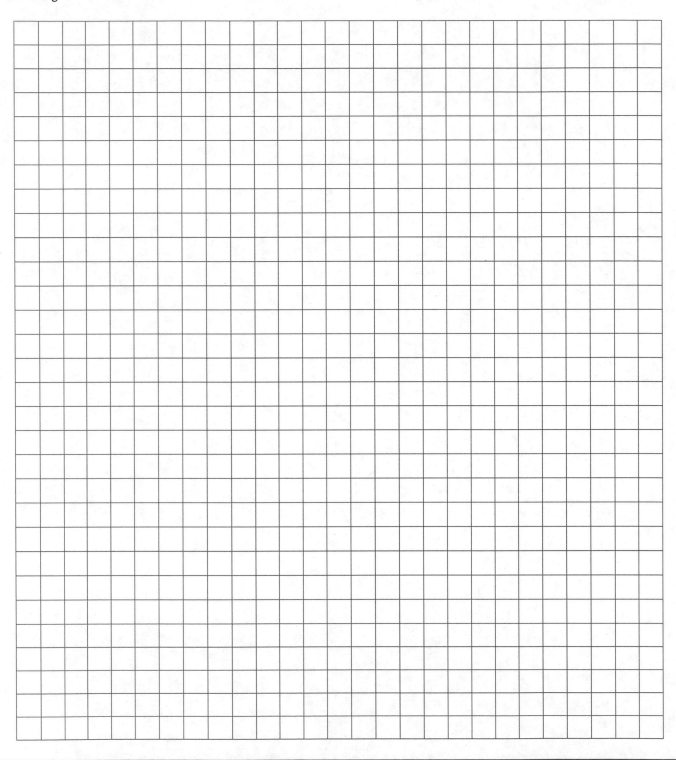

Invented by: _____ Date: _____

Invented by: _____ Date: _____

The above confidential information is witnessed and understood by:

_____ Date: _____

_____ Date: _____

Record of Conception of Invention

Ramifications:

_____

_____

_____

_____

_____

Novel features:

_____

_____

_____

_____

_____

_____

Closest known prior art:

_____

_____

_____

_____

_____

Advantages of my invention:

_____

_____

_____

_____

_____

_____

_____

_____

Invented by: _____ Date: _____

Invented by: _____ Date: _____

The above confidential information is witnessed and understood by:

_____ Date: _____

_____ Date: _____

Record of Conception of Invention

Additional conceptions and ramifications:

_____
_____
_____
_____
_____
_____
_____
_____
_____
_____
_____
_____
_____
_____
_____
_____
_____
_____
_____
_____
_____
_____
_____
_____
_____
_____
_____
_____
_____
_____
_____

Invented by: _____ Date: _____

Invented by: _____ Date: _____

The above confidential information is witnessed and understood by:

_____ Date: _____

Date: _____

Record of Conception of Invention

Additional conceptions and ramifications:

_____

_____

_____

_____

_____

_____

_____

_____

_____

_____

_____

_____

_____

_____

_____

_____

_____

_____

_____

_____

_____

_____

_____

_____

_____

_____

_____

_____

_____

_____

_____

_____

_____

Invented by: _____ Date: _____

Invented by: _____ Date: _____

The above confidential information is witnessed and understood by:

_____ Date: _____

_____ Date: _____

Record of Conception of Invention

Additional conceptions and ramifications:

_____

_____

_____

_____

_____

_____

_____

_____

_____

_____

_____

_____

_____

_____

_____

_____

_____

_____

_____

_____

_____

_____

_____

_____

_____

_____

_____

_____

_____

_____

_____

_____

Invented by: _____ Date: _____

Invented by: _____ Date: _____

The above confidential information is witnessed and understood by:

_____ Date: _____

_____ Date: _____

Record of Building and Testing of Invention

Drawing:

Invented by: _____ Date: _____

Invented by: _____ Date: _____

The above confidential information is witnessed and understood by:

_____ Date: _____

_____ Date: _____

Record of Building and Testing of Invention

Drawing:

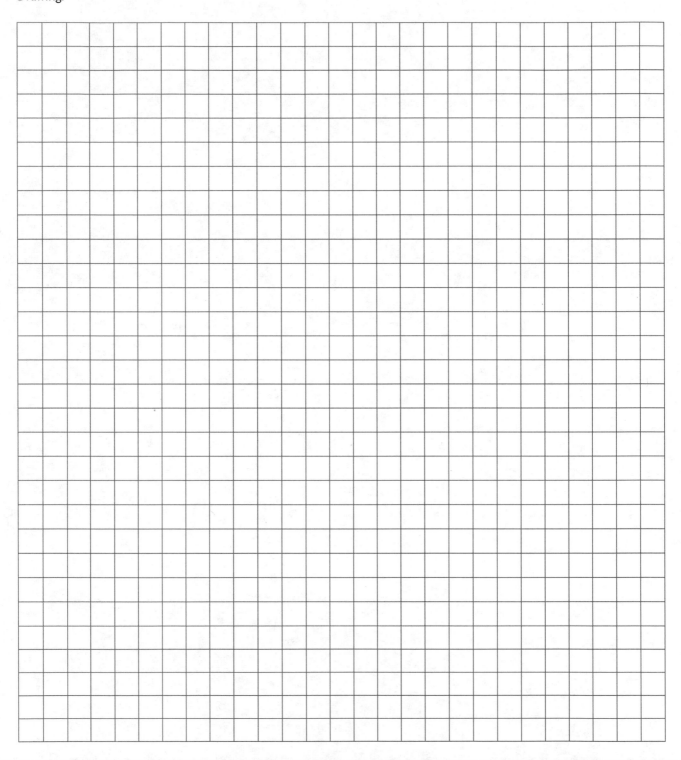

Invented by: _____ Date: _____

Invented by: _____ Date: _____

The above confidential information is witnessed and understood by:

_____ Date: _____

_____ Date: _____

Record of Building and Testing of Invention

Drawing:

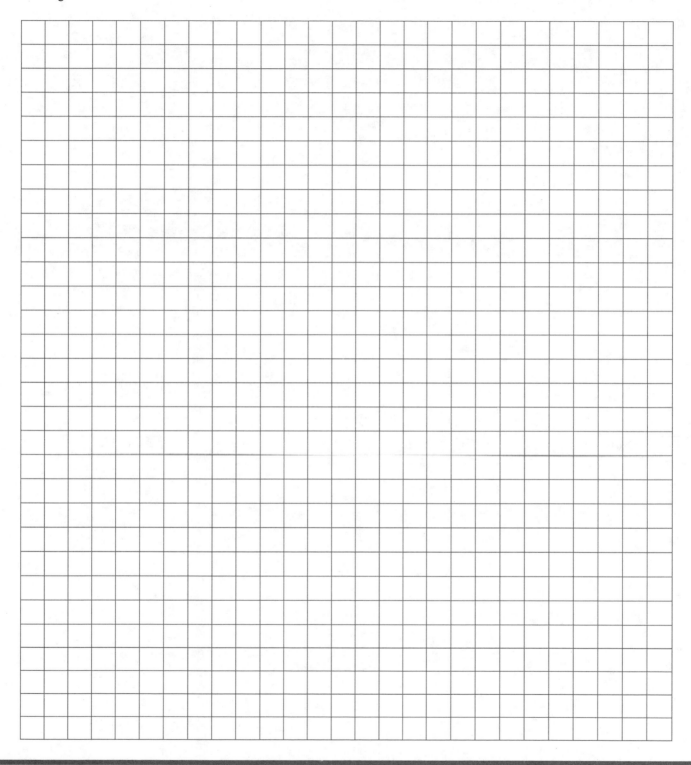

Invented by: _____ Date: _____

Invented by: _____ Date: _____

The above confidential information is witnessed and understood by:

_____ Date: _____

_____ Date: _____

Record of Building and Testing of Invention

Drawing:

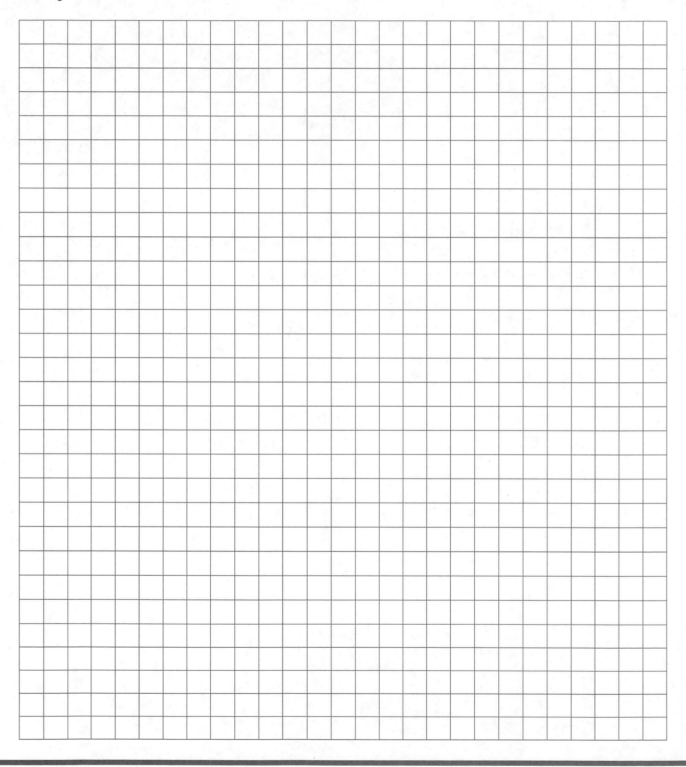

Invented by: _____ Date: _____

Invented by: _____ Date: _____

The above confidential information is witnessed and understood by:

_____ Date: _____

_____ Date: _____

Record of Building and Testing of Invention

Drawing:

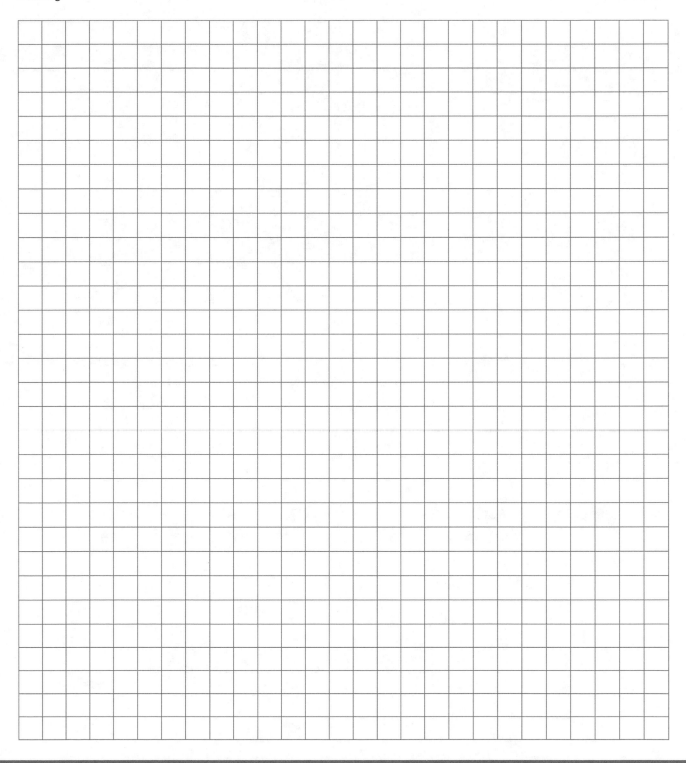

Invented by: _____ Date: _____

Invented by: _____ Date: _____

The above confidential information is witnessed and understood by:

_____ Date: _____

_____ Date: _____

Record of Building and Testing of Invention

Drawing:

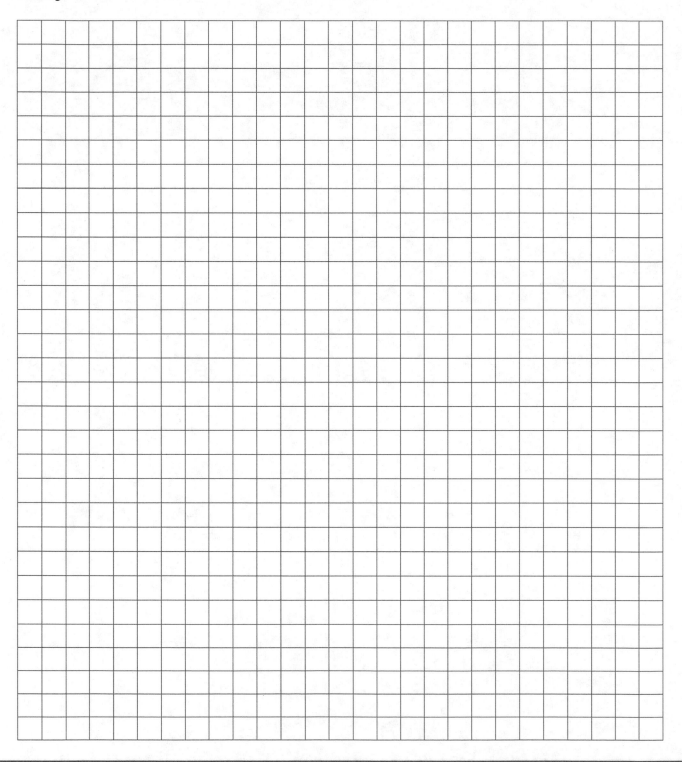

Invented by: _____ Date: _____

Invented by: _____ Date: _____

The above confidential information is witnessed and understood by:

_____ Date: _____

_____ Date: _____

Record of Building and Testing of Invention

Drawing:

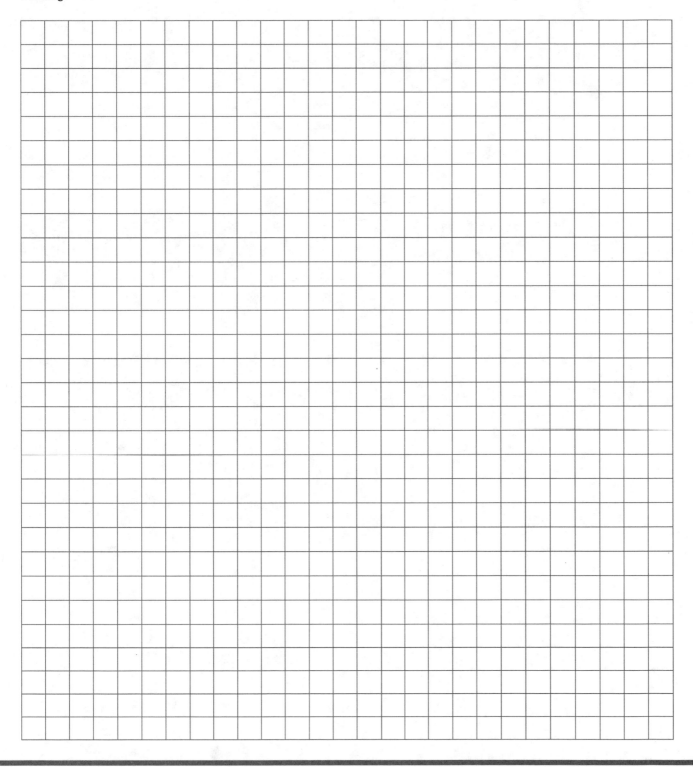

Invented by: _____ Date: _____

Invented by: _____ Date: _____

The above confidential information is witnessed and understood by:

_____ Date: _____

_____ Date: _____

Record of Building and Testing of Invention

Drawing:

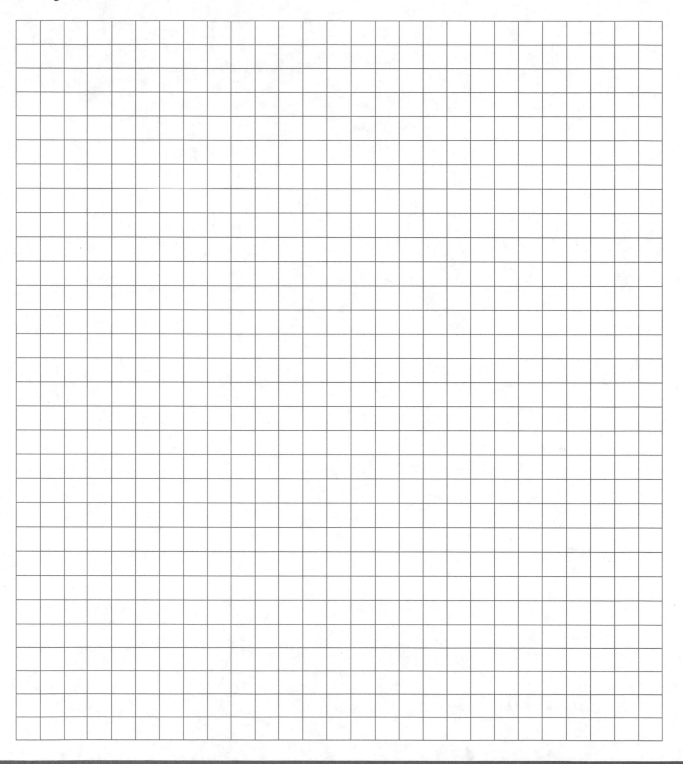

Invented by: _____ Date: _____

Invented by: _____ Date: _____

The above confidential information is witnessed and understood by:

_____ Date: _____

_____ Date: _____

Record of Building and Testing of Invention

Drawing:

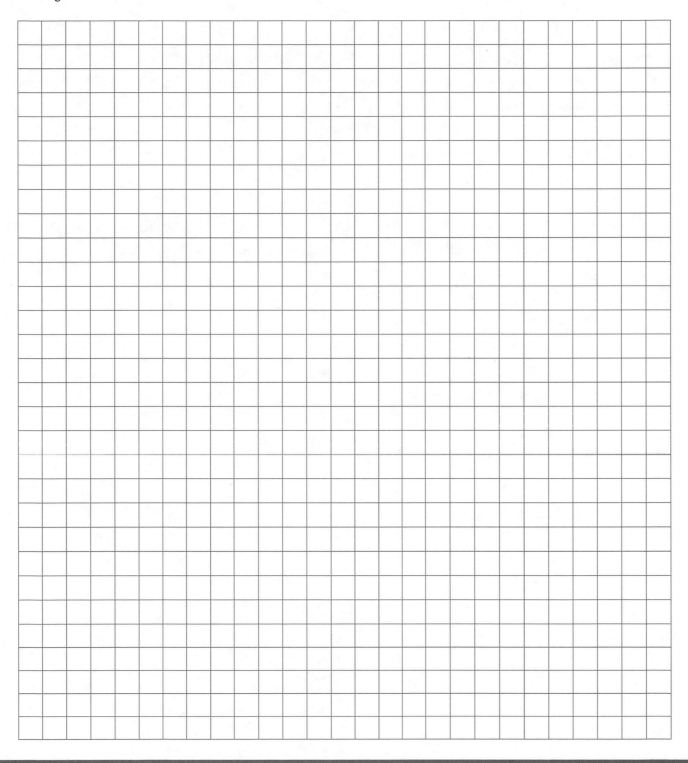

Invented by: _____ Date: _____

Invented by: _____ Date: _____

The above confidential information is witnessed and understood by:

_____ Date: _____

_____ Date: _____

Record of Building and Testing of Invention

Drawing:

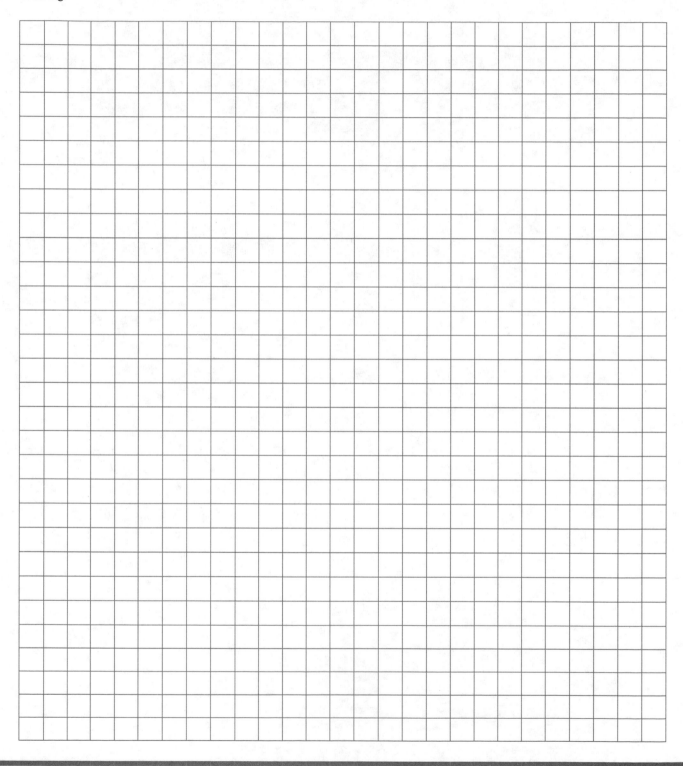

Invented by: _____   Date: _____

Invented by: _____   Date: _____

The above confidential information is witnessed and understood by:

_____   Date: _____

_____   Date: _____

Record of Building and Testing of Invention

Drawing:

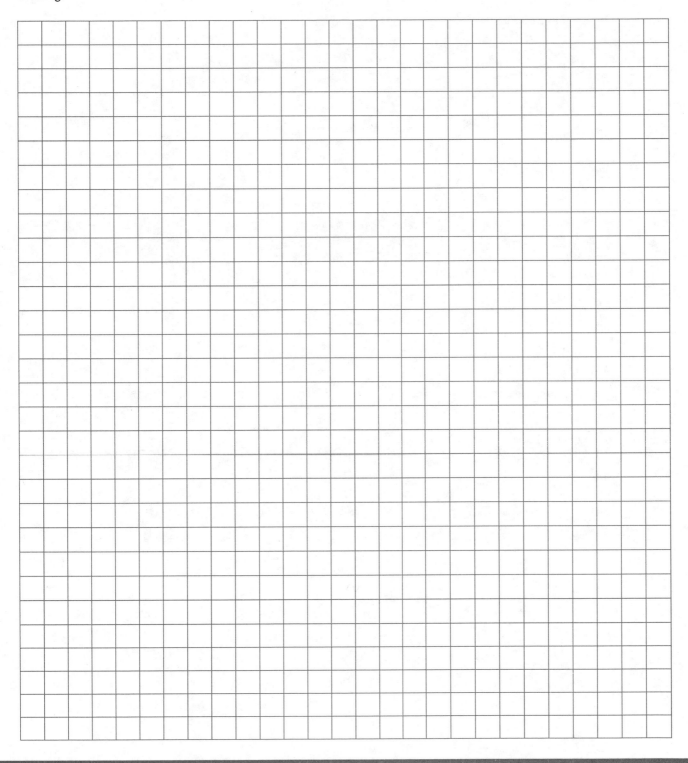

Invented by: _____ Date: _____

Invented by: _____ Date: _____

The above confidential information is witnessed and understood by:

_____ Date: _____

_____ Date: _____

Record of Building and Testing of Invention

Drawing:

Invented by: _____ Date: _____

Invented by: _____ Date: _____

The above confidential information is witnessed and understood by:

_____ Date: _____

_____ Date: _____

Record of Building and Testing of Invention

Drawing:

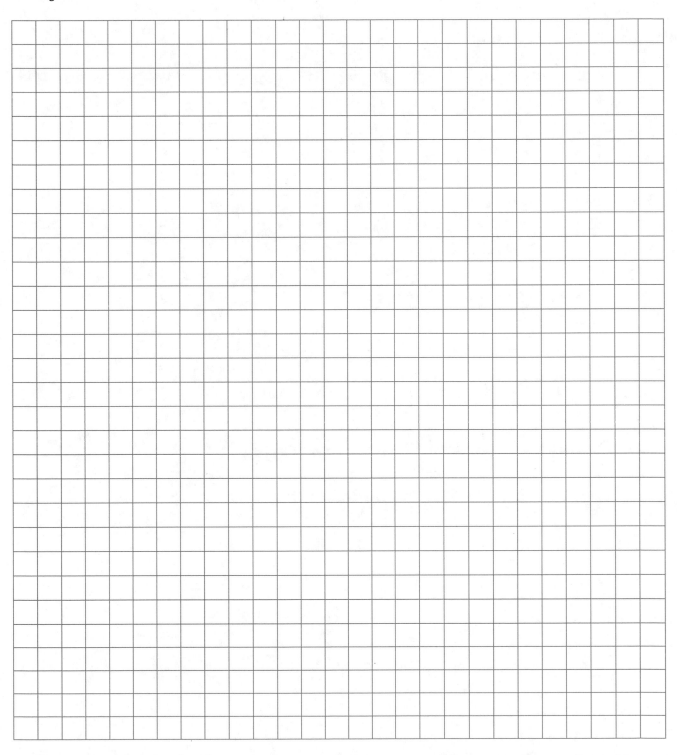

Invented by: _____ Date: _____

Invented by: _____ Date: _____

The above confidential information is witnessed and understood by:

_____ Date: _____

_____ Date: _____

Record of Building and Testing of Invention

Drawing:

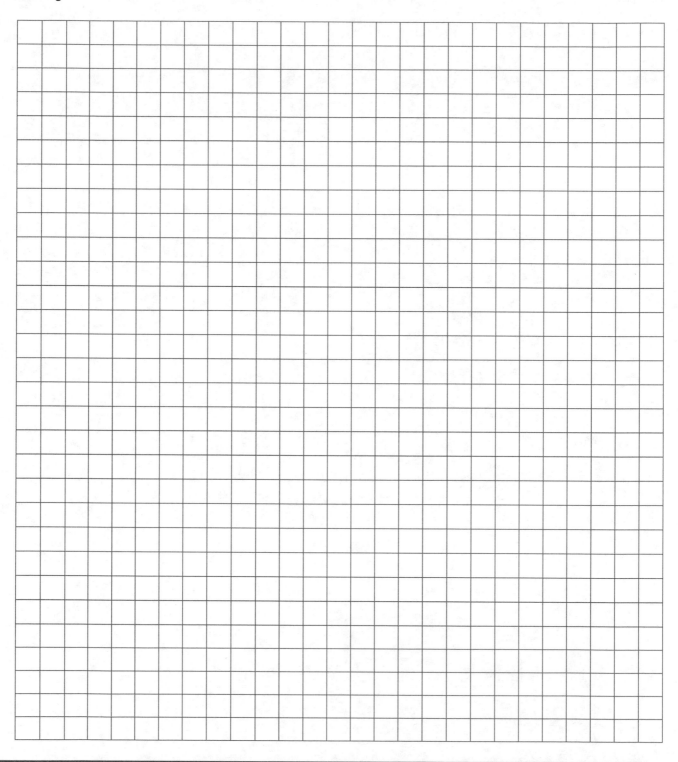

Invented by: _____ Date: _____

Invented by: _____ Date: _____

The above confidential information is witnessed and understood by:

_____ Date: _____

_____ Date: _____

Record of Building and Testing of Invention

Drawing:

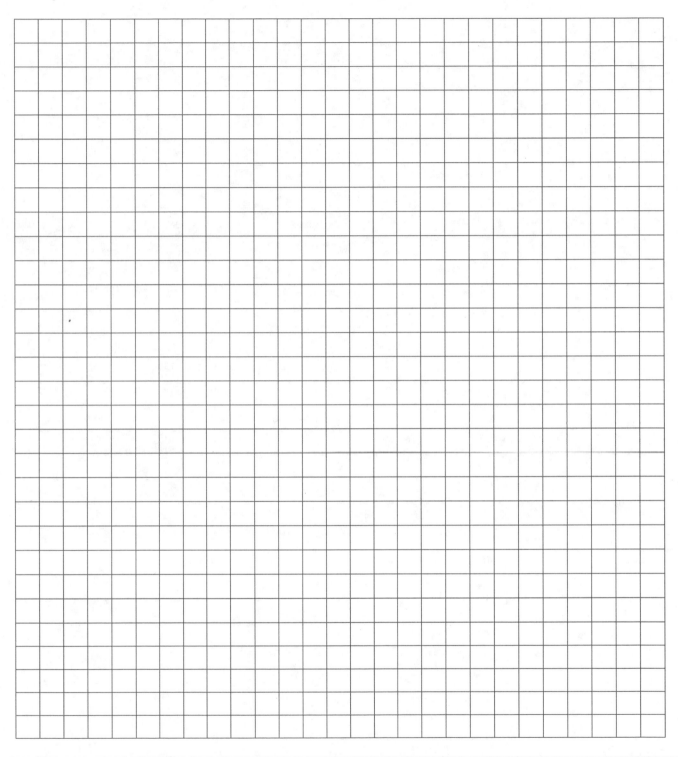

Invented by: _____ Date: _____

Invented by: _____ Date: _____

The above confidential information is witnessed and understood by:

_____ Date: _____

_____ Date: _____

Record of Building and Testing of Invention

Drawing:

Invented by: _____ Date: _____

Invented by: _____ Date: _____

The above confidential information is witnessed and understood by:

_____ Date: _____

_____ Date: _____

Record of Building and Testing of Invention

Drawing:

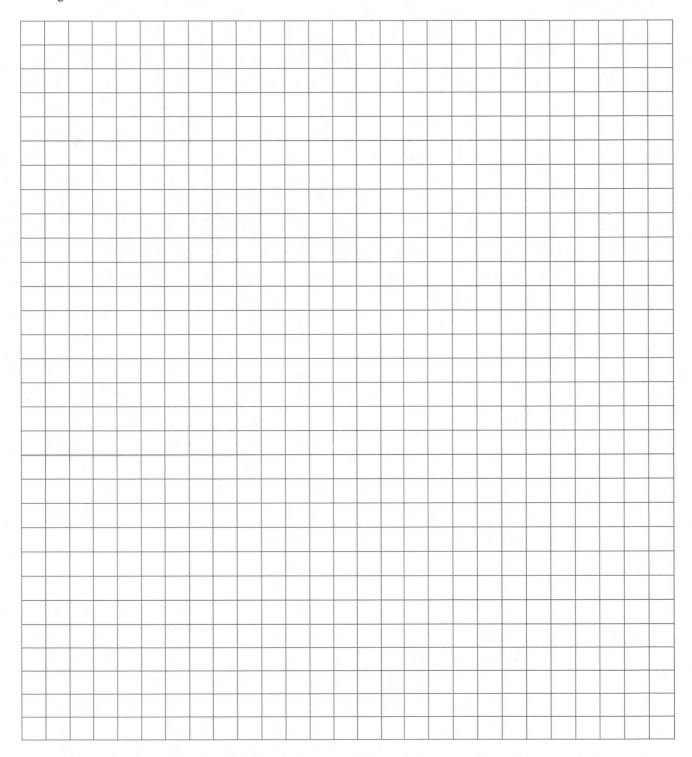

Invented by: _____ Date: _____

Invented by: _____ Date: _____

The above confidential information is witnessed and understood by:

_____ Date: _____

_____ Date: _____

Record of Building and Testing of Invention

Drawing:

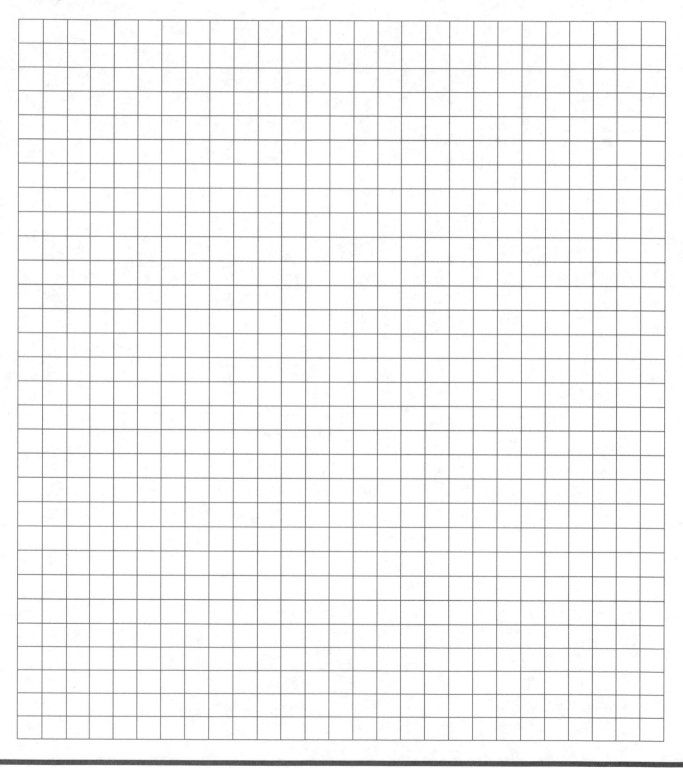

Invented by: _____ Date: _____

Invented by: _____ Date: _____

The above confidential information is witnessed and understood by:

_____ Date: _____

_____ Date: _____

Record of Building and Testing of Invention

Drawing:

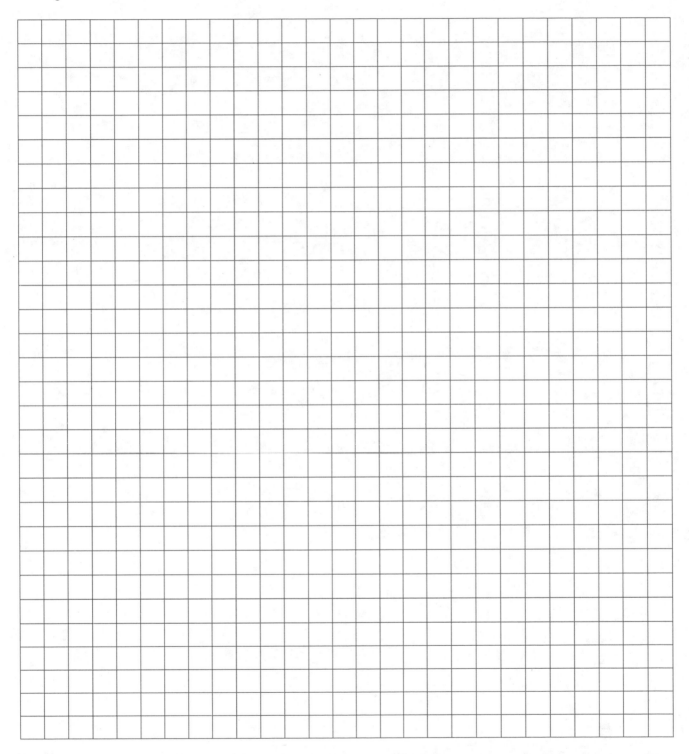

Invented by: _____ Date: _____

Invented by: _____ Date: _____

The above confidential information is witnessed and understood by:

_____ Date: _____

_____ Date: _____

Record of Building and Testing of Invention

Drawing:

Invented by: _____ Date: _____

Invented by: _____ Date: _____

The above confidential information is witnessed and understood by:

_____ Date: _____

_____ Date: _____

Record of Building and Testing of Invention

Drawing:

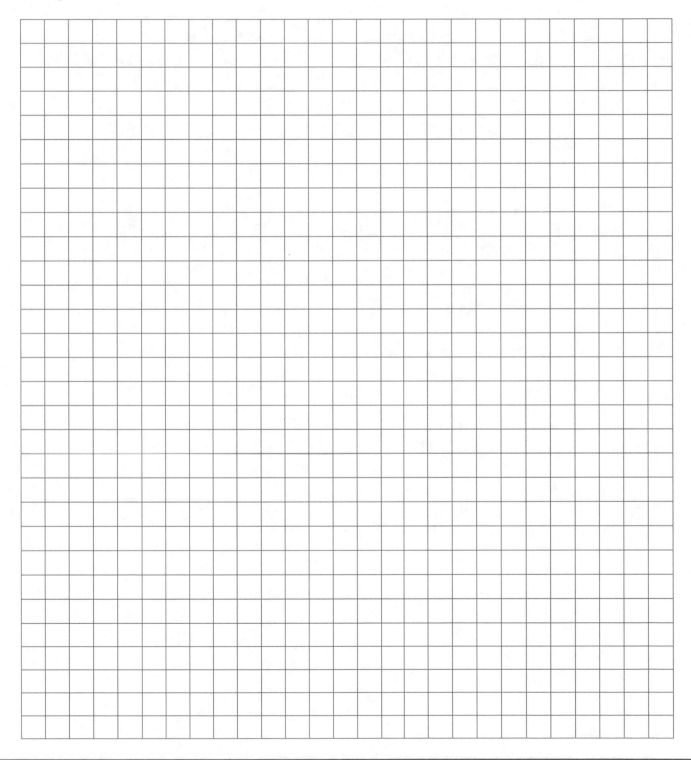

Invented by: _____ Date: _____

Invented by: _____ Date: _____

The above confidential information is witnessed and understood by:

_____ Date: _____

_____ Date: _____

Record of Building and Testing of Invention

Drawing:

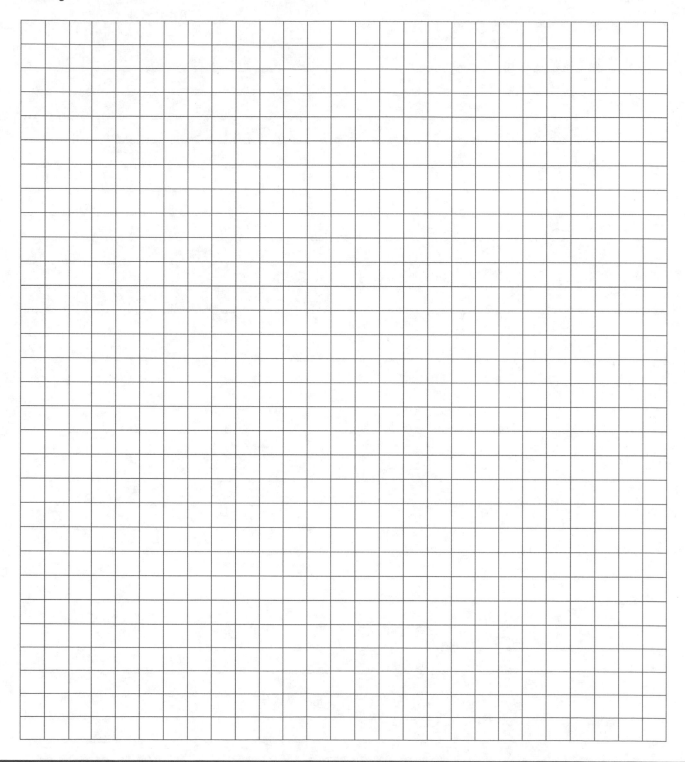

Invented by: _____ Date: _____

Invented by: _____ Date: _____

The above confidential information is witnessed and understood by:

_____ Date: _____

_____ Date: _____

Record of Building and Testing of Invention

Drawing:

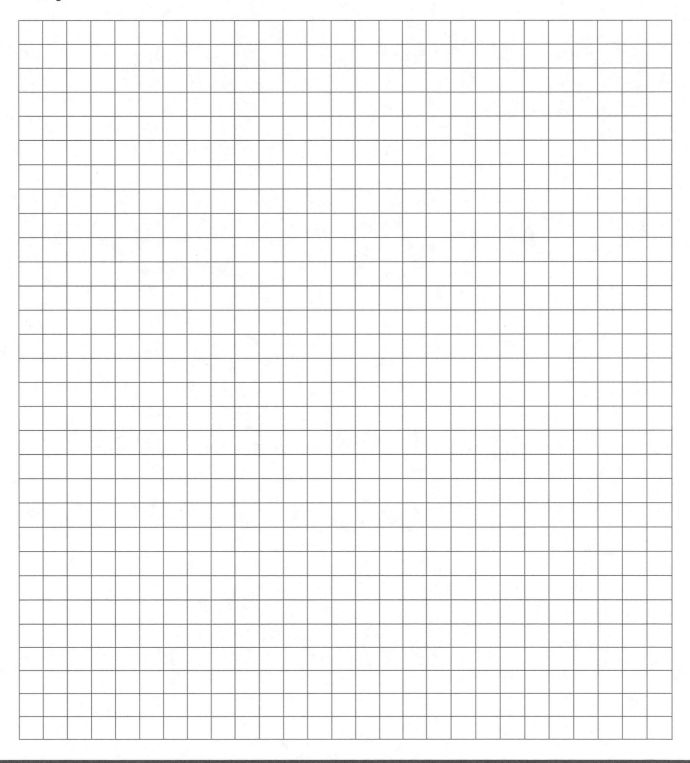

Invented by: _____ Date: _____

Invented by: _____ Date: _____

The above confidential information is witnessed and understood by:

_____ Date: _____

_____ Date: _____

Record of Building and Testing of Invention

Drawing:

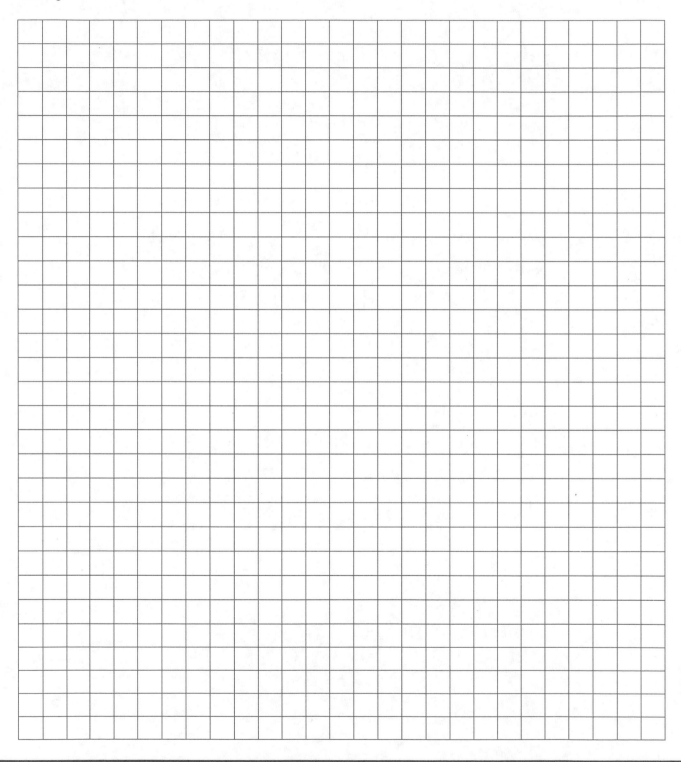

Invented by: _____ Date: _____

Invented by: _____ Date: _____

The above confidential information is witnessed and understood by:

_____ Date: _____

_____ Date: _____

Other Possible Applications of Invention

1. Alternative application and change required:

_____

_____

_____

_____

2. Alternative application and change required:

_____

_____

_____

_____

3. Alternative application and change required:

_____

_____

_____

_____

4. Alternative application and change required:

_____

_____

_____

_____

5. Alternative application and change required:

_____

_____

_____

_____

Invented by: _____ Date: _____

Invented by: _____ Date: _____

The above confidential information is witnessed and understood by:

_____ Date: _____

_____ Date: _____

Trademark Conception and Protection

Distinctive Name/Design & Goods/Service:

Distinctive Name/Design & Goods/Service:

Invented by: _____ Date: _____

Invented by: _____ Date: _____

The above confidential information is witnessed and understood by:

_____ Date: _____

_____ Date: _____

Trademark Conception and Protection

Distinctive Name/Design & Goods/Service:

Distinctive Name/Design & Goods/Service:

Invented by: _____ Date: _____

Invented by: _____ Date: _____

The above confidential information is witnessed and understood by:

_____ Date: _____

_____ Date: _____

Distinctive Design Conception

Drawing:

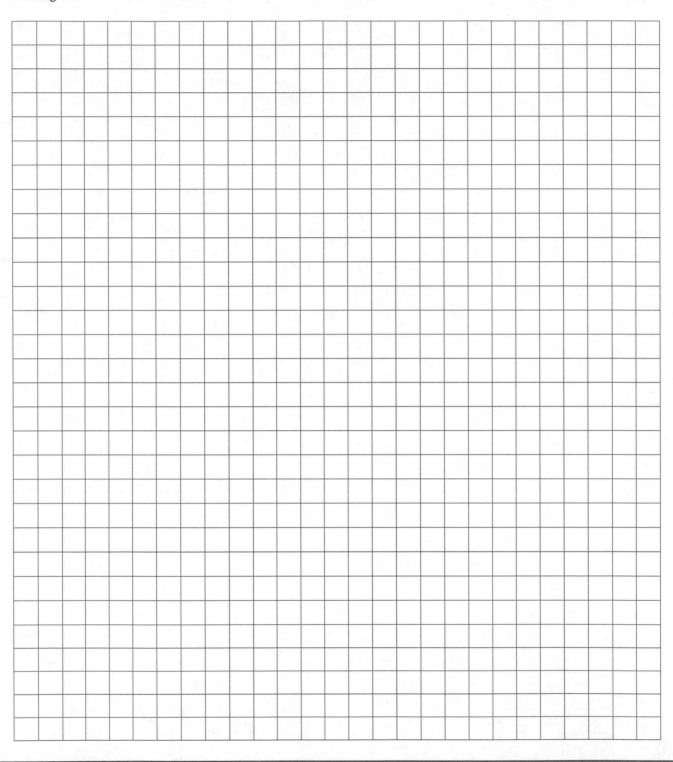

Invented by: _____ Date: _____

Invented by: _____ Date: _____

The above confidential information is witnessed and understood by:

_____ Date: _____

_____ Date: _____

Distinctive Design Conception

Drawing:

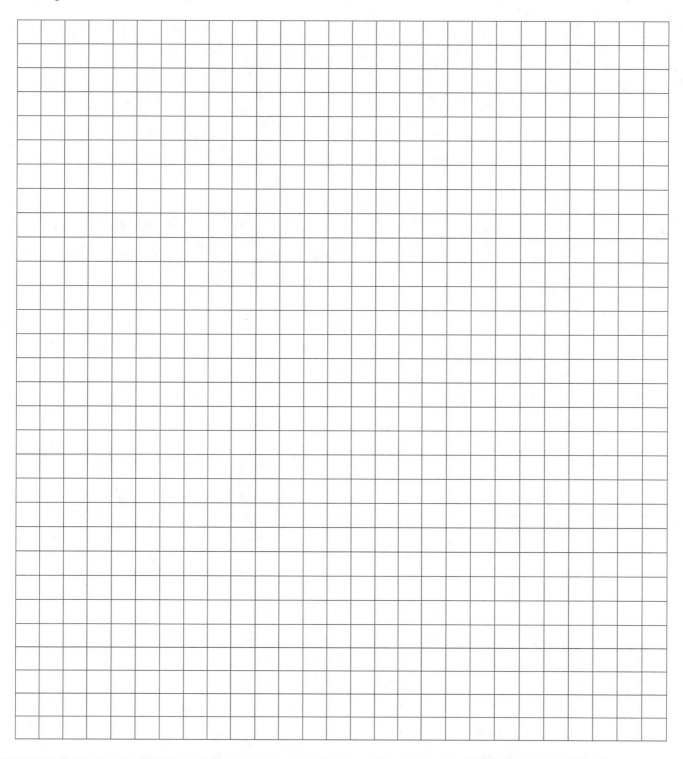

Invented by: _____ Date: _____

Invented by: _____ Date: _____

The above confidential information is witnessed and understood by:

_____ Date: _____

_____ Date: _____

Distinctive Design Conception

Drawing:

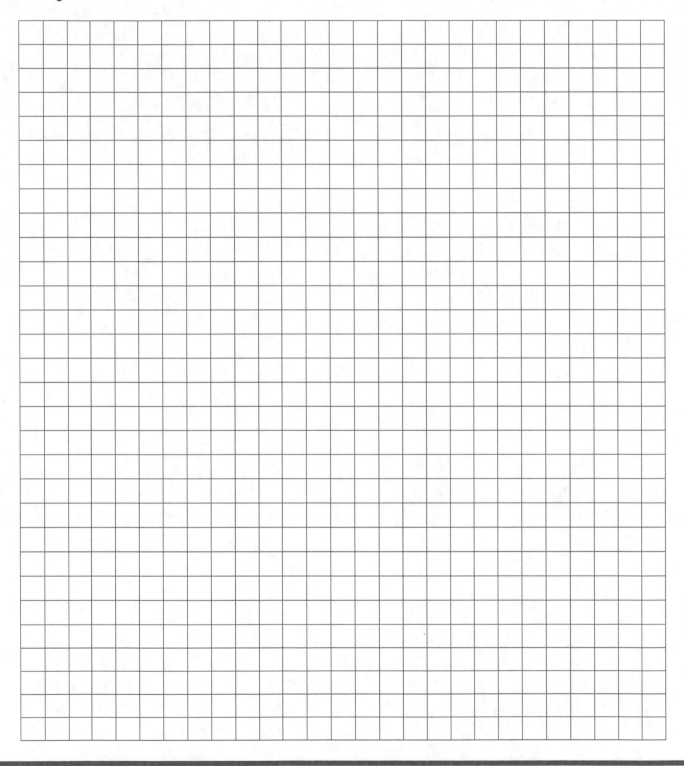

Invented by: _____ Date: _____

Invented by: _____ Date: _____

The above confidential information is witnessed and understood by:

_____ Date: _____

_____ Date: _____

Distinctive Design Conception

Drawing:

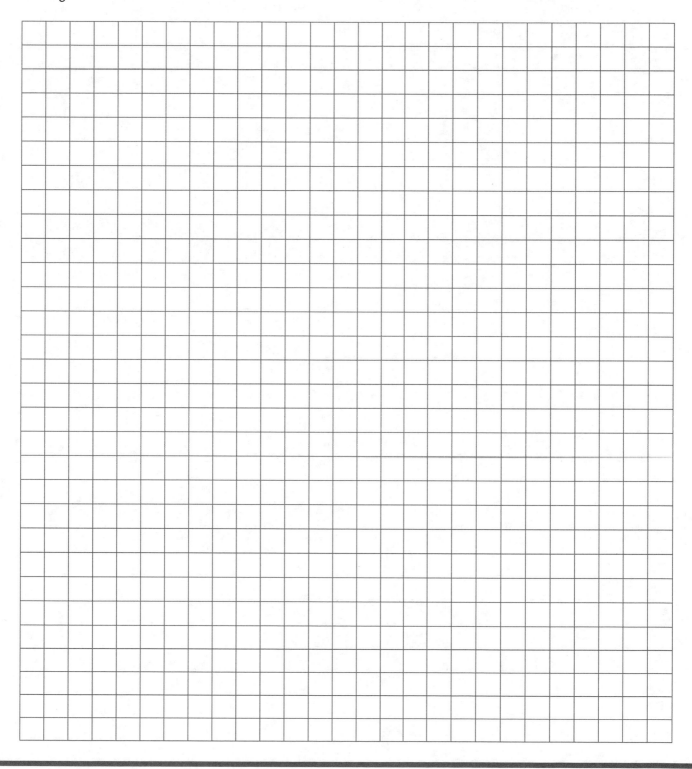

Invented by: _____ Date: _____

Invented by: _____ Date: _____

The above confidential information is witnessed and understood by:

_____ Date: _____

_____ Date: _____

Distinctive Design Conception

Drawing:

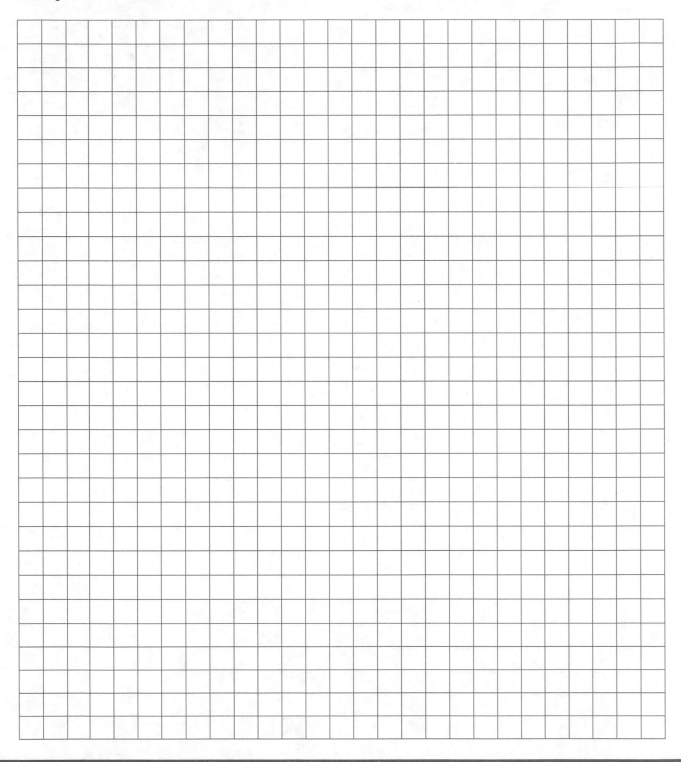

Invented by: _____ Date: _____

Invented by: _____ Date: _____

The above confidential information is witnessed and understood by:

_____ Date: _____

_____ Date: _____

Distinctive Design Conception

Drawing:

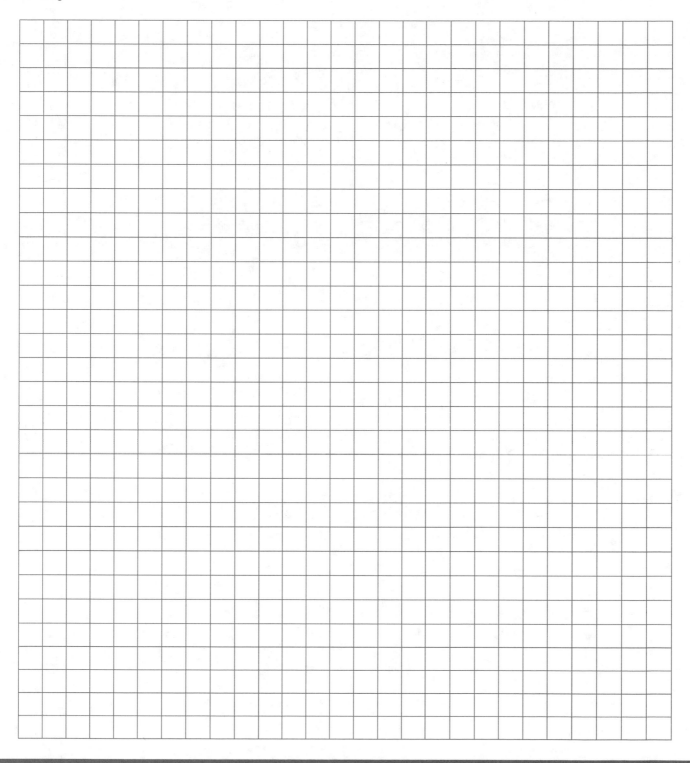

Invented by: _____ Date: _____

Invented by: _____ Date: _____

The above confidential information is witnessed and understood by:

_____ Date: _____

_____ Date: _____

Distinctive Design Conception

Drawing:

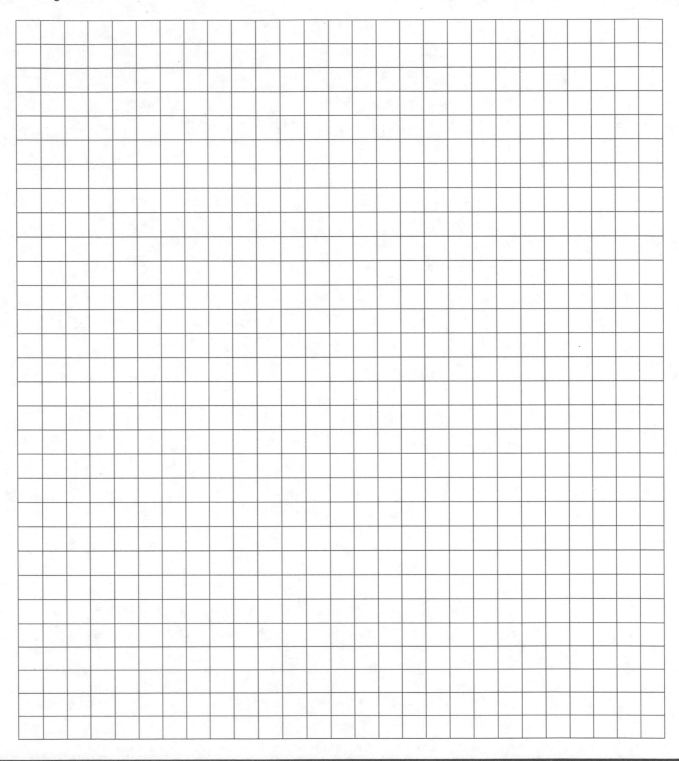

Invented by: _____ Date: _____

Invented by: _____ Date: _____

The above confidential information is witnessed and understood by:

_____ Date: _____

_____ Date: _____

Distinctive Design Conception

Drawing:

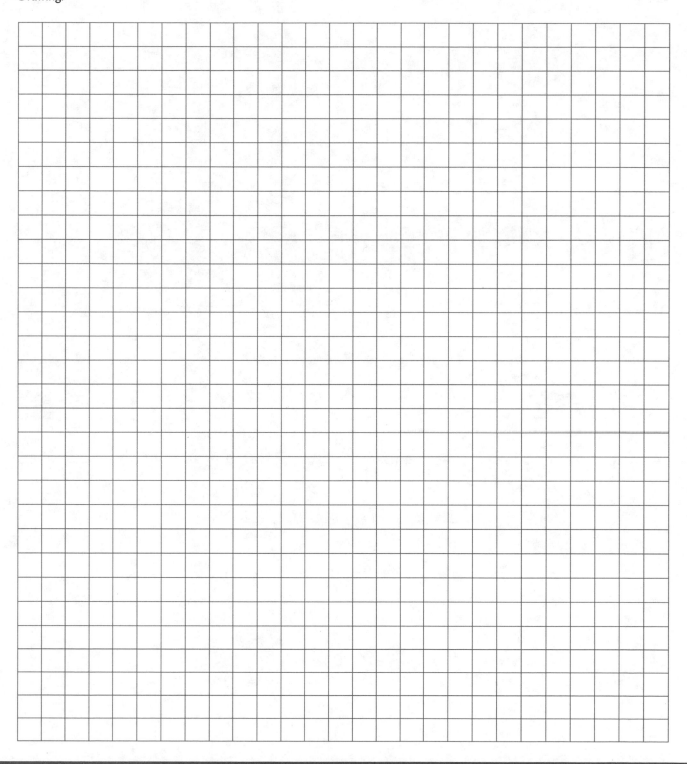

Invented by: _____ Date: _____

Invented by: _____ Date: _____

The above confidential information is witnessed and understood by:

_____ Date: _____

_____ Date: _____

Distinctive Design Conception

Drawing:

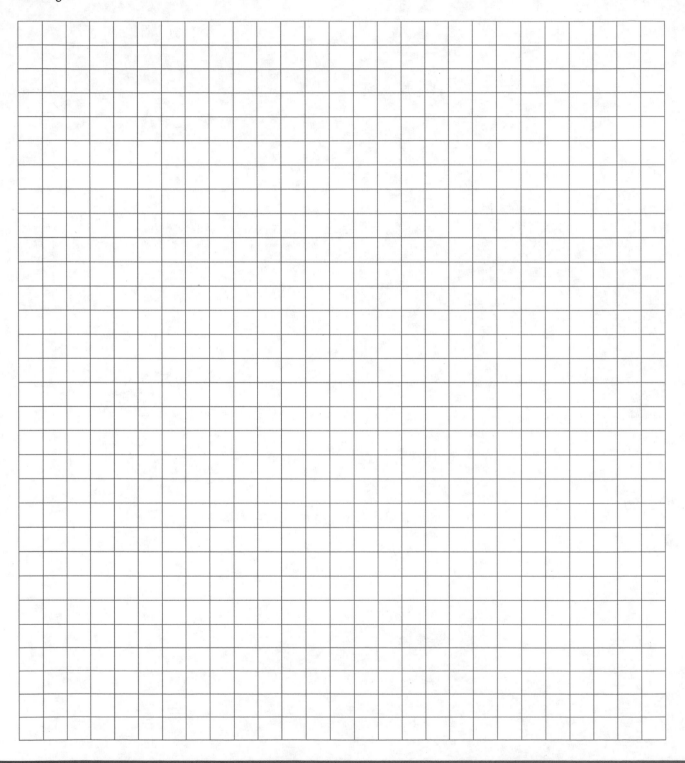

Invented by: _____ Date: _____

Invented by: _____ Date: _____

The above confidential information is witnessed and understood by:

_____ Date: _____

_____ Date: _____

Distinctive Design Conception

Drawing:

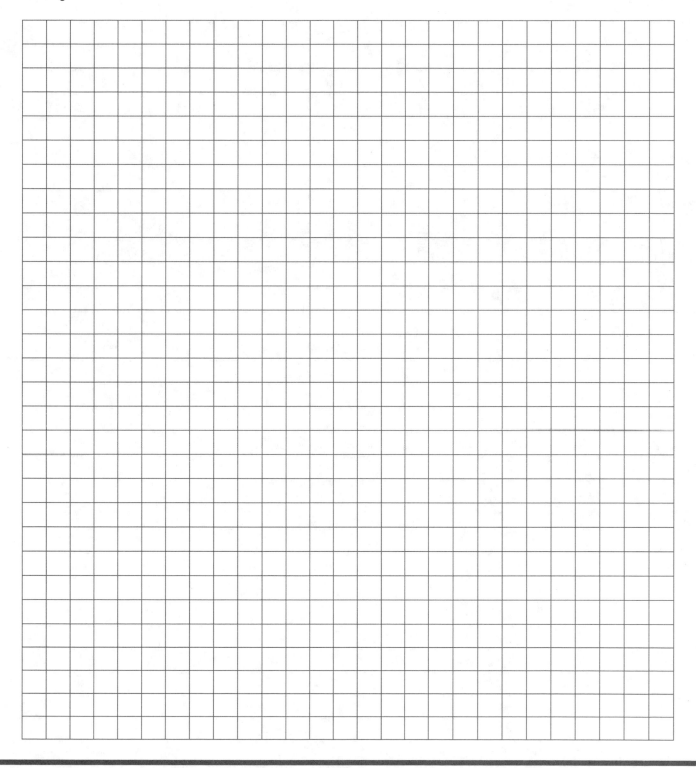

Invented by: _____ Date: _____

Invented by: _____ Date: _____

The above confidential information is witnessed and understood by:

_____ Date: _____

_____ Date: _____

Distinctive Design Conception

Drawing:

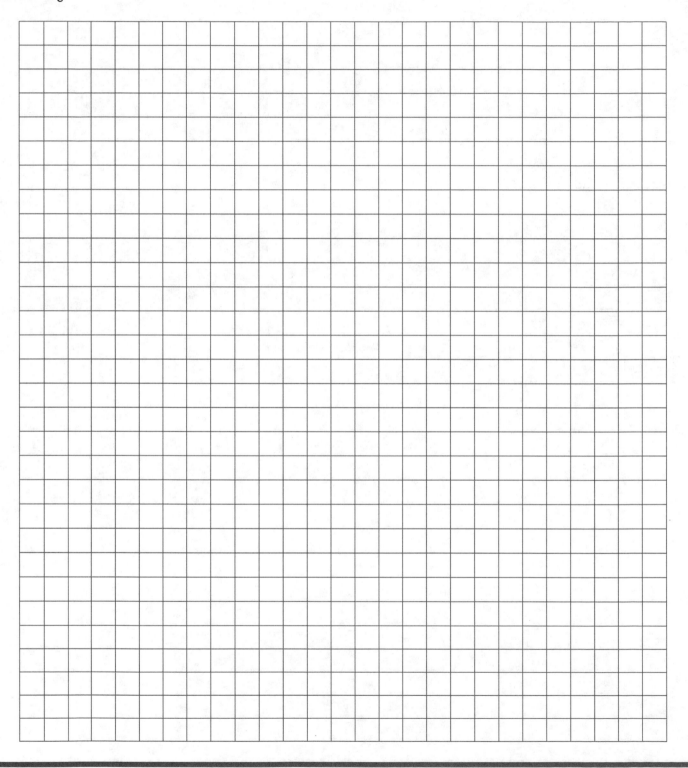

Invented by: _____ Date: _____

Invented by: _____ Date: _____

The above confidential information is witnessed and understood by:

_____ Date: _____

_____ Date: _____

Worksheets

Prior Art Search

Steps	**Date**

1. My earliest provable date of invention:

   _____ _____

   _____ _____

2. Date of the first public use, offer for sale, public disclosure, or commercial disclosure of my invention:

   _____ _____

   _____ _____

3. Publications searched:

   a._____ _____

   b._____ _____

   c._____ _____

   d._____ _____

   e._____ _____

   f._____ _____

   g._____ _____

4. Search of similar products (include stores visited):

   a._____ _____

   _____

   b._____ _____

   _____

   c._____ _____

   _____

   d._____ _____

   _____

   e._____ _____

   _____

   f._____ _____

   _____

   g._____ _____

   _____

Prior Art Search

Steps   Date

1. My earliest provable date of invention:

   _____   _____

   _____   _____

2. Date of the first public use, offer for sale, public disclosure, or commercial disclosure of my invention:

   _____   _____

   _____   _____

3. Publications searched:

   a._____   _____

   b._____   _____

   c._____   _____

   d._____   _____

   e._____   _____

   f. _____   _____

   g._____   _____

4. Search of similar products (include stores visited):

   a._____   _____

   _____

   b._____   _____

   _____

   c._____   _____

   _____

   d._____   _____

   _____

   e._____   _____

   _____

   f. _____   _____

   _____

   g._____   _____

   _____

Prior Art Search

Steps   **Date**

1. My earliest provable date of invention:

   _____   _____

   _____   _____

2. Date of the first public use, offer for sale, public disclosure, or commercial disclosure of my invention:

   _____   _____

   _____   _____

3. Publications searched:

   a._____   _____

   b._____   _____

   c._____   _____

   d._____   _____

   e._____   _____

   f._____   _____

   g._____   _____

4. Search of similar products (include stores visited):

   a._____   _____

   _____

   b._____   _____

   _____

   c._____   _____

   _____

   d._____   _____

   _____

   e._____   _____

   _____

   f._____   _____

   _____

   g._____   _____

   _____

Patentability Checklist

My invention is a new and useful*:

☐ Process or method   ☐ Composition of matter (includes new life forms)

☐ Machine (includes electrical circuits)   ☐ New use of one of the above

☐ Article of manufacture

These Novel Physical Features**   Produce   These New Unexpected Results

a. _____   a. _____

b. _____   b. _____

c. _____   c. _____

d. _____   d. _____

* As long as you can fit your invention into one or more of these categories, it doesn't matter which category you choose. They do overlap to some extent.

** Remember that a novel physical feature can be a novel combination of old physical features.

Patentability Checklist

My invention is a new and useful:

☐ Process or method

☐ Machine (includes electrical circuits)

☐ Article of manufacture

☐ Composition of matter (includes new life forms)

☐ New use of one of the above

These Novel Physical Features — Produce — These New Unexpected Results

a. _____

_____

_____

_____

_____

_____

b. _____

_____

_____

_____

_____

_____

c. _____

_____

_____

_____

_____

_____

d. _____

_____

_____

_____

_____

a. _____

_____

_____

_____

_____

_____

b. _____

_____

_____

_____

_____

_____

c. _____

_____

_____

_____

_____

_____

d. _____

_____

_____

_____

_____

Patentability Checklist

My invention is a new and useful:

- ☐ Process or method
- ☐ Machine (includes electrical circuits)
- ☐ Article of manufacture
- ☐ Composition of matter (includes new life forms)
- ☐ New use of one of the above

These Novel Physical Features   Produce   These New Unexpected Results

a. _____

_____

_____

_____

_____

b. _____

_____

_____

_____

_____

c. _____

_____

_____

_____

_____

d. _____

_____

_____

_____

_____

a. _____

_____

_____

_____

_____

b. _____

_____

_____

_____

_____

c. _____

_____

_____

_____

_____

d. _____

_____

_____

_____

_____

Provisional Patent Application Checklist

_____
Date

A. Application

☐ 1. A description of the invention and its operation, which clearly teaches how to make and use all embodiments of the invention that you might later want to claim. (This should be the equivalent of the information supplied in the Invention Description and Operation Description of the Specification in a regular patent application (RPA).)

☐ 2. Drawing sheets, if necessary to describe invention.

☐ 3. Although it's not necessary, we recommend that your PPA include all the parts of a Specification included in an RPA.

☐ 4. Although it's not necessary, we recommend that your PPA contain at least one claim.

☐ 5. A completed Provisional Patent Application Cover including Express Mail section (see Appendix V: Tear-Out Forms).

☐ 6. A check for the specified fee, payable to the Commissioner for Patents (see Appendix IV: Fee Schedule) or, if paying by credit card, enclose Credit Card Payment Form.

☐ 7. A stamped receipt postcard with your name and address on the front.

☐ 8. Envelope addressed to:
Mail Stop Patent Application
Commissioner for Patents
P.O. Box 1450
Alexandria, VA 22313-1450

Patent Application Checklist

A. Application   Date: _____

☐ 1. Return Receipt Postcard addressed to you with all papers listed on back

☐ 2. Check or Money Order for correct filing fee (basic fee and fee for any excess claims) or, if paying by credit card, enclose Credit Card Payment Form

☐ 3. Transmittal Letter and Fee Transmittal

☐ 4. Drawing sheets

☐ 5. Specification

☐ 6. Claims

☐ 7. Abstract

☐ 8. Patent Application Declaration (PAD)

☐ 9. Information Disclosure Statement and PTO-1449 with references attached (if you're filing it with your application; otherwise IDS must be sent within three months)

☐ 10. Petition to Make Special (optional to speed application processing)

☐ 11. Assignment if needed

☐ 12. Disclosure Document Reference Letter if you previously filed a Disclosure Document

☐ 13. Envelope addressed to:
Mail Stop Patent Application
Commissioner for Patents
P.O. Box 1450
Alexandria, VA 22313-1450

B. Amendment   Date: _____

☐ 1. All pages completed?

☐ 2. All points in Office Action answered?

☐ 3. If number of claims is increased, is any necessary additional fee enclosed?

☐ 4. Certificate of Mailing included?

☐ 5. Amendment mailed on time or Petition to Extend with fee included?

☐ 6. If Petition to Extend is included, is it properly completed with proper fee?

☐ 7. Amendment signed and dated by proper party(ies)?

☐ 8. Envelope properly addressed and stamped?

☐ 9. Stamped, addressed, properly completed return postcard enclosed?

☐ 10. Enough file copies made?

Patent Application Checklist

C. Paying Issue Fee   Date: _____

☐ 1. Issue Fee Transmittal form filled out and signed?

☐ 2. If paying by check, is check for correct amount attached and signed?

☐ 3. If paying by credit card, is Credit Card Payment Form enclosed?

☐ 4. Postcard attached, stamped, addressed?

☐ 5. Any needed drawing corrections made?

☐ 6. Certificate of Mailing attached, completed, signed, dated?

☐ 7. Mailed on time? (Three-month period is not extendable.)

☐ 8. Stamped, addressed, properly completed return postcard enclosed?

☐ 9. Enough file copies made?

Design Patent Application Checklist

☐ 1. Design Patent Application   Date: _____

☐ 2. The Drawing(s)   Date: _____

☐ 3. Patent Application Declaration   Date: _____

☐ 4. Filing Fee   Date: _____

☐ 5. Receipt Postcard   Date: _____

☐ 6. Information Disclosure Statement and List of Prior Art Cited   Date: _____

Trademark Use and Registration

1. Final version of trademark conceived (documented in Section A4) Date: _____

2. Trademark search completed Date: _____

   a. Name of searcher

   b. Federally registered trademarks

   c. State registered trademarks

   d. Trade journals and product lists

      i. _____

     ii. _____

    iii. _____

    iv. _____

     v. _____

    vi. _____

   vii. _____

  viii. _____

3. First use of trademark

   a. Intrastate Date: _____

   b. Interstate Date: _____

   c. Foreign Date: _____

Trademark Use and Registration

4. Registration of trademark with PTO*   Date: _____

    a. Date regular application filed (trademark already in use)   Date: _____

    b. Date application based upon intent to use filed   Date: _____

    c. Date Amendment to Allege Use filed   Date: _____

    d. Date registration granted   Date: _____

    e. Registration # _____   Date: _____

    f. ☐ Principal Register   ☐ Supplemental Register

    g. Class and description of goods:

    _____

    _____

    _____

    _____

5. Renewal of federal registration

    a. §§ 8/15 Declarations due by   Date: _____

    b. Renewal due by   Date: _____

---

* State trademark registration also exists. If you aren't using your invention across states, consider placing it on your state's trademark register.

Record of Contacts

Name & Title: _____

Date: _____   Agreement Signed: ☐ Yes   ☐ No

Address & Phone: _____

_____

_____

Comments: _____

_____

_____

Follow up? _____

_____

Name & Title: _____

Date: _____   Agreement Signed: ☐ Yes   ☐ No

Address & Phone: _____

_____

_____

Comments: _____

_____

_____

Follow up? _____

_____

Name & Title: _____

Date: _____   Agreement Signed: ☐ Yes   ☐ No

Address & Phone: _____

_____

_____

Comments: _____

_____

_____

Follow up? _____

_____

Record of Contacts

Name & Title: _____

Date: _____   Agreement Signed: ☐ Yes   ☐ No

Address & Phone: _____

_____

_____

Comments: _____

_____

_____

Follow up? _____

_____

Name & Title: _____

Date: _____   Agreement Signed: ☐ Yes   ☐ No

Address & Phone: _____

_____

_____

Comments: _____

_____

_____

Follow up? _____

_____

Name & Title: _____

Date: _____   Agreement Signed: ☐ Yes   ☐ No

Address & Phone: _____

_____

_____

Comments: _____

_____

_____

Follow up? _____

_____

Record of Contacts

Name & Title: _____

Date: _____   Agreement Signed: ☐ Yes ☐ No

Address & Phone: _____

_____

_____

Comments: _____

_____

_____

Follow up? _____

_____

Name & Title: _____

Date: _____   Agreement Signed: ☐ Yes ☐ No

Address & Phone: _____

_____

_____

Comments: _____

_____

_____

Follow up? _____

_____

Name & Title: _____

Date: _____   Agreement Signed: ☐ Yes ☐ No

Address & Phone: _____

_____

_____

Comments: _____

_____

_____

Follow up? _____

_____

Record of Contacts

Name & Title: _____

Date: _____   Agreement Signed: ☐ Yes ☐ No

Address & Phone: _____

_____

_____

Comments: _____

_____

_____

Follow up? _____

_____

Name & Title: _____

Date: _____   Agreement Signed: ☐ Yes ☐ No

Address & Phone: _____

_____

_____

Comments: _____

_____

_____

Follow up? _____

_____

Name & Title: _____

Date: _____   Agreement Signed: ☐ Yes ☐ No

Address & Phone: _____

_____

_____

Comments: _____

_____

_____

Follow up? _____

_____

Record of Contacts

Name & Title: _____

Date: _____   Agreement Signed: ☐ Yes ☐ No

Address & Phone: _____

_____

_____

Comments: _____

_____

_____

Follow up? _____

_____

Name & Title: _____

Date: _____   Agreement Signed: ☐ Yes ☐ No

Address & Phone: _____

_____

_____

Comments: _____

_____

_____

Follow up? _____

_____

Name & Title: _____

Date: _____   Agreement Signed: ☐ Yes ☐ No

Address & Phone: _____

_____

_____

Comments: _____

_____

_____

Follow up? _____

_____

Legal Protection Summary

1. Conception recorded, signed, dated, and witnessed — Date: _____

2. Disclosure of conception signed, dated, recorded, and witnessed — Date: _____

3. Disclosure document filed (optional) — Date: _____

4. Building and testing recorded, signed, dated, and witnessed — Date: _____

5. Provisional Patent Application filed (optional) — Date: _____

6. Patent application filed — Date: _____

7. Patent pending notice on invention — ☐ Yes   ☐ No

8. Patent application published — Date: _____

9. Patent application allowed — Date: _____

10. Foreign patent application(s) filed

    a. _____ Date: _____

    b. _____ Date: _____

    c. _____ Date: _____

    d. _____ Date: _____

    e. _____ Date: _____

11. Trade secret without patent application — ☐ Yes   ☐ No

12. First trademark use — Date: _____

13. State trademark registration — Date: _____

14. Trademark registration with PTO — Date: _____

15. Design patent application filed — Date: _____

16. Design patent approved — Date: _____

17. Copyright notice on design, artwork, or written materials — ☐ Yes   ☐ No

18. Copyright registered — Date: _____

19. Sold invention before filing for patent — Date: _____

Positive and Negative Factors Evaluation

Inventor(s): _____

Invention: _____

Factor	Weight (−100 to +100)	Factor	Weight (−100 to +100)
1. Cost	_____	35. Legality	_____
2. Weight	_____	36. Operability	_____
3. Size	_____	37. Development	_____
4. Safety/Health	_____	38. Profitability	_____
5. Speed	_____	39. Obsolescence	_____
6. Ease of Use	_____	40. Incompatibility	_____
7. Ease of Production	_____	41. Product Liability Risk	_____
8. Durability	_____	42. Market Dependence	_____
9. Repairability	_____	43. Difficulty of Distribution	_____
10. Novelty	_____	44. Service Requirements	_____
11. Convenience/Social Benefit	_____	45. New Tooling Required	_____
12. Reliability	_____	46. Inertia Must Be Overcome	_____
13. Ecology	_____	47. Too Advanced Technically	_____
14. Salability	_____	48. Substantial Learning Required	_____
15. Appearance	_____	49. Difficult to Promote	_____
16. Viewability	_____	50. Lack of Market	_____
17. Precision	_____	51. Crowded Field	_____
18. Noise	_____	52. Commodities	_____
19. Odor	_____	53. Combination Products	_____
20. Taste	_____	54. Entrenched Competition	_____
21. Market Size	_____	55. Instant Anachronism	_____
22. Trend of Demand	_____	56. Prototype Availability	_____
23. Seasonal Demand	_____	57. Broad Patent Coverage Available	_____
24. Difficulty of Market Penetration	_____	58. High Sales Anticipated	_____
25. Potential Competition	_____	59. Visibility of Invention in Final Product	_____
26. Quality	_____	60. Ease of Packaging	_____
27. Excitement	_____	61. Youth Market	_____
28. Markup	_____	62. Part of a Current Fad	_____
29. Inferior Performance	_____	63. Will a Contingent Fee Litigator Take Your Case?	_____
30. "Sexy" Packaging	_____		
31. Miscellaneous	_____	Total Positive	_____
32. Long Life Cycle	_____	Less: Total Negative	_____
33. Related Product Addability	_____	NET:	_____
34. Satisfies Existing Need	_____		

Signed: _____

Date: _____

Positive and Negative Factors Evaluation

Inventor(s): _____   Invention: _____

_____

Factor	Weight (−100 to +100)	Factor	Weight (−100 to +100)
1. Cost	_____	35. Legality	_____
2. Weight	_____	36. Operability	_____
3. Size	_____	37. Development	_____
4. Safety/Health	_____	38. Profitability	_____
5. Speed	_____	39. Obsolescence	_____
6. Ease of Use	_____	40. Incompatibility	_____
7. Ease of Production	_____	41. Product Liability Risk	_____
8. Durability	_____	42. Market Dependence	_____
9. Repairability	_____	43. Difficulty of Distribution	_____
10. Novelty	_____	44. Service Requirements	_____
11. Convenience/Social Benefit	_____	45. New Tooling Required	_____
12. Reliability	_____	46. Inertia Must Be Overcome	_____
13. Ecology	_____	47. Too Advanced Technically	_____
14. Salability	_____	48. Substantial Learning Required	_____
15. Appearance	_____	49. Difficult to Promote	_____
16. Viewability	_____	50. Lack of Market	_____
17. Precision	_____	51. Crowded Field	_____
18. Noise	_____	52. Commodities	_____
19. Odor	_____	53. Combination Products	_____
20. Taste	_____	54. Entrenched Competition	_____
21. Market Size	_____	55. Instant Anachronism	_____
22. Trend of Demand	_____	56. Prototype Availability	_____
23. Seasonal Demand	_____	57. Broad Patent Coverage Available	_____
24. Difficulty of Market Penetration	_____	58. High Sales Anticipated	_____
25. Potential Competition	_____	59. Visibility of Invention in Final Product	_____
26. Quality	_____	60. Ease of Packaging	_____
27. Excitement	_____	61. Youth Market	_____
28. Markup	_____	62. Part of a Current Fad	_____
29. Inferior Performance	_____	63. Will a Contingent Fee Litigator Take Your Case?	_____
30. "Sexy" Packaging	_____		
31. Miscellaneous	_____	Total Positive	_____
32. Long Life Cycle	_____	Less: Total Negative	_____
33. Related Product Addability	_____	NET:	_____
34. Satisfies Existing Need	_____		

Signed: _____   Date: _____

Positive and Negative Factors Evaluation

Inventor(s): _____   Invention: _____

_____   _____

Factor	Weight (−100 to +100)	Factor	Weight (−100 to +100)
1. Cost	_____	35. Legality	_____
2. Weight	_____	36. Operability	_____
3. Size	_____	37. Development	_____
4. Safety/Health	_____	38. Profitability	_____
5. Speed	_____	39. Obsolescence	_____
6. Ease of Use	_____	40. Incompatibility	_____
7. Ease of Production	_____	41. Product Liability Risk	_____
8. Durability	_____	42. Market Dependence	_____
9. Repairability	_____	43. Difficulty of Distribution	_____
10. Novelty	_____	44. Service Requirements	_____
11. Convenience/Social Benefit	_____	45. New Tooling Required	_____
12. Reliability	_____	46. Inertia Must Be Overcome	_____
13. Ecology	_____	47. Too Advanced Technically	_____
14. Salability	_____	48. Substantial Learning Required	_____
15. Appearance	_____	49. Difficult to Promote	_____
16. Viewability	_____	50. Lack of Market	_____
17. Precision	_____	51. Crowded Field	_____
18. Noise	_____	52. Commodities	_____
19. Odor	_____	53. Combination Products	_____
20. Taste	_____	54. Entrenched Competition	_____
21. Market Size	_____	55. Instant Anachronism	_____
22. Trend of Demand	_____	56. Prototype Availability	_____
23. Seasonal Demand	_____	57. Broad Patent Coverage Available	_____
24. Difficulty of Market Penetration	_____	58. High Sales Anticipated	_____
25. Potential Competition	_____	59. Visibility of Invention in Final Product	_____
26. Quality	_____	60. Ease of Packaging	_____
27. Excitement	_____	61. Youth Market	_____
28. Markup	_____	62. Part of a Current Fad	_____
29. Inferior Performance	_____	63. Will a Contingent Fee Litigator Take Your Case?	_____
30. "Sexy" Packaging	_____		
31. Miscellaneous	_____	Total Positive	_____
32. Long Life Cycle	_____	Less: Total Negative	_____
33. Related Product Addability	_____	NET:	_____
34. Satisfies Existing Need	_____		

Signed: _____   Date: _____

Potential User Survey

1. Name: _____ Date: _____

   Agreement signed: ☐ Yes ☐ No

   Comments: _____

   _____

   _____

   _____

   _____

   _____

   _____

   _____

   _____

   _____

   _____

   _____

   Signed: _____ Date: _____

2. Name: _____ Date: _____

   Agreement signed: ☐ Yes ☐ No

   Comments: _____

   _____

   _____

   _____

   _____

   _____

   _____

   _____

   _____

   _____

   _____

   _____

   Signed: _____ Date: _____

Potential User Survey

3. Name: _____ Date: _____

    Agreement signed: ☐ Yes ☐ No

    Comments: _____

_____

_____

_____

_____

_____

_____

_____

_____

_____

_____

_____

Signed: _____ Date: _____

4. Name: _____ Date: _____

    Agreement signed: ☐ Yes ☐ No

    Comments: _____

_____

_____

_____

_____

_____

_____

_____

_____

_____

_____

Signed: _____ Date: _____

Potential User Survey

5. Name: _____ Date: _____

   Agreement signed: ☐ Yes ☐ No

   Comments: _____

   _____

   _____

   _____

   _____

   _____

   _____

   _____

   _____

   _____

   _____

   _____

   Signed: _____ Date: _____

6. Name: _____ Date: _____

   Agreement signed: ☐ Yes ☐ No

   Comments: _____

   _____

   _____

   _____

   _____

   _____

   _____

   _____

   _____

   _____

   _____

   _____

   Signed: _____ Date: _____

Potential User Survey

7. Name: _____ Date: _____

Agreement signed: ☐ Yes ☐ No

Comments: _____

_____

_____

_____

_____

_____

_____

_____

_____

_____

_____

Signed: _____ Date: _____

8. Name: _____ Date: _____

Agreement signed: ☐ Yes ☐ No

Comments: _____

_____

_____

_____

_____

_____

_____

_____

_____

_____

_____

Signed: _____ Date: _____

Potential User Survey

9. Name: _____ Date: _____

    Agreement signed: ☐ Yes ☐ No

    Comments: _____

    _____

    _____

    _____

    _____

    _____

    _____

    _____

    _____

    _____

    _____

    _____

    Signed: _____ Date: _____

10. Name: _____ Date: _____

    Agreement signed: ☐ Yes ☐ No

    Comments: _____

    _____

    _____

    _____

    _____

    _____

    _____

    _____

    _____

    _____

    _____

    _____

    Signed: _____ Date: _____

Regional Buying Patterns of Related Products

Product Name	Source of Information	Sales for Last Year Surveyed	Sales Projected
Region: _____	_____	_____	_____
Product A _____	_____	_____	_____
Product B _____	_____	_____	_____
Product C _____	_____	_____	_____
Product D _____	_____	_____	_____
Product E _____	_____	_____	_____
Region: _____	_____	_____	_____
Product A _____	_____	_____	_____
Product B _____	_____	_____	_____
Product C _____	_____	_____	_____
Product D _____	_____	_____	_____
Product E _____	_____	_____	_____
Region: _____	_____	_____	_____
Product A _____	_____	_____	_____
Product B _____	_____	_____	_____
Product C _____	_____	_____	_____
Product D _____	_____	_____	_____
Product E _____	_____	_____	_____
Region: _____	_____	_____	_____
Product A _____	_____	_____	_____
Product B _____	_____	_____	_____
Product C _____	_____	_____	_____
Product D _____	_____	_____	_____
Product E _____	_____	_____	_____
Region: _____	_____	_____	_____
Product A _____	_____	_____	_____
Product B _____	_____	_____	_____
Product C _____	_____	_____	_____
Product D _____	_____	_____	_____
Product E _____	_____	_____	_____

Regional Buying Patterns of Related Products

Product Name	Source of Information	Sales for Last Year Surveyed	Sales Projected
Region:			
Product A			
Product B			
Product C			
Product D			
Product E			
Region:			
Product A			
Product B			
Product C			
Product D			
Product E			
Region:			
Product A			
Product B			
Product C			
Product D			
Product E			
Region:			
Product A			
Product B			
Product C			
Product D			
Product E			
Region:			
Product A			
Product B			
Product C			
Product D			
Product E			

Regional Buying Patterns of Related Products

Product Name	Source of Information	Sales for Last Year Surveyed	Sales Projected
Region: _____	_____	_____	_____
Product A _____	_____	_____	_____
Product B _____	_____	_____	_____
Product C _____	_____	_____	_____
Product D _____	_____	_____	_____
Product E _____	_____	_____	_____
Region: _____	_____	_____	_____
Product A _____	_____	_____	_____
Product B _____	_____	_____	_____
Product C _____	_____	_____	_____
Product D _____	_____	_____	_____
Product E _____	_____	_____	_____
Region: _____	_____	_____	_____
Product A _____	_____	_____	_____
Product B _____	_____	_____	_____
Product C _____	_____	_____	_____
Product D _____	_____	_____	_____
Product E _____	_____	_____	_____
Region: _____	_____	_____	_____
Product A _____	_____	_____	_____
Product B _____	_____	_____	_____
Product C _____	_____	_____	_____
Product D _____	_____	_____	_____
Product E _____	_____	_____	_____
Region: _____	_____	_____	_____
Product A _____	_____	_____	_____
Product B _____	_____	_____	_____
Product C _____	_____	_____	_____
Product D _____	_____	_____	_____
Product E _____	_____	_____	_____

Predictions for Targeted Buying Groups

Potential Purchasers	Age	Sex	Other	Predicted % of Sales
Group 1				
Group 2				
Group 3				

	Source of Information	Last Year Surveyed	Projected

GROUP 1

% of Population

Region 1			
Region 2			
Region 3			

Disposable Income

Region 1			
Region 2			
Region 3			

GROUP 2

% of Population

Region 1			
Region 2			
Region 3			

Disposable Income

Region 1			
Region 2			
Region 3			

GROUP 3

% of Population

Region 1			
Region 2			
Region 3			

Disposable Income

Region 1			
Region 2			
Region 3			

Predictions for Targeted Buying Groups

	Potential Purchasers	Age	Sex	Other	Predicted % of Sales
Group 1					
Group 2					
Group 3					

	Source of Information	Last Year Surveyed	Projected

GROUP 1

% of Population

Region 1			
Region 2			
Region 3			

Disposable Income

Region 1			
Region 2			
Region 3			

GROUP 2

% of Population

Region 1			
Region 2			
Region 3			

Disposable Income

Region 1			
Region 2			
Region 3			

GROUP 3

% of Population

Region 1			
Region 2			
Region 3			

Disposable Income

Region 1			
Region 2			
Region 3			

Predictions for Targeted Buying Groups

Potential Purchasers	Age	Sex	Other	Predicted % of Sales
Group 1				
Group 2				
Group 3				

	Source of Information	Last Year Surveyed	Projected

GROUP 1

% of Population

Region 1			
Region 2			
Region 3			

Disposable Income

Region 1			
Region 2			
Region 3			

GROUP 2

% of Population

Region 1			
Region 2			
Region 3			

Disposable Income

Region 1			
Region 2			
Region 3			

GROUP 3

% of Population

Region 1			
Region 2			
Region 3			

Disposable Income

Region 1			
Region 2			
Region 3			

Conclusions Regarding Marketing Trends

The demand for my product will likely increase because of these factors:

_____

_____

_____

_____

_____

_____

_____

_____

_____

The demand could decrease because of these factors:

_____

_____

_____

_____

_____

_____

_____

_____

To take advantage of the positive trends and overcome any projected negative developments, I propose to market my product in the following ways:

_____

_____

_____

_____

_____

_____

_____

_____

_____

_____

_____

_____

Conclusions Regarding Marketing Trends

The demand for my product will likely increase because of these factors:

_____

_____

_____

_____

_____

_____

_____

_____

The demand could decrease because of these factors:

_____

_____

_____

_____

_____

_____

_____

_____

To take advantage of the positive trends and overcome any projected negative developments, I propose to market my product in the following ways:

_____

_____

_____

_____

_____

_____

_____

_____

_____

_____

_____

Conclusions Regarding Marketing Trends

The demand for my product will likely increase because of these factors:

_____

_____

_____

_____

_____

_____

_____

_____

The demand could decrease because of these factors:

_____

_____

_____

_____

_____

_____

_____

_____

To take advantage of the positive trends and overcome any projected negative developments, I propose to market my product in the following ways:

_____

_____

_____

_____

_____

_____

_____

_____

_____

_____

_____

Manufacturer/Distributor Evaluation

If I Want to Distribute It Myself

1. Items needed

    a. Facilities: _____

    _____

    b. Inventory: _____

    _____

    c. Employees: _____

    _____

    d. New skills: _____

    _____

    e. Advertising: _____

    _____

2. Funds needed: _____

    _____

3. Distribution options: _____

    _____

4. Sales volume desired: _____

    _____

5. Time needed to achieve sales volume: _____

    _____

6. Liability risks: _____

    _____

7. Time needed to recover costs: _____

    _____

8. Percent per unit that would be paid to an existing distributor: __

    _____

Conclusions: _____

_____

_____

_____

_____

_____

Manufacturer/Distributor Evaluation

If I Want to Distribute It Myself

1. Items needed

   a. Facilities: _____

   _____

   b. Inventory: _____

   _____

   c. Employees: _____

   _____

   d. New skills: _____

   _____

   e. Advertising: _____

2. Funds needed: _____

   _____

3. Distribution options: _____

   _____

4. Sales volume desired: _____

   _____

5. Time needed to achieve sales volume: _____

   _____

6. Liability risks: _____

   _____

7. Time needed to recover costs: _____

   _____

8. Percent per unit that would be paid to an existing distributor: _____

   _____

Conclusions: _____

_____

_____

_____

_____

_____

Choosing the Right Company

Choice Number _____

a. Name and Location: _____

_____

_____

b. Officers:

_____

_____

_____

c. Current Products:

_____

_____

d. Sales Volume:

_____

e. Advertising Budget:

_____

f. Other:

_____

Choice Number _____

a. Name and Location: _____

_____

_____

b. Officers:

_____

_____

_____

c. Current Products:

_____

_____

d. Sales Volume:

_____

e. Advertising Budget:

_____

f. Other:

_____

Choosing the Right Company

Choice Number _____

a. Name and Location: _____

_____

_____

b. Officers:

_____

_____

_____

c. Current Products:

_____

_____

d. Sales Volume:

_____

e. Advertising Budget:

_____

f. Other:

_____

Choice Number_____

a. Name and Location: _____

_____

_____

b. Officers:

_____

_____

_____

c. Current Products:

_____

_____

d. Sales Volume:

_____

e. Advertising Budget:

_____

f. Other:

_____

Choosing the Right Company

Choice Number _____

a. Name and Location: _____

_____

_____

b. Officers:

_____

_____

_____

c. Current Products:

_____

_____

d. Sales Volume:

_____

e. Advertising Budget:

_____

f. Other:

_____

Choice Number _____

a. Name and Location: _____

_____

_____

b. Officers:

_____

_____

_____

c. Current Products:

_____

_____

d. Sales Volume:

_____

e. Advertising Budget:

_____

f. Other:

_____

Choosing the Right Company

Choice Number _____

a. Name and Location: _____

_____

_____

b. Officers:

_____

_____

_____

c. Current Products:

_____

_____

d. Sales Volume:

_____

e. Advertising Budget:

_____

f. Other:

_____

Choice Number _____

a. Name and Location: _____

_____

_____

b. Officers:

_____

_____

_____

c. Current Products:

_____

_____

d. Sales Volume:

_____

e. Advertising Budget:

_____

f. Other:

_____

Choosing the Right Company

Choice Number _____

a. Name and Location: _____

_____

_____

b. Officers:

_____

_____

_____

c. Current Products:

_____

_____

d. Sales Volume:

_____

e. Advertising Budget:

_____

f. Other:

_____

Choice Number _____

a. Name and Location: _____

_____

_____

b. Officers:

_____

_____

_____

c. Current Products:

_____

_____

d. Sales Volume:

_____

e. Advertising Budget:

_____

f. Other:

_____

Budget

Purpose	High Estimate	Middle Estimate	Low Estimate
1. Build working model			
Parts			
Labor			
Subtotal			
2. Testing			
Parts			
Labor			
Subtotal			
3. Obtain legal protection			
Labor			
Legal fees			
Subtotal			
4. Test marketing			
Survey			
Number of units			
Advertising/publicity			
Subtotal			
5. Establish production			
Facilities			
Materials			
Employees			
Subtotal			
6. Other			
7. Grand total			

Budget

Purpose	High Estimate	Middle Estimate	Low Estimate
1. Build working model			
Parts			
Labor			
Subtotal			
2. Testing			
Parts			
Labor			
Subtotal			
3. Obtain legal protection			
Labor			
Legal fees			
Subtotal			
4. Test marketing			
Survey			
Number of units			
Advertising/publicity			
Subtotal			
5. Establish production			
Facilities			
Materials			
Employees			
Subtotal			
6. Other			
7. Grand total			

Budget

Purpose	High Estimate	Middle Estimate	Low Estimate
1. Build working model			
Parts			
Labor			
Subtotal			
2. Testing			
Parts			
Labor			
Subtotal			
3. Obtain legal protection			
Labor			
Legal fees			
Subtotal			
4. Test marketing			
Survey			
Number of units			
Advertising/publicity			
Subtotal			
5. Establish production			
Facilities			
Materials			
Employees			
Subtotal			
6. Other			
7. Grand total			

Checklist for Selling Invention/Seeking Capital

☐ Made working model

☐ Obtained legal protection

☐ Test-marketed

☐ Prepared business plan

☐ Return on investment projected

☐ Recruited management team

    ☐ President or CEO

    ☐ Accounting

    ☐ Marketing

    ☐ Engineering

☐ Surveyed manufacturers

☐ Surveyed capital sources

☐ Letter requesting appointment for presentation

    ☐ 1st presentation

    ☐ 2nd presentation

    ☐ 3rd presentation

☐ Phone call confirming appointment

    ☐ 1st presentation

    ☐ 2nd presentation

    ☐ 3rd presentation

Checklist for Selling Invention/Seeking Capital

Personal Presentation Notes

a. Advantages of my invention:

_____

_____

_____

_____

_____

b. Anticipation of possible questions:

_____

_____

_____

_____

_____

c. Profit potential:

_____

_____

_____

_____

_____

d. Demonstration:

_____

_____

_____

_____

_____

e. Trial presentation (rehearsal):

_____

_____

_____

_____

_____

Funding Sources and Results

1. Relatives/Friends

a. Name _____ Response _____

_____

b. Name _____ Response _____

_____

c. Name _____ Response _____

_____

d. Name _____ Response _____

_____

e. Name _____ Response _____

_____

2. Banks

a. Name _____ Response _____

_____

b. Name _____ Response _____

_____

c. Name _____ Response _____

_____

d. Name _____ Response _____

_____

e. Name _____ Response _____

_____

Funding Sources and Results

3. Government Programs

a. Name _____ Response _____

_____

b. Name _____ Response _____

_____

c. Name _____ Response _____

_____

d. Name _____ Response _____

_____

e. Name _____ Response _____

_____

4. Venture Capital Companies

a. Name _____ Response _____

_____

b. Name _____ Response _____

_____

c. Name _____ Response _____

_____

d. Name _____ Response _____

_____

e. Name _____ Response _____

_____

Glossary

Section A contains a glossary of words used to describe parts and functions of inventions. Section B contains a glossary of patent terms and their definitions as used in patent law.

A. Glossary of Useful Technical Terms

This glossary[1] provides a list of useful words to describe the hardware, parts, and functions of your invention in the specification and claims. The most esoteric of these words are briefly defined. While some definitions are similar, this is due to space limitations; all words have nuances in meanings.

If you're looking for a word to describe a certain part, look through the list for a likely prospect and then check a dictionary for its precise meaning. If you can't find the right word here, look in your search patents, in *What's What* or another visual dictionary, or in a thesaurus. If you can't find an appropriate word, you'll probably be able to get away with "member" or "means-plus-a-function" language. Also, for new fields, you may invent words, preferably using Latin or Greek roots, as Farnsworth did with "television," or by extending the meaning of words from analogous devices (for example, "base" for a part of a transistor). Very technical or specialized fields have their own vocabulary (for example, "catamenial" in medicine, "syzygy" in astronomy); look in appropriate tutorial texts for these. The words are grouped loosely by the following functions:

1. Structure
2. Mounting and Fastening
3. Springs
4. Numbers
5. Placement
6. Voids
7. Shape
8. Materials and Properties
9. Optics
10. Fluid Flow
11. Electronics
12. Movement
13. Rotation/Machine

[1] Expanded and used with kind permission and thanks from a list originally prepared by Louis B. Applebaum, Esq., of Newport, R.I.

1. Structure

annulus (ring)

apron

apse (dome)

arbor (shaft)

arm

bail (arch wire)

band

barrel

bascale (seesaw)

base

beam
 —cantilever
 —simple

belt

bib

blade

blower

board

bob (hanging weight)

body

bollard (thick post)

boom

boss (projection)

bougie (body-insertion member)

boule (pear-shaped)

branch

breech (back part)

bunker

caisson

canard (front wing)

carriage

case

channel

charger (shallow dish)

chase

chord

cincture (encircling band)

clew (sail part)

column

configuration

container

conveyor

cornice (horiz. top of structure)

cover

cupola (projection)

cylinder

dasher (plunger, churn)

derrick

detent

device

dibble (pointed tool)

die

disparate (dissimilar)

diversion

doctor blade (scraper)

dog (holder)

drum

echelon (staggered line)

element

enclosure

fence (stop on tool)

felly (rim of spoked wheel)

fillet (narrow strip)

fin

finger

finial (ornament)

flange

fluke (triangular part)

flute (groove on shaft)

frame

fret

frit (vitreous substance)

frustrum (cut-off area)

furcate (branch)

futtock (curved ship timber)

gaff (hook, spar)

gauge

generatrix (path traced)

gnomon (sundial upright)

graticulate (squares)

grommet

groove

gusset (triangular insert)

handle

head

header (base, support conduit)

homologous

horn

housing

hub

jacket

jaw

jib (crane arm)

knocker (clapper)

lagging (support)

ledger (horizonal support)

leg

lip

list (margin strip)

lobe

magazine

mandrel (tapered axle)

manifold

marge (edge)

marginate (w/margin)

medium

member

mullion (dividing strip)

nacelle (pod)

napiform (turnip-shaped)

neck

obcordate (heart shaped)

object

outcrop

panel

parietal (wall)

particle

partition

piece

piston

placket (slit in garment)

platform

plug

plunger

pontoon

portion

post

pounce (fine powder)

projection

purlin (horiz. rafter support)

putlog (horiz. support above ledger)

race

raceway

rank (row, series, range)

rib

riddle (sieve)

riffles (obstructions)

ring

rod

sash (frame)

screed (guide strip)

scroll

sear (catch)

shell

shoe

shoulder

skeleton

sleeve

sluice (channel)

snare

snorkel

spar (pole, support)

spline (projection on shaft)

spoke

sprag (spoke stop)

spur

stanchion

station

stay

stem

stent (stretcher)

step

stepped

stile (dividing strip)

stop

strake (ship plank)

strip

strut

tang (shank, tool)

tare (net weight)

tine

tip

tongue

trace (pivoted rod)

tracery (scrolling)

track

trave (crossbar)

truss

tuft

turret

tuyere (air pipe)

upright

vang (guy)

volar (palm, sole)

wall

ward (ridge or notch)

warp

woof (weft)

ziggurat (pyramid with terraces)

2. Mounting & Fastening

attach

billet (tip of belt)

bolt

bonnet

braze

busing

cable

camber

caster

clamp

cleat (reinforcer)

clevis (U-shaped pin)

colligate (bound together)

connection

couple

coupling

cribbing (support)

demountably

docking

dowel

engage

fay (join tightly)

ferrule (barrel)

ferruminate (attach, solder)

fix

funicular (ropelike)

gib (holding member)

gland (sliding holder)

guy wire

harp (lamp shade support)

hold

holder

hook

imbricate (regular overlap)

joint
  —universal

keeper

key

latch

lock

lug

matrix

mount

nail

nut

pin

plinth (base)

pricket (holding spike)

pylon (support)

ribband (holds ribs)

rivet

scarf (notched joint)

screw

seam

seat

secure

set

sheathed

sliding

snare/loop

solder

spike

springably

support

thill (horse joinder stake)

thrust

toe-in

tweld

3. Springs

air

bias
  —element

coil

compressed

elastic

expanded

helical
  —compression
  —tension

leaf

press

relaxed

resilient

springably

torsional

urge

4. Numbers

argument

caboodle (collection, bunch)

compound

congeries (collection, aggregation)

difference

dividend

divisor

equation

formula

index

lemma

minuend

modulo

multiplicand

multiplicity

multiplier

plurality

power

product

quotient

remainder

sheaf

subtrahend

variable

5. Placement (Relation)

adjacent

aft

aligned

angle

aposition (facing)

array

attached

axial

bottom

close

complementary

concentric

contiguous

contracted

course

crest

disposed

distal

divided

edge

engaged

equitant (overlap in two ranks)

evert (inside out)

extended

external

face

fiducial (reference)

film

fore

horizontal

imbricate (overlapping series)

incline

integral

intermediate

internal

interposed

juxtaposed

layer

located

lower

mating

meshing

mesial (between)

normal

oblique

obtuse

offset

open

opposed

overlapping

parallel

perpendicular

pitched

positioned

projecting

prolapsed (out of place)

proximal

proximate

raked (pitched)

reference

removable

resting

rim

row

sandwich

section

slant

spacer

staggered

superimposed

supported

surface

surrounding

symmetrical

tilt

top

ubiety (located in a place)

vernier (9:10 gauge)

vertical

6. Voids

aperture

bore

cavity

chamber

concavity

cutout

dimple

duct

embrasure (slant opening)

engraved

filister (groove)

foramen (opening)

fossa (depression)

furrow (groove)

gain (notch)

gap

groove

hole

hollow

infold

intaglinated (engraved)

invaginate (enclosed, turned in)

lumen (bore of tube)

lunette (crescent opening)

mortise (cutout)

nock (notch on arrow)

notch

opening

orifice

passage

placket (garment slit)

polled (dehorned)

rabbet (groove)

raceway

recess

rifling (spiral groove)

separation

slit

slot

spandrel (triangular gap above arch side)

sulcus (groove)

ullage (lost liquid)

via (path)

void

wicket (small door or gate)

7. Shape

acclivity (slope)

acicular (needle-shaped)

agonic (no angle)

annular

anticline (peak)

applanation

arch

arcuate

barrel

bevel

bifurcated (two branches)

bight (bend)

botryoidal (like a bunch of grapes)

bucket

buckled

chamfer (beveled)

channel

circular

coin

concave

congruent (same shape)

conical

convex

convoluted (curled in)

corner (inside, outside)

corrugated

crest

crimp

crispate (curled)

cup

cusp (projection)

cylinder

depression

dihedral (two-faced)

direction

disc

dome

draw (depression)

drawing (pulling out)

elliptical

fairing (streamlined)

fin

flange

fold

fork

fossa (groove)

fundus (base)

furcate (branched)

goffer (ridges or pleats)

helical

hook

incurvate (curved in)

invaginate (sheathed, folded in)

line

lobe

lozenge (diamond-shaped)

lune (crescent)

mammilated (nipple-shaped)

navicular (boat-shaped)

notch

oblate (flattened)

oblong

ogive (pointed arch)

orb (globe)

oval

parabolic

parallelogram

plane

prolate (cigar-shaped)

rectangular

reticulated (gridlike)

rhomboid (nonequal adjacent sides)

rhombus (equal adjacent sides)

rick-rock

rill (long narrow valley)

round

salient (standing out)

serrated

setaceous (bristlelike)

sheet

shelf

sinusoidal

skive (shaven)

slab

spall (broken chips)

spherical

spica (overlapping reverse spirals)

square

stamped

striated (grooved or ridged)

swaged (flattened)

swale (depression)

syncline (V-shaped)

taper terminus (end)

tesselated (tiled)

topology (unchangeable geometry)

tortuous (twisting)

tram (on wheels)

trefoil (three-leaved)

triangular

trihedral (3-sided)

trough

tubular

tumescence (detumescence)

turbinate (top/spiral shaped)

twist

upset (distorted)

vermiculate (worm-eaten)

volute (spiral)

wafer

web

wedge

whorl (spiral)

xyresic (razor-sharp)

8. Materials & Properties

adhesive

alluvial (sand or clay deposited by water)

concrete

cork

dappled (spotted)

denier (gauge)

dense

elastic

enlarged

fabric

fiber

flexible

foraminous

frit (fused glass)

haptic (sense of touch)

humectant (moistener)

insulation

intenerate (soften)

liquid

material

metal

nappy

opaque

pied (splotched)

placer (glacial deposit)

plastic

porous

prill

refractory

resilient

rigid

rubber

sand

screen

shirred (gathered)

smectic (cleaning)

stratified (layered)

strong

sturdy

translucent

transparent

wood

xerotic (dry)

9. Optics

aniseikonic (unequal sizes)

astigmatic

bezel

bulb
 —fluorescent
 —incandescent

fresnel

lamp

light
 —beam
 —ray

opaque

parallax (change in direction)

pellicle

pellucid (clear)

reflection

refraction

schlieren (streaks)

translucent

transmission

transparent

window

10. Fluid Flow

accumulator

afferent (to center)

aspirator

bellows

bibb (valve)

bung (hole or stopper)

cock (valve)

conduit

confluent (flow together)

connector

convection

cylinder
 —piston
 —rod

dashpot

diaphragm

discharge

dispenser

efferent (away from center)

filter

fitting

flue

gasket

hose

hydraulic

medium

navicular (like boat)

nozzle

obturator (blocker)

outlet

pipe

plunger

poppet (axial valve)

port
  —inlet
  —outlet

pump
  —centrifugal
  —gear
  —piston
  —reservoir
  —seal
  —siphon
  —tank
  —vane

sparge (spray)

sprue (vent tube)

suctorial (sucking)

sufflate (inflate)

swash (channel barrier)

tube

valve
  —ball
  —check
  —control
  —gate
  —shutoff

wattle (intertwined wall)

weir (dam)

wicket (gate or door)

11. Electronics

adder

amplifier

astable

capacitance

clipping

conductor

contact

control element

demodulator

diode

electrode

electromagnet

filament

flip flop

gate (AND, OR, etc.)

impedance

inductance

insulator

integrated circuit

laser

lead

light emitting diode

line cord

liquid crystal

maser

memory

motor

multiplier

multivibrator

oscillator

pixel (CRT spot)

power supply

raster

read-and-write memory

read-only memory

resistance

sampling

Schmitt trigger

shift register

Shottky diode

socket

solenoid

switch

terminal

thermistor

transformer

transistor

triode

valve

varistor

wire

Zener diode

12. Movement

alternate

articulate (jointed)

avulsion (tear away)

cam

compression

cyclic

detent (click)

downward

draft (pull)

drag

drift pin

drill

eccentric

emergent

epicyclic (on circle)

equilibrate (bring into equilibrium)

escapement

extensible

extrude

grinding

impact

inclined plane

inertia

interval

lag

lead

lever

linkage
  —parallel

longitudinal

machine

meeting

nutate (to and fro)

pressing

propelling

pulverize

sagging

sequacious (regular)

severing

shuttle (to & fro member)

skive (peel)

slidable

snub (stop)

straight line
  —motion

terminating

toggle

torque

traction

transverse

traversing

triturate (grind to powder)

trochoid (roll on circle)

urging

vibrating

wedge

13. Rotation/Machine

antifriction
  —ball
  —needle
  —roller
  —tapered

arbor (shaft)

bell crank

brake
  —band
  —disk
  —shoe

bushing

cam

chain

clevis (circular holder)

clutch
  —centrifugal
  —one-way
  —sprag (stop)
  —toothed

cog (tooth)

connecting rod

crank arm

drive
  —belt
  —pulley
  —sheave
  —toothed

flexible coupling

friction

fulcrum

gear
  —bevel
  —crown
  —internal

  —noncircular
  —pinion
  —right angle
  —spur
  —wheel
  —worm

gin (hoist, pile driver, pump)

guide

gudgeon (axle)

intermittent
  —escapement
  —geneva
  —pawl
  —pendulum
  —ratchet

jack

journal

mandrel

orbit

pinion (small wheel)

pintle (axle)

pivot

pulley

radial

radius bar

screw

seal

sheave (pulley)

spindle

sprocket

swash (wobble) plate

tappet (valve cam)

trunnion

variable speed

vertiginous (turning)

ward (ridge or notch)

winch

yoke

B. Glossary of Patent Terms

abstract a concise, one-paragraph summary of the patent. It details the structure, nature, and purpose of the invention. The abstract is used by the PTO and the public to quickly determine the gist of what is being disclosed.

abandonment 1. allowing a pending, active patent application to be removed from the PTO's active files and treated as if the inventor has given up all claims to a patent on the invention. An inventor can expressly abandon an application by letter or allow an application to go abandoned by not timely replying to an office action. 2. treating an invention as if the inventor has lost all interest in exploiting it, usually by not developing it or by not filing a patent application on it for a very long time.

actual damages (also known as compensatory damages) in a lawsuit, money awarded to one party to cover actual injury or economic loss. Actual damages are intended to put the injured party in the position he or she was in prior to the injury.

answer a written response to a complaint (the opening papers in a lawsuit) in which the defendant admits or denies the allegations and may provide a list of defenses.

best mode the inventor's principal and preferred method of embodying the invention.

Board of Appeals and Patent Interferences (BAPI) a tribunal of judges at the PTO that hears appeals from final Office Actions.

cease and desist letter correspondence from the owner of a proprietary work that requests the cessation of all infringing activity.

clear and convincing proof evidence that is highly probable and free from serious doubt.

complaint papers filed with a court clerk by the plaintiff to initiate a lawsuit by setting out facts and legal claims (usually called causes of action).

compositions of matter items such as chemical compositions, conglomerates, aggregates, or other chemically significant substances that are usually supplied in bulk (solid or particulate), liquid, or gaseous form.

conception the mental part of inventing, including how an invention is formulated or how a problem is solved.

confidentiality agreement (also known as a nondisclosure agreement) a contract in which one or both parties agree not to disclose certain information.

continuation application a new patent application that allows the applicant to re-present an invention and get a second or third bite at the apple. The applicant can file a new application (known as a "continuation") while the original (or "parent") application is still pending. A continuation application consists of the same invention, cross-referenced to the parent application and a new set of claims. The applicant retains the filing date of the parent application for purposes of determining the relevancy of prior art.

Continuation-in-Part (CIP) less common than a continuation application, this form of extension application is used when a portion or all of an earlier patent application is continued and new matter (not disclosed in the earlier application) is included. CIP applications are used when an applicant wants to present an improvement but is prevented from adding a pending application to it because of the prohibition against adding "new matter."

Continuing Prosecution Application (CPA) a patent application that is like a continuation application in effect, but no new application need be filed. The applicant merely pays another filing fee, submits new claims, and files a CPA request form. CPAs can only be used for applications filed prior to 2000 May 29. Applications after that date must use the Request for Continued Examination.

contributory infringement occurs when a material component of a patented invention is sold with knowledge that the component is designed for an unauthorized use. This type of infringement cannot occur unless there is a direct infringement. In other words, it is not enough to sell infringing parts; those parts must be used in an infringing invention.

copyright the legal right to exclude others, for a limited time, from copying, selling, performing, displaying, or making derivative versions of a work of authorship such as a writing, music, or artwork.

counterclaim a legal claim usually asserted by the defendant against an opposing party, usually the plaintiff.

Court of Appeals for the Federal Circuit (CAFC) the federal appeals court that specializes in patent appeals. If the Board of Appeals and Patent Interferences rejects an application appeal, an applicant can further appeal to the CAFC within 60 days of the decision. If the CAFC upholds the PTO, the applicant can request the United States Supreme Court hear the case (although the Supreme Court rarely hears patent appeals).

date of invention the earliest of the following dates: (a) the date an inventor filed the patent application (provisional or regular), (b) the date an inventor can prove that the invention was built and tested in the U.S. or a country that is a member of the North American Free Trade Association (NAFTA) or the World Trade Organization (WTO), or (c) the date an inventor can prove that the invention was conceived in a NAFTA or WTO country, provided the inventor can also prove diligence in building and testing it or filing a patent application on it.

declaratory relief a request that the court sort out the rights and legal obligations of the parties in the midst of an actual controversy.

deposit date the date the PTO receives a patent application.

deposition oral or written testimony of a party or witness and given under oath.

design patent covers the unique, ornamental, or visible shape or design of a nonnatural object.

divisional application a patent application used when an applicant wants to protect several inventions claimed in the original application. The official definition is "a later application for a distinct or independent invention, carved out of a pending application and disclosing and claiming only subject matter disclosed in the earlier or parent application" (MPEP 201.06). A divisional application is entitled to the filing date of the parent case for purposes of overcoming prior art. The divisional application must be filed while the parent is pending. A divisional application can be filed as a CPA.

Doctrine of Equivalents (DoE) a form of patent infringement that occurs when an invention performs substantially the same function in substantially the same manner and obtains the same result as the patented invention. A court analyzes each element of the patented invention separately. Under a recent Supreme Court decision, the DoE must be applied on an element-by-element basis to the claims.

double patenting when an applicant has obtained a patent and has filed a second application containing the same invention, the second application will be rejected. If the second application resulted in a patent, that patent will be invalidated. Two applications contain the same invention when the two inventions are literally the same or the second invention is an obvious modification of the first invention.

embodiment a physical version of an invention as described in a patent application; a patent application may describe several embodiments of an invention, but is supposed to state the one that the inventor considers the **best mode** as of the filing date; see **ramification**.

enhanced damages (treble damages) in exceptional infringement cases, financial damages may be increased, at the discretion of the court, up to triple the award for actual damages (known as "enhanced damages").

examiner's answer a brief submitted by a patent examiner in response to an applicant's brief in an appeal to the PTO's Board of Patent Appeals and Interferences.

exclusive jurisdiction the sole authority of a court to hear a certain type of case.

exhaustion *see* **first sale doctrine**.

ex parte (Latin: one party only) refers to legal proceedings where only one party is present or represented.

experimental use doctrine a rule excusing an inventor from the one-year bar provided that the alleged sale or public use was primarily for the purpose of perfecting or testing the invention.

file wrapper estoppel (or prosecution history estoppel) affirmative defense used in patent infringement litigation that precludes the patent owner from asserting rights that were disclaimed during the patent application process. The term is derived from the fact that the official file in which a patent is contained at the Patent and Trademark Office is known as a "file wrapper." All statements, admissions, correspondence, or documentation relating to the invention are placed in the file wrapper. Estoppel means that a party is prevented from acting contrary to a former statement or action when someone else has relied to the party's detriment on the prior statement or action.

final office action the examiner's response to the applicant's first amendment. The final office action is supposed to end the prosecution stage but a "final action" is rarely final.

first Office Action (sometimes called an "official letter" or "OA") response from the patent examiner after the initial examination of the application. It is very rare that an application is allowed in the first Office Action. More often, the examiner rejects some or all of the claims.

first sale doctrine (also known as the exhaustion doctrine) once a patented product (or product resulting from a patented process) is sold or licensed, the patent owner's rights are exhausted and the owner has no further rights as to the resale of that particular article.

generic (genus) an entire group or class, or a group of related items or species.

grace period a period in which an action may be taken even though the normal period for taking action has passed.

indirect infringement occurs either when someone is persuaded to make, use, or sell a patented invention without authorization (inducing infringement); or when a material component of a patented invention is sold with knowledge that the component is designed for an unauthorized use (contributory infringement). An indirect infringement cannot occur unless there is a direct infringement. In other words, it is not enough to sell infringing parts; those parts must be used in an infringing invention.

infringement an invention is infringing if it is a literal copy of a patented invention or if it performs substantially the same function in substantially the same manner and obtains the same result as the patented invention. *See* **doctrine of equivalents**

injunction a court order requiring that a party halt a particular activity. In the case of patent infringement, a court can order all infringing activity be halted at the end of a trial (a permanent injunction) or the patent owner can attempt to halt the infringing activity immediately, rather than wait for a trial (a preliminary injunction). A court uses two factors to determine whether to grant a preliminary injunction: (1) Is the plaintiff likely to succeed in the lawsuit? and (2) Will the plaintiff suffer irreparable harm if the injunction is not granted? The patent owner may seek relief for a very short injunction known as a temporary restraining order or TRO, which usually lasts only a few days or weeks. A temporary restraining order may be granted without notice to the infringer if it appears that immediate damage will result—for example, that evidence will be destroyed.

interference a costly, complex PTO proceeding that determines who will get a patent when two or more applicants are claiming the same invention. It is basically a method of sorting out priority of inventorship. Occasionally an interference may involve a patent that has been in force for less than one year.

inter partes (Latin: between parties) refers to legal proceedings where all parties to the action are represented.

interrogatories written questions that must be answered under oath.

invention any new article, machine, composition, or process or new use developed by a human.

jury instructions explanations of the legal rules that the jury must use in reaching a verdict.

lab notebook a system of documenting an invention that usually includes descriptions of the invention and novel features; procedures used in the building and testing of the invention; drawings, photos, or sketches of the invention; test results and conclusions; discussions of any known prior-art references; and additional documentation such as correspondence and purchase receipts.

literal infringement occurs if a defendant makes, sells, or uses the invention defined in the plaintiff's patent claim. In other words, the infringing product includes each and every component, part, or step in the patented invention. It is a literal infringement because the defendant's device is actually the *same* invention in the patent claim.

machine a device or things used for accomplishing a task; usually involves some activity or motion performed by working parts.

magistrate an officer of the court who may exercise some of the authority of a federal district court judge, including the authority to conduct a jury or nonjury trial.

manufactures (sometimes termed "articles of manufacture") items that have been made by human hands or by machines; may have working or moving parts as prime features.

means-plus-function clause (or means for clause) a provision in a patent claim in which the applicant does not specifically describe the structure of one of the items in the patent and instead describes the function of the item. Term is derived from the fact that the clause usually starts with the word "means."

new matter any technical information, including dimensions, materials, etc., that was not present in the patent application as originally filed. An applicant can never add new matter to an application (PTO Rule 118).

new-use invention a new and unobvious process or method for using an old and known invention.

nonobviousness a standard of patentability that requires that an invention produce "unusual and surprising results." In 1966, the U.S. Supreme Court established the steps for determining unobviousness in the case of *Graham v. John Deere*, 383 U.S. 1 (1966).

Notice of Allowance a document issued when the examiner is convinced that the application meets the requirements of patentability. An issue fee is due within three months.

objection a disapproval made by an examiner to a nonsubstantive matter, such as an unclear drawing or dependent claim having a rejected claim.

objects and advantages a phrase used to explain "what the invention accomplishes." Usually, the objects are also the invention's advantages, since those aspects are intended to be superior over prior art.

Office Action (OA, also known as Official Letter or Examiner's Action) correspondence (usually including forms and a letter) from a patent examiner that describes what is wrong with the application and why it cannot be allowed. Generally, an OA will reject claims, list defects in the specifications or drawings, raise objections, or cite and enclose copies of relevant prior art demonstrating a lack of novelty or nonobviousness.

on-sale bar prevents an inventor from acquiring patent protection if the application is filed more than one year from the date of sale, use, or offer of sale of the invention in the United States.

one-year rule a rule that requires an inventor to file a patent application within one year after selling, offering for sale, or commercially or publicly using or describing an invention. If an inventor fails to file within one year of such occurrence the inventor is barred from obtaining a patent.

patent a grant from a government that confers upon an inventor the right to exclude others from making, using, selling, importing, or offering an invention for sale for a fixed period of time.

patent application a set of papers that describe an invention and that are suitable for filing in a patent office in order to apply for a patent on the invention.

Patent Application Declaration (PAD) a declaration that identifies the inventor or joint inventors and provides an attestation by the applicant that the inventor understands the contents of the claims and specification and has fully disclosed all material information. The PTO provides a form for the PAD.

patent misuse a defense in patent infringement that prevents a patent owner who has abused patent law from enforcing patent rights. Common examples of misuse are violation of the antitrust laws or unethical business practices.

patent pending (also known as the "pendency period") time between filing a patent application (or PPA) and issuance of the patent. The inventor has no patent rights during this period. However, when and if the patent later issues, the inventor will obtain the right to prevent the continuation of any infringing activity that started during the pendency period. If the application has been published by the PTO during the pendency period and the infringer had notice, the applicant may later seek royalties for these infringements during the pendency period. It's a criminal offense to use the words "patent applied for" or "patent pending" (they mean the same thing) in any advertising if there's no active, applicable regular or provisional patent application on file.

patent prosecution the process of shepherding a patent application through the Patent and Trademark Office.

Patent Rules of Practice administrative regulations located in Volume 37 of the Code of Federal Regulations (37 CFR § 1).

pendency period. *See* **patent pending**

permanent injunction a durable injunction issued after a final judgment on the merits of the case; permanently restrains the defendant from engaging in the infringing activity.

Petition to Make Special an applicant can, under certain circumstances, have an application examined sooner than the normal course of PTO examination (one to three years). This is accomplished by filing a Petition to Make Special (PTMS), together with a Supporting Declaration.

plant patent covers plants that can be reproduced through the use of grafts and cuttings (asexual reproduction).

power of attorney a document that gives another person legal authority to act on one's behalf. If an attorney is preparing an application on behalf of an inventor, a power of attorney should be executed to authorize the patent attorney or agent to act on behalf of the inventor. The power of attorney form may be combined with the Patent Application Declaration.

prima facie (Latin: on its face) at first sight, obvious.

prior art the state of knowledge existing or publicly available either before the date of an invention or more than one year prior to the patent application date.

process (sometimes referred to as a "method") a way of doing or making things that involves more than purely mental manipulations.

Provisional Patent Application (PPA) an interim document that clearly explains how to make and use the invention. The PPA is equivalent to a reduction to practice (see below). If a regular patent application is filed within one year of filing the PPA, the inventor can use the PPA's filing date for the purpose of deciding whether a reference is prior art. In addition to an early filing date, an inventor may claim patent pending status for the one-year period following the filing of the PPA.

ramification a version or variation of an invention that is different from a main version or **best mode**.

reduction to practice the point at which the inventor can demonstrate that the invention works for its intended purpose. Reduction to practice can be accomplished by building and testing the invention (actual reduction to practice) or by preparing a patent application or provisional patent application that shows how to make and use the invention and that it works (constructive reduction to practice). In the event of a dispute or a challenge at the PTO, invention documentation is essential in order to prove the "how and when" of conception and reduction to practice.

reissue application an application used to correct information in a patent. It is usually filed when a patent owner believes the claims are not broad enough, the claims are too broad (the applicant discovered a new reference), or there are significant errors in the specification. In these cases, the applicant seeks to correct the patent by filing an application to get the applicant's original patent reissued at any time during its term. The reissue patent will take the place of the applicant's original patent and expire the same time as the original patent would have expired. If the applicant wants to broaden the claims of the patent through a reissue application, the applicant must do so within two years from the date the original patent issued. There is a risk in filing a reissue application because all of the claims of the original patent will be examined and can be rejected.

rejection a disapproval made by an examiner to a substantive matter such as a claim that is deemed obvious over the prior art.

repair doctrine affirmative defense based on the right of an authorized licensor of a patented device to repair and replace unpatented components. It also includes the right to sell materials used to repair or replace a patented invention. The defense does not apply for completely rebuilt inventions, unauthorized inventions, or items that are made or sold without authorization of the patent owner.

reply a brief submitted by a patent applicant in response to an examiner's answer.

request for admission request for a party to the lawsuit to admit the truthfulness of a statement.

Request for Continued Examination (RCE) a paper filed when a patent applicant wishes to continue prosecuting an application that has received a final **Office Action**. Filing the RCE with another filing fee effectively removes the final action so that the applicant can submit further amendments—for example, new claims, new arguments, a new declaration, or new references.

request for production of documents the way a party to a lawsuit obtains documents or other physical evidence from the other side.

reverse doctrine of equivalents (or negative doctrine of equivalents) a rarely used affirmative defense to patent infringement in which, even if there is a literal infringement, the court will excuse the defendant's conduct if the infringing device has a different function or result than the patented invention. The doctrine is applied when the allegedly infringing device performs the same function in a substantially different way.

sequence listing an attachment to a patent application used if a biotech invention includes a sequence listing of a nucleotide or amino acid sequence. The applicant attaches this information on separate sheets of paper and refers to the sequence listing in the application (see PTO Rule 77). If there is no sequence listing, the applicant states "Nonapplicable."

small entity a status that enables small businesses, independent inventors, and nonprofit companies to pay a reduced application fee. There are three types of small entities: (1) independent inventors, (2) nonprofit companies, and (3) small businesses. To qualify, an independent inventor must either own all rights, or have transferred—or be obligated to transfer—rights to a small business or nonprofit organization. Nonprofit organizations are defined and listed in the Code of Federal Regulations and usually are educational institutions or charitable organizations. A small-entity business is one with fewer than 500 employees. The number of employees is computed by averaging the number of full- and part-time employees during a fiscal year.

species one of a group of related individual items collectively subordinate to a genus.

specification a patent application disclosure made by the inventor and drafted so that an individual skilled in the art to which the invention pertains could, when reading the patent, make and use the invention without needing further experiment. A **specification** is constructed of several sections. Collectively, these sections form a narrative that describes and distinguishes the invention. If it can later be proved that the inventor knew of a better way (or "best mode") and failed to disclose it, that failure could result in the loss of patent rights.

statute of limitations the legally prescribed time limit in which a lawsuit must be filed. In patent law there is no time limit (statute of limitations) for filing a patent infringement lawsuit, but monetary damages can be recovered only for infringements committed during the six years prior to the filing the lawsuit. For example, if a patent owner sues after ten years of infringement, the owner cannot recover monetary damages for the first four years of infringement. Despite the fact that there is no law setting a time limit, courts will not permit a patent owner to sue for infringement if the owner has waited an unreasonable time to file the lawsuit ("laches").

Statutory Invention Registration (SIR) a document that allows an applicant who abandons an application to prevent anyone else from getting a valid patent on the same invention. This is accomplished by converting the patent application to a SIR.

statutory subject matter an invention that falls into one of the five statutory classes: process (method), machine, article of manufacture, composition, or a "new use" of one of the first four.

substitute application essentially a duplicate of an abandoned patent application. (See MPEP § 201.09.) The disadvantage of a substitute application is that the applicant doesn't get the benefit of the filing date of the previously abandoned patent application, which could be useful, because any prior art occurring after the filing date of the earlier case can be used against the substitute case. If the applicant's substitute application issues into a patent, the patent will expire 20 years from the filing date of the substitute.

successor liability responsibility for infringement that is borne by a company that has purchased another company that is liable for infringements. In order for successor liability to occur, there must be an agreement between the companies to assume liability or a merger between the companies, or the purchaser must be a "continuation" of the purchased business. If the sale is made to escape liability and lacks any of the foregoing characteristics, liability will still attach.

summons a document served with the complaint that tells the defendant he or she has been sued, has a certain time limit in which to respond, and must appear in court on a stated date.

temporary restraining order (TRO) a court order that tells one party to do or stop doing something—for example, to stop infringing. A TRO is issued after the aggrieved party appears before a judge. Once the TRO is issued, the court holds a second hearing where the other side can tell his or her story and the court can decide whether to make the TRO permanent by issuing an injunction. The TRO is often granted *ex parte* (without allowing the other side to respond), and for that reason is short in duration and remains in effect only until the court has an opportunity to schedule a hearing for the preliminary injunction.

traverse to argue against.

tying a form of patent misuse in which, as a condition of a transaction, the buyer of a patented device must also purchase an additional product. For example, in one case a company had a patent on a machine that deposited salt tablets in canned food. Purchasers of the machine were also required to buy salt tablets from the patent owner. A party that commits patent misuse may have its patent invalidated, may have to pay monetary damages, or both.

utility patent the main type of patent, which covers inventions that function in a unique manner to produce a utilitarian result.

verified statement a statement made under oath or a declaration. A false verified statement is punishable as perjury.

vicarious liability legal responsibility that results when a business such as a corporation or partnership is liable for infringements committed by employees or agents. This liability attaches when the agent acts under the authority or direction of the business, an employee acts within the scope of employment, or the business benefits from, or adopts or approves the infringing activity.

voir dire ("speak the truth") process by which attorneys and judges question potential jurors in order to determine whether they may be fair and impartial.

Fee Schedule

> **CAUTION**
> To see all current fees go to the PTO website (www.uspto.gov), then click "Patents," then "Tutorial/Fees," then "Current FY2008 Fee Schedule." If you file by EFS-Web (strongly recommended), all current fees are also on the Fee-Payment pages. If you underpay any fee, the PTO imposes a stiff surcharge. The USPTO's filing fee is currently

broken into three parts (filing, search, and examination). These fees are itemized on the PTO's Fee Transmittal Form (PTO/SB/17), but since the total must be paid at the time of filing, the listing below includes only the total fee. Two fees separated by a slash refer to large entity/small entity; a single fee applies to both entities. PTO fees are listed in order for the patenting process.

Service or Item	Fee ($)	Form/Chapter
PTO Fees (Rule):		
Printed Copy of Patent or Patent Order Coupon Utility/Design; Also for Copy of SIR (19(a))	3	Ch. 6
Copy of Plant Patent in Color/Utility With Color Drawings (19(a))	15	
Application Filing Fees:		
Utility Patent (incl. search and exam fees) (16(a))*	1,030/515	10-1, 14-1
Utility Patent Electronic Filing (incl. search and exam fees)*	1,030/435	
Design Patent (incl. search and exam fees) (16(f))*	440/220	10-8
Plant Patent (incl. search and exam fees) (16(g))*	680/340	Ch. 10
Provisional Patent Appn., Filing (16(r))	210/105	Ch. 3
Prov. Appn. Late Filing Fee or Cover Sheet (16(l))	50/25	Ch. 3
Prov. Appn. Correct Inventors or Convert RPA to PPA (17(q))	50	Ch. 3
Reissue Patent (incl. search and exam)	1,430/715	Ch. 14
Fee for Each Independent Claim Over Three (16(b))	210/105	10-1, 14-1
Fee for Each Claim Over 20 (Independent or Dependent) (16(c))	50/25	Ch. 10
Surcharge—Multiple Dependent Claims in Any Application (16(d))	370/185	Ch. 10
Surcharge If Filing Fee or Declaration Late (16(e))	130/65	Ch. 10
Recording Assignment per Application or Patent Involved (21(h))	40	10-1
Surcharge If Any Check Bounces (21(m))	50	Ch. 10
Size Fee (if application is over 100 sheets)	260/130	Ch. 10
Request for Continued Examination	820/410	Ch. 14

* Although these fees have three components (filing, search, and exam—see Form 10-3), all components must be paid in one lump sum, indicated in the "Fee ($)" column.

Service or Item	Fee ($)	Form/Chapter
Petitions to Commissioner:		
To Accept Color Drawings (17(k)), Regarding Inventorship	130	Ch. 10
Maintenance Fees, Interferences, Foreign Filing Licenses, Access to Records, Foreign Priority Papers, and Misc.	130	Ch. 13
Amendments After Issue Fee, Defer/Withdraw a Case From Issue (17(k,l))	130	10-7
To Make Application Special (where fee required) (17(l))	200	Ch. 10
Expedited Examination of Design Application (Rocket Docket) (17(k))	900	Ch. 10
Extra Special Petitions (17f)	400	
Petition to Revive Abandoned Appication:		
Unavoidable Delay (17(l))	510/255	Ch. 13
Unintentional Delay (17(m))	1,540/770	Ch. 13
Extensions to Reply to Office Actions:		
1st Month (17(a))	120/60	13-5
2nd Month (17(b))	460/230	13-5
3rd Month (17(c))	1,050/525	13-5
4th Month (17(d))	1,640/820	13-5
5th Month (17(d)) (no extension over six months)	2,230/1,115	13-5
Appeal to Board of Appeals & Patent Interferences:		
Filing Notice of Appeal (17(b)) or Brief (17(c))	510/255	Ch. 13
Oral Hearing (17(g))	1,030/515	Ch. 13
Application Issue and Post-Issue Fees:		
Utility Patent (18(a))	1,440/720	Ch. 13
Utility Patent Publication Fee (18(d))	300	Chs. 8-10, 13
Prior Art Citation Fee Against Published Appn. (17(p))	180	Ch. 13
Design Patent (18(b))	820/410	Ch. 13
Plant Patent (18(c))	1,130/565	Ch. 13
Certificate to Correct Patent (Applicant's Mistake) (20(a))	100	15-1
Reexamination Fee Ex Parte (20(c))	2,520	Ch. 15
Reexamination Fee Inter Partes (20(c)(2))	8,800	
Utility Patent Maintenance Fees:		
I (3.5 years—pays for yrs 4 thru 8) (20(e))	930/465	15-3
II (7.5 years—pays for yrs 9 thru 12) (20(f))	2,360/1,180	15-3
III (11.5 years—pays for yrs 13 thru 17) (20(g))	3,910/1,955	15-3
Late Charge (in 6-month grace period) (20(h))	130/65	15-3
Petition to Revive (after patent expires)—unintentional delay (20(i))	1,640	Ch. 15
Petition to Revive (after patent expires)—unavoidable delay (20(i))	700	Ch. 15

Service or Item	Fee ($)	Form/Chapter
Other Fees:		
Certified Copy Patent Application as Filed (19(b))	25	Ch. 12
Certified Copy of File & Contents—Issued Patent (19(b)(2)) up to 400 pp.	200	Ch. 15
Certified Copy of Patent Assignment Record (19(b)(3))	25	Ch. 14
Disclaimer of Claims or Terminal Part of Term of Patent (20(d))	130/65	
Dedication of Entire Term or Terminal Part of Term of Patent	No charge	
Late IDS Fee (before or after final action) (17(p))	180	Ch. 13
Trademark Application Filing (in PTO) on Paper	375	Ch. 1
Trademark Application Filing (in PTO) via the Internet	325	Ch. 1
Trademark Application Filing (in PTO) via the Internet Using Standard Goods Terms (TEAS+)	275	Ch. 1
Trademark Application Filing (in California)	70	Ch. 1
Copyright Application Filing (in Copyright Office)	45	Ch. 1
PCT and Foreign Fees (Always check just before filing; these fees change frequently):		
Transmittal Fee	300	Ch. 12
Search Fees:		
In U.S. PTO		
—no corres. prior U.S. appn. filed	1,800	Ch. 12
—corres. prior U.S. appn. filed	1,800	Ch. 12
In European Patent Office	2,197	Ch. 12
In Korean Intellectual Property Office	232	Ch. 12
International Fees:		
Basic (First 30 Pages)	1,163*	Ch. 12
Each Additional Sheet Over 30	12	Ch. 12
Chapter II Fees:		
Handling Fee	155	Ch. 12
Examination Fee: In U.S. PTO (assuming a patent search is done by the U.S. PTO, as described in Chapter 1)	600–750	
Filing a European or Japanese Pat. Appn., incl. agent's fee, approx.	5,000–7,000	Ch. 12

* $1,008 if PCT-EASY software used.

Tear-Out Forms

n Appendix V we provide you with tear-out copies of the following:

- Consultant's Work Agreement. If you do use a consultant (for example, a model maker), you should take precautions to protect the confidentiality and proprietary status of your invention. There's no substitute for checking out your consultant carefully by asking for references (assuming you don't already know the consultant). In addition, have your consultant sign a copy of the Consultant's Work Agreement. For more information on this subject, see Chapter 4 of *Patent It Yourself.*

- Proprietary Materials Agreement. This agreement is designed for use when you disclose significant details about an unpatented invention to potential developers, investors, evaluators, or partners. The form binds the recipient of the information to confidentiality so you can preserve your invention as a trade secret up until the time your patent is made public.

- Joint Owners' Agreement. Problems commonly arise in situations where there are two or more inventors or owners of a patent application or patent. These include questions as to who is entitled to commercially exploit the invention, financial shares, what type of accounting must be performed on partnership books, etc. Fortunately, most of these problems can be eliminated by the use of a Joint Owners' Agreement (JOA). More information on joint ownership issues is available in Chapter 16 of *Patent It Yourself.*

- Assignment of Invention and Patent Application. To make a transfer of ownership in the arcane patent world, you must sign an "assignment"—a legal document that the law will recognize as effective to make the transfer of ownership. An assignment for transferring ownership of an invention is provided. A cover sheet and fee must be submitted to the PTO with any assignment to be recorded. More information about this procedure and about assignment of patent rights is available in Chapter 16 of *Patent It Yourself.* The assignment document presented here, like the Joint Owners' Agreement, is but one of many possible alternatives. If you use it, you may want to change a number of provisions to fit your situation. Also, keep in mind, a consultation with a patent attorney is advisable if you wish to fully understand how this agreement will affect your rights.

- Universal License Agreement. This agreement can be used to exclusively or nonexclusively license your invention as well as to license know-how. It can also be used to grant a potential licensee an option to evaluate your invention for a given period in return for a payment. Most companies will either prefer to use their own license agreement or to make one up from scratch, but you can use the Universal License Agreement for purposes of comparison.

- Invention Disclosure Statement. This form is used to document conception when filing under the Disclosure Document Program. (See Chapter 2, Section C, of this book or Chapter 3 of *Patent it Yourself.*)

- Provisional Patent Application Cover Letter. This is a cover letter for filing a provisional patent application (See Chapter 2, Section E, of this book or Chapter 3 of *Patent it Yourself.*)

Consultant's Work Agreement

1. **Parties:** This Work Agreement is made between the following parties:

   Name(s): _____

   Address(es): _____

   _____

   (hereinafter "Contractor"), and

   Name(s): _____

   Address(es): _____

   _____

   (hereinafter "Consultant").

2. **Name of Project:**

   _____

   _____

3. **Work to Be Performed by Consultant:**

   _____

   _____

4. **Work/Payment Schedule:**

   _____

   _____

5. **Date:** This Agreement shall be effective as of the latter date below written.

6. **Recitals:** Contractor has one or more ideas relating to the above project and desires to have such project developed more completely, as specified in the above statement of Work. Consultant has certain skills desired by Contractor relating to performance of the above Work.

7. **Performance:** Consultant will perform the above work for Contractor in accordance with the above-scheduled Work/Payment Schedule, and Contractor will make the above-scheduled payments to Consultant. Any changes to the Work to Be Performed or the Work/Payment Schedule shall be described in a writing referring to this Agreement and signed and dated by both parties. Time is of the essence of this Agreement, and if Consultant fails to perform according to the above work schedule, contractor may (a) void this agreement and pay consultant 50% of what would otherwise be due, or (b) require that Consultant pay contractor a penalty of $ _____ per day.

8. **Intellectual Property:** All intellectual property, including trademarks, writings, information, trade secrets, inventions, discoveries, or improvements, whether or not registrable or patentable, which are conceived, constructed, or written by Consultant and arise out of or are related to work and services performed under this agreement, are, or shall become and remain the sole and exclusive property of Contractor, whether or not such intellectual property is conceived during the time such work and services are performed or billed.

9A. **Protection of Intellectual Property:** Contractor and Consultant recognize that under U.S. patent laws, all patent applications must be filed in the name of the true and actual inventor(s) of the subject matter sought to be patented. Thus if Consultant makes any patentable inventions relating to the above project, Consultant agrees to be named as an applicant in any U.S. patent application(s) filed on such invention(s). Actual ownership of such patent applications shall be governed by clause 8.

9B. Consultant shall promptly disclose to Contractor in writing all information pertaining to any intellectual property generated or conceived by Consultant under this Agreement. Consultant hereby assigns and agrees to assign all of Consultant's rights to such intellectual property, including patent rights and foreign priority rights. Consultant hereby expressly agrees, without further charge for time, to do all things and sign all documents deemed by Contractor to be necessary or appropriate to invest in intellectual property, including obtaining for and vesting in Contractor all U.S. and foreign patents and patent applications which Contractor desires to obtain to cover such intellectual property, provided that Contractor shall bear all expenses relating thereto. All reasonable local travel time and expenses shall be borne by Consultant.

10. Trade Secrets: Consultant recognizes that all information relating to the above Project disclosed to Consultant by Contractor, and all information generated by Consultant in the performance of the above Work, is a valuable trade secret of Contractor and Consultant shall treat all such information as strictly confidential, during and after the performance of Work under this Agreement. Specifically Consultant shall not reveal, publish, or communicate any such information to anyone other than Contractor, and shall safeguard all such information from access to anyone other than Contractor, except upon the express written authorization of Contractor. This clause shall not apply to any information which Consultant can document in writing is presently in or enters the public domain from a bona fide source other than Consultant.

11. Return of Property: Consultant agrees to return all written materials and objects received from Contractor, to deliver to Contractor all objects and a copy (and all copies and originals if requested by Contractor) of all written materials resulting from or relating to work performed under this Agreement, and not to deliver to any person, organization, or publisher, or cause to be published, any such written material without prior written authorization.

12. Conflicts of Interest: Consultant recognizes a fiduciary obligation to Contractor arising out of the work and services performed under this agreement and accordingly will not offer Consultant's service to or perform services for any competitor, potential or actual, of Contractor for the above Project, or perform any other acts which may result in any conflict of interest by Consultant, during and after the term of this Agreement.

13. Mediation and Arbitration: If any dispute arises under this Agreement, the parties shall negotiate in good faith to settle such dispute. If the parties cannot resolve such dispute themselves, then either party may submit the dispute to mediation by a mediator approved by both parties. If the parties cannot agree to any mediator, or if either party does not wish to abide by any decision of the mediator, they shall submit the dispute to arbitration by any mutually acceptable arbitrator, or the American Arbitration Association (AAA). If the AAA is selected, the arbitration shall take place under the auspices of the nearest branch of such to both parties. The costs of the arbitration proceeding shall be borne according to the decision of the arbitrator, who may apportion costs equally, or in accordance with any finding or fault or lack of good faith of either party. The arbitrator's award shall be nonappealable and enforceable in any court of competent jurisdiction.

14. Governing Law: This Agreement shall be governed by and interpreted under and according to the laws of the State of _____ .

15. Signatures: The parties have indicated their agreement to all of the above terms by signing this Agreement on the respective dates below indicated. Each party has received an original signed copy hereof.

Contractor: _____ Date: _____

Consultant: _____ Date: _____

Consultant's Work Agreement

1. **Parties:** This Work Agreement is made between the following parties:

   Name(s): _____

   Address(es): _____

   _____

   (hereinafter "Contractor"), and

   Name(s): _____

   Address(es): _____

   _____

   (hereinafter "Consultant").

2. **Name of Project:**

   _____

   _____

3. **Work to Be Performed by Consultant:**

   _____

   _____

4. **Work/Payment Schedule:**

   _____

   _____

5. **Date:** This Agreement shall be effective as of the latter date below written.

6. **Recitals:** Contractor has one or more ideas relating to the above project and desires to have such project developed more completely, as specified in the above statement of Work. Consultant has certain skills desired by Contractor relating to performance of the above Work.

7. **Performance:** Consultant will perform the above work for Contractor in accordance with the above-scheduled Work/Payment Schedule, and Contractor will make the above-scheduled payments to Consultant. Any changes to the Work to Be Performed or the Work/Payment Schedule shall be described in a writing referring to this Agreement and signed and dated by both parties. Time is of the essence of this Agreement, and if Consultant fails to perform according to the above work schedule, contractor may (a) void this agreement and pay consultant 50% of what would otherwise be due, or (b) require that Consultant pay contractor a penalty of $ _____ per day.

8. **Intellectual Property:** All intellectual property, including trademarks, writings, information, trade secrets, inventions, discoveries, or improvements, whether or not registrable or patentable, which are conceived, constructed, or written by Consultant and arise out of or are related to work and services performed under this agreement, are, or shall become and remain the sole and exclusive property of Contractor, whether or not such intellectual property is conceived during the time such work and services are performed or billed.

9A. **Protection of Intellectual Property:** Contractor and Consultant recognize that under U.S. patent laws, all patent applications must be filed in the name of the true and actual inventor(s) of the subject matter sought to be patented. Thus if Consultant makes any patentable inventions relating to the above project, Consultant agrees to be named as an applicant in any U.S. patent application(s) filed on such invention(s). Actual ownership of such patent applications shall be governed by clause 8.

9B. Consultant shall promptly disclose to Contractor in writing all information pertaining to any intellectual property generated or conceived by Consultant under this Agreement. Consultant hereby assigns and agrees to assign all of Consultant's rights to such intellectual property, including patent rights and foreign priority rights. Consultant hereby expressly agrees, without further charge for time, to do all things and sign all documents deemed by Contractor to be necessary or appropriate to invest in intellectual property, including obtaining for and vesting in Contractor all U.S. and foreign patents and patent applications which Contractor desires to obtain to cover such intellectual property, provided that Contractor shall bear all expenses relating thereto. All reasonable local travel time and expenses shall be borne by Consultant.

10. Trade Secrets: Consultant recognizes that all information relating to the above Project disclosed to Consultant by Contractor, and all information generated by Consultant in the performance of the above Work, is a valuable trade secret of Contractor and Consultant shall treat all such information as strictly confidential, during and after the performance of Work under this Agreement. Specifically Consultant shall not reveal, publish, or communicate any such information to anyone other than Contractor, and shall safeguard all such information from access to anyone other than Contractor, except upon the express written authorization of Contractor. This clause shall not apply to any information which Consultant can document in writing is presently in or enters the public domain from a bona fide source other than Consultant.

11. Return of Property: Consultant agrees to return all written materials and objects received from Contractor, to deliver to Contractor all objects and a copy (and all copies and originals if requested by Contractor) of all written materials resulting from or relating to work performed under this Agreement, and not to deliver to any person, organization, or publisher, or cause to be published, any such written material without prior written authorization.

12. Conflicts of Interest: Consultant recognizes a fiduciary obligation to Contractor arising out of the work and services performed under this agreement and accordingly will not offer Consultant's service to or perform services for any competitor, potential or actual, of Contractor for the above Project, or perform any other acts which may result in any conflict of interest by Consultant, during and after the term of this Agreement.

13. Mediation and Arbitration: If any dispute arises under this Agreement, the parties shall negotiate in good faith to settle such dispute. If the parties cannot resolve such dispute themselves, then either party may submit the dispute to mediation by a mediator approved by both parties. If the parties cannot agree to any mediator, or if either party does not wish to abide by any decision of the mediator, they shall submit the dispute to arbitration by any mutually acceptable arbitrator, or the American Arbitration Association (AAA). If the AAA is selected, the arbitration shall take place under the auspices of the nearest branch of such to both parties. The costs of the arbitration proceeding shall be borne according to the decision of the arbitrator, who may apportion costs equally, or in accordance with any finding or fault or lack of good faith of either party. The arbitrator's award shall be nonappealable and enforceable in any court of competent jurisdiction.

14. Governing Law: This Agreement shall be governed by and interpreted under and according to the laws of the State of _____ .

15. Signatures: The parties have indicated their agreement to all of the above terms by signing this Agreement on the respective dates below indicated. Each party has received an original signed copy hereof.

Contractor: _____ Date: _____

Consultant: _____ Date: _____

Consultant's Work Agreement

1. **Parties:** This Work Agreement is made between the following parties:

   Name(s): _____

   Address(es): _____

   _____

   (hereinafter "Contractor"), and

   Name(s): _____

   Address(es): _____

   _____

   (hereinafter "Consultant").

2. **Name of Project:**

   _____

   _____

3. **Work to Be Performed by Consultant:**

   _____

   _____

4. **Work/Payment Schedule:**

   _____

   _____

5. **Date:** This Agreement shall be effective as of the latter date below written.

6. **Recitals:** Contractor has one or more ideas relating to the above project and desires to have such project developed more completely, as specified in the above statement of Work. Consultant has certain skills desired by Contractor relating to performance of the above Work.

7. **Performance:** Consultant will perform the above work for Contractor in accordance with the above-scheduled Work/Payment Schedule, and Contractor will make the above-scheduled payments to Consultant. Any changes to the Work to Be Performed or the Work/Payment Schedule shall be described in a writing referring to this Agreement and signed and dated by both parties. Time is of the essence of this Agreement, and if Consultant fails to perform according to the above work schedule, contractor may (a) void this agreement and pay consultant 50% of what would otherwise be due, or (b) require that Consultant pay contractor a penalty of $ _____ per day.

8. **Intellectual Property:** All intellectual property, including trademarks, writings, information, trade secrets, inventions, discoveries, or improvements, whether or not registrable or patentable, which are conceived, constructed, or written by Consultant and arise out of or are related to work and services performed under this agreement, are, or shall become and remain the sole and exclusive property of Contractor, whether or not such intellectual property is conceived during the time such work and services are performed or billed.

9A. **Protection of Intellectual Property:** Contractor and Consultant recognize that under U.S. patent laws, all patent applications must be filed in the name of the true and actual inventor(s) of the subject matter sought to be patented. Thus if Consultant makes any patentable inventions relating to the above project, Consultant agrees to be named as an applicant in any U.S. patent application(s) filed on such invention(s). Actual ownership of such patent applications shall be governed by clause 8.

9B. Consultant shall promptly disclose to Contractor in writing all information pertaining to any intellectual property generated or conceived by Consultant under this Agreement. Consultant hereby assigns and agrees to assign all of Consultant's rights to such intellectual property, including patent rights and foreign priority rights. Consultant hereby expressly agrees, without further charge for time, to do all things and sign all documents deemed by Contractor to be necessary or appropriate to invest in intellectual property, including obtaining for and vesting in Contractor all U.S. and foreign patents and patent applications which Contractor desires to obtain to cover such intellectual property, provided that Contractor shall bear all expenses relating thereto. All reasonable local travel time and expenses shall be borne by Consultant.

10. Trade Secrets: Consultant recognizes that all information relating to the above Project disclosed to Consultant by Contractor, and all information generated by Consultant in the performance of the above Work, is a valuable trade secret of Contractor and Consultant shall treat all such information as strictly confidential, during and after the performance of Work under this Agreement. Specifically Consultant shall not reveal, publish, or communicate any such information to anyone other than Contractor, and shall safeguard all such information from access to anyone other than Contractor, except upon the express written authorization of Contractor. This clause shall not apply to any information which Consultant can document in writing is presently in or enters the public domain from a bona fide source other than Consultant.

11. Return of Property: Consultant agrees to return all written materials and objects received from Contractor, to deliver to Contractor all objects and a copy (and all copies and originals if requested by Contractor) of all written materials resulting from or relating to work performed under this Agreement, and not to deliver to any person, organization, or publisher, or cause to be published, any such written material without prior written authorization.

12. Conflicts of Interest: Consultant recognizes a fiduciary obligation to Contractor arising out of the work and services performed under this agreement and accordingly will not offer Consultant's service to or perform services for any competitor, potential or actual, of Contractor for the above Project, or perform any other acts which may result in any conflict of interest by Consultant, during and after the term of this Agreement.

13. Mediation and Arbitration: If any dispute arises under this Agreement, the parties shall negotiate in good faith to settle such dispute. If the parties cannot resolve such dispute themselves, then either party may submit the dispute to mediation by a mediator approved by both parties. If the parties cannot agree to any mediator, or if either party does not wish to abide by any decision of the mediator, they shall submit the dispute to arbitration by any mutually acceptable arbitrator, or the American Arbitration Association (AAA). If the AAA is selected, the arbitration shall take place under the auspices of the nearest branch of such to both parties. The costs of the arbitration proceeding shall be borne according to the decision of the arbitrator, who may apportion costs equally, or in accordance with any finding or fault or lack of good faith of either party. The arbitrator's award shall be nonappealable and enforceable in any court of competent jurisdiction.

14. Governing Law: This Agreement shall be governed by and interpreted under and according to the laws of the State of _____ .

15. Signatures: The parties have indicated their agreement to all of the above terms by signing this Agreement on the respective dates below indicated. Each party has received an original signed copy hereof.

Contractor: _____ Date: _____

Consultant: _____ Date: _____

Consultant's Work Agreement

1. **Parties:** This Work Agreement is made between the following parties:

   Name(s): _____

   Address(es): _____

   _____

   (hereinafter "Contractor"), and

   Name(s): _____

   Address(es): _____

   _____

   (hereinafter "Consultant").

2. **Name of Project:**

   _____

   _____

3. **Work to Be Performed by Consultant:**

   _____

   _____

4. **Work/Payment Schedule:**

   _____

   _____

5. **Date:** This Agreement shall be effective as of the latter date below written.

6. **Recitals:** Contractor has one or more ideas relating to the above project and desires to have such project developed more completely, as specified in the above statement of Work. Consultant has certain skills desired by Contractor relating to performance of the above Work.

7. **Performance:** Consultant will perform the above work for Contractor in accordance with the above-scheduled Work/Payment Schedule, and Contractor will make the above-scheduled payments to Consultant. Any changes to the Work to Be Performed or the Work/Payment Schedule shall be described in a writing referring to this Agreement and signed and dated by both parties. Time is of the essence of this Agreement, and if Consultant fails to perform according to the above work schedule, contractor may (a) void this agreement and pay consultant 50% of what would otherwise be due, or (b) require that Consultant pay contractor a penalty of $ _____ per day.

8. **Intellectual Property:** All intellectual property, including trademarks, writings, information, trade secrets, inventions, discoveries, or improvements, whether or not registrable or patentable, which are conceived, constructed, or written by Consultant and arise out of or are related to work and services performed under this agreement, are, or shall become and remain the sole and exclusive property of Contractor, whether or not such intellectual property is conceived during the time such work and services are performed or billed.

9A. **Protection of Intellectual Property:** Contractor and Consultant recognize that under U.S. patent laws, all patent applications must be filed in the name of the true and actual inventor(s) of the subject matter sought to be patented. Thus if Consultant makes any patentable inventions relating to the above project, Consultant agrees to be named as an applicant in any U.S. patent application(s) filed on such invention(s). Actual ownership of such patent applications shall be governed by clause 8.

9B. Consultant shall promptly disclose to Contractor in writing all information pertaining to any intellectual property generated or conceived by Consultant under this Agreement. Consultant hereby assigns and agrees to assign all of Consultant's rights to such intellectual property, including patent rights and foreign priority rights. Consultant hereby expressly agrees, without further charge for time, to do all things and sign all documents deemed by Contractor to be necessary or appropriate to invest in intellectual property, including obtaining for and vesting in Contractor all U.S. and foreign patents and patent applications which Contractor desires to obtain to cover such intellectual property, provided that Contractor shall bear all expenses relating thereto. All reasonable local travel time and expenses shall be borne by Consultant.

10. **Trade Secrets:** Consultant recognizes that all information relating to the above Project disclosed to Consultant by Contractor, and all information generated by Consultant in the performance of the above Work, is a valuable trade secret of Contractor and Consultant shall treat all such information as strictly confidential, during and after the performance of Work under this Agreement. Specifically Consultant shall not reveal, publish, or communicate any such information to anyone other than Contractor, and shall safeguard all such information from access to anyone other than Contractor, except upon the express written authorization of Contractor. This clause shall not apply to any information which Consultant can document in writing is presently in or enters the public domain from a bona fide source other than Consultant.

11. **Return of Property:** Consultant agrees to return all written materials and objects received from Contractor, to deliver to Contractor all objects and a copy (and all copies and originals if requested by Contractor) of all written materials resulting from or relating to work performed under this Agreement, and not to deliver to any person, organization, or publisher, or cause to be published, any such written material without prior written authorization.

12. **Conflicts of Interest:** Consultant recognizes a fiduciary obligation to Contractor arising out of the work and services performed under this agreement and accordingly will not offer Consultant's service to or perform services for any competitor, potential or actual, of Contractor for the above Project, or perform any other acts which may result in any conflict of interest by Consultant, during and after the term of this Agreement.

13. **Mediation and Arbitration:** If any dispute arises under this Agreement, the parties shall negotiate in good faith to settle such dispute. If the parties cannot resolve such dispute themselves, then either party may submit the dispute to mediation by a mediator approved by both parties. If the parties cannot agree to any mediator, or if either party does not wish to abide by any decision of the mediator, they shall submit the dispute to arbitration by any mutually acceptable arbitrator, or the American Arbitration Association (AAA). If the AAA is selected, the arbitration shall take place under the auspices of the nearest branch of such to both parties. The costs of the arbitration proceeding shall be borne according to the decision of the arbitrator, who may apportion costs equally, or in accordance with any finding or fault or lack of good faith of either party. The arbitrator's award shall be nonappealable and enforceable in any court of competent jurisdiction.

14. **Governing Law:** This Agreement shall be governed by and interpreted under and according to the laws of the State of _____ .

15. **Signatures:** The parties have indicated their agreement to all of the above terms by signing this Agreement on the respective dates below indicated. Each party has received an original signed copy hereof.

Contractor: _____ Date: _____

Consultant: _____ Date: _____

Consultant's Work Agreement

1. **Parties:** This Work Agreement is made between the following parties:

   Name(s): _____

   Address(es): _____

   _____

   (hereinafter "Contractor"), and

   Name(s): _____

   Address(es): _____

   _____

   (hereinafter "Consultant").

2. **Name of Project:**

   _____

   _____

3. **Work to Be Performed by Consultant:**

   _____

   _____

4. **Work/Payment Schedule:**

   _____

   _____

5. **Date:** This Agreement shall be effective as of the latter date below written.

6. **Recitals:** Contractor has one or more ideas relating to the above project and desires to have such project developed more completely, as specified in the above statement of Work. Consultant has certain skills desired by Contractor relating to performance of the above Work.

7. **Performance:** Consultant will perform the above work for Contractor in accordance with the above-scheduled Work/Payment Schedule, and Contractor will make the above-scheduled payments to Consultant. Any changes to the Work to Be Performed or the Work/Payment Schedule shall be described in a writing referring to this Agreement and signed and dated by both parties. Time is of the essence of this Agreement, and if Consultant fails to perform according to the above work schedule, contractor may (a) void this agreement and pay consultant 50% of what would otherwise be due, or (b) require that Consultant pay contractor a penalty of $ _____ per day.

8. **Intellectual Property:** All intellectual property, including trademarks, writings, information, trade secrets, inventions, discoveries, or improvements, whether or not registrable or patentable, which are conceived, constructed, or written by Consultant and arise out of or are related to work and services performed under this agreement, are, or shall become and remain the sole and exclusive property of Contractor, whether or not such intellectual property is conceived during the time such work and services are performed or billed.

9A. **Protection of Intellectual Property:** Contractor and Consultant recognize that under U.S. patent laws, all patent applications must be filed in the name of the true and actual inventor(s) of the subject matter sought to be patented. Thus if Consultant makes any patentable inventions relating to the above project, Consultant agrees to be named as an applicant in any U.S. patent application(s) filed on such invention(s). Actual ownership of such patent applications shall be governed by clause 8.

9B. Consultant shall promptly disclose to Contractor in writing all information pertaining to any intellectual property generated or conceived by Consultant under this Agreement. Consultant hereby assigns and agrees to assign all of Consultant's rights to such intellectual property, including patent rights and foreign priority rights. Consultant hereby expressly agrees, without further charge for time, to do all things and sign all documents deemed by Contractor to be necessary or appropriate to invest in intellectual property, including obtaining for and vesting in Contractor all U.S. and foreign patents and patent applications which Contractor desires to obtain to cover such intellectual property, provided that Contractor shall bear all expenses relating thereto. All reasonable local travel time and expenses shall be borne by Consultant.

10. **Trade Secrets:** Consultant recognizes that all information relating to the above Project disclosed to Consultant by Contractor, and all information generated by Consultant in the performance of the above Work, is a valuable trade secret of Contractor and Consultant shall treat all such information as strictly confidential, during and after the performance of Work under this Agreement. Specifically Consultant shall not reveal, publish, or communicate any such information to anyone other than Contractor, and shall safeguard all such information from access to anyone other than Contractor, except upon the express written authorization of Contractor. This clause shall not apply to any information which Consultant can document in writing is presently in or enters the public domain from a bona fide source other than Consultant.

11. **Return of Property:** Consultant agrees to return all written materials and objects received from Contractor, to deliver to Contractor all objects and a copy (and all copies and originals if requested by Contractor) of all written materials resulting from or relating to work performed under this Agreement, and not to deliver to any person, organization, or publisher, or cause to be published, any such written material without prior written authorization.

12. **Conflicts of Interest:** Consultant recognizes a fiduciary obligation to Contractor arising out of the work and services performed under this agreement and accordingly will not offer Consultant's service to or perform services for any competitor, potential or actual, of Contractor for the above Project, or perform any other acts which may result in any conflict of interest by Consultant, during and after the term of this Agreement.

13. **Mediation and Arbitration:** If any dispute arises under this Agreement, the parties shall negotiate in good faith to settle such dispute. If the parties cannot resolve such dispute themselves, then either party may submit the dispute to mediation by a mediator approved by both parties. If the parties cannot agree to any mediator, or if either party does not wish to abide by any decision of the mediator, they shall submit the dispute to arbitration by any mutually acceptable arbitrator, or the American Arbitration Association (AAA). If the AAA is selected, the arbitration shall take place under the auspices of the nearest branch of such to both parties. The costs of the arbitration proceeding shall be borne according to the decision of the arbitrator, who may apportion costs equally, or in accordance with any finding or fault or lack of good faith of either party. The arbitrator's award shall be nonappealable and enforceable in any court of competent jurisdiction.

14. **Governing Law:** This Agreement shall be governed by and interpreted under and according to the laws of the State of _____ .

15. **Signatures:** The parties have indicated their agreement to all of the above terms by signing this Agreement on the respective dates below indicated. Each party has received an original signed copy hereof.

Contractor: _____ Date: _____

Consultant: _____ Date: _____

Proprietary Materials Agreement

(Keep Confidential/Non-Disclosure Agreement)

PROPRIETARY MATERIALS (items, documents, or models loaned—describe or identify fully, including number of sheets):

_____

_____

_____

_____

PROPRIETARY MATERIALS loaned by (name and address):

_____

_____

_____ ("LENDER")

PROPRIETARY MATERIALS loaned to (name and address):

_____

_____ ("BORROWER")

BORROWER acknowledges and agrees as follows:

(1) BORROWER:

[BORROWER *cross out (a) and initial (b), or vice versa, as appropriate*]

(a) has received the above Proprietary Materials from LENDER (_____)

(b) understands that LENDER will immediately send the above PROPRIETARY MATERIALS to BORROWER upon LENDER'S receipt, from BORROWER, of a signed copy of this Agreement (_____)

(2) These PROPRIETARY MATERIALS contain valuable proprietary information of LENDER. This proprietary information constitutes a trade secret of LENDER and loss or outside disclosure of these materials or the information contained within these materials will harm LENDER economically.

(3) BORROWER acknowledges that these PROPRIETARY MATERIALS are furnished to BORROWER under the following conditions:

(a) These PROPRIETARY MATERIALS and the information they contain shall be used by BORROWER solely to review or evaluate a proposal or information from, supply a quotation to, or provide a component or item for LENDER.

(b) BORROWER agrees not to disclose these PROPRIETARY MATERIALS or the information they contain except to any persons within BORROWER'S organization having a good faith "need to know" same for the purpose of fulfilling the terms of this Agreement. If necessary, BORROWER may make additional copies of this Agreement and have each such person sign a copy of this Agreement and furnish such copy(ies) to LENDER.

(c) BORROWER and all persons within BORROWER'S organization shall exercise a high degree of care to safeguard these PROPRIETARY MATERIALS and the information they contain from access or disclosure to all unauthorized persons.

(d) BORROWER shall not make any copies of these PROPRIETARY MATERIALS except upon written permission of LENDER and BORROWER shall return all PROPRIETARY MATERIALS (including any copies made) to LENDER at any time upon request by LENDER.

(4) These terms shall not apply to any information which BORROWER can document becomes part of the general public knowledge without fault of BORROWER or comes into BORROWER'S possession in good faith without restriction.

BORROWER: _____
(Name of Organization or Individual)

BY: _____
(Name and Title)

Date: _____ / _____ / _____

Other persons within BORROWER'S organization obtaining access to PROPRIETARY MATERIALS:

_____   _____ / _____ / _____

Print Name: _____

_____   _____ / _____ / _____

Print Name: _____

Proprietary Materials Agreement

(Keep Confidential/Non-Disclosure Agreement)

PROPRIETARY MATERIALS (items, documents, or models loaned—describe or identify fully, including number of sheets):

_____

_____

_____

_____

PROPRIETARY MATERIALS loaned by (name and address):

_____

_____

_____ ("LENDER")

PROPRIETARY MATERIALS loaned to (name and address):

_____

_____ ("BORROWER")

BORROWER acknowledges and agrees as follows:

(1) BORROWER:

[BORROWER cross out (a) and initial (b), or vice versa, as appropriate]

(a) has received the above Proprietary Materials from LENDER (_____)

(b) understands that LENDER will immediately send the above PROPRIETARY MATERIALS to BORROWER upon LENDER'S receipt, from BORROWER, of a signed copy of this Agreement (_____)

(2) These PROPRIETARY MATERIALS contain valuable proprietary information of LENDER. This proprietary information constitutes a trade secret of LENDER and loss or outside disclosure of these materials or the information contained within these materials will harm LENDER economically.

(3) BORROWER acknowledges that these PROPRIETARY MATERIALS are furnished to BORROWER under the following conditions:

(a) These PROPRIETARY MATERIALS and the information they contain shall be used by BORROWER solely to review or evaluate a proposal or information from, supply a quotation to, or provide a component or item for LENDER.

(b) BORROWER agrees not to disclose these PROPRIETARY MATERIALS or the information they contain except to any persons within BORROWER'S organization having a good faith "need to know" same for the purpose of fulfilling the terms of this Agreement. If necessary, BORROWER may make additional copies of this Agreement and have each such person sign a copy of this Agreement and furnish such copy(ies) to LENDER.

(c) BORROWER and all persons within BORROWER'S organization shall exercise a high degree of care to safeguard these PROPRIETARY MATERIALS and the information they contain from access or disclosure to all unauthorized persons.

(d) BORROWER shall not make any copies of these PROPRIETARY MATERIALS except upon written permission of LENDER and BORROWER shall return all PROPRIETARY MATERIALS (including any copies made) to LENDER at any time upon request by LENDER.

(4) These terms shall not apply to any information which BORROWER can document becomes part of the general public knowledge without fault of BORROWER or comes into BORROWER'S possession in good faith without restriction.

BORROWER: _____
(Name of Organization or Individual)

BY: _____
(Name and Title)

Date: _____ / _____ / _____

Other persons within BORROWER'S organization obtaining access to PROPRIETARY MATERIALS:

_____   _____ / _____ / _____

Print Name: _____

_____   _____ / _____ / _____

Print Name: _____

Proprietary Materials Agreement

(Keep Confidential/Non-Disclosure Agreement)

PROPRIETARY MATERIALS (items, documents, or models loaned—describe or identify fully, including number of sheets):

_____

_____

_____

_____

PROPRIETARY MATERIALS loaned by (name and address):

_____

_____

_____ ("LENDER")

PROPRIETARY MATERIALS loaned to (name and address):

_____

_____ ("BORROWER")

BORROWER acknowledges and agrees as follows:

(1) BORROWER:

   [BORROWER cross out (a) and initial (b), or vice versa, as appropriate]

   (a) has received the above Proprietary Materials from LENDER (_____)

   (b) understands that LENDER will immediately send the above PROPRIETARY MATERIALS to BORROWER upon LENDER'S receipt, from BORROWER, of a signed copy of this Agreement (_____)

(2) These PROPRIETARY MATERIALS contain valuable proprietary information of LENDER. This proprietary information constitutes a trade secret of LENDER and loss or outside disclosure of these materials or the information contained within these materials will harm LENDER economically.

(3) BORROWER acknowledges that these PROPRIETARY MATERIALS are furnished to BORROWER under the following conditions:

   (a) These PROPRIETARY MATERIALS and the information they contain shall be used by BORROWER solely to review or evaluate a proposal or information from, supply a quotation to, or provide a component or item for LENDER.

   (b) BORROWER agrees not to disclose these PROPRIETARY MATERIALS or the information they contain except to any persons within BORROWER'S organization having a good faith "need to know" same for the purpose of fulfilling the terms of this Agreement. If necessary, BORROWER may make additional copies of this Agreement and have each such person sign a copy of this Agreement and furnish such copy(ies) to LENDER.

(c) BORROWER and all persons within BORROWER'S organization shall exercise a high degree of care to safeguard these PROPRIETARY MATERIALS and the information they contain from access or disclosure to all unauthorized persons.

(d) BORROWER shall not make any copies of these PROPRIETARY MATERIALS except upon written permission of LENDER and BORROWER shall return all PROPRIETARY MATERIALS (including any copies made) to LENDER at any time upon request by LENDER.

(4) These terms shall not apply to any information which BORROWER can document becomes part of the general public knowledge without fault of BORROWER or comes into BORROWER'S possession in good faith without restriction.

BORROWER: _____
(Name of Organization or Individual)

BY: _____
(Name and Title)

Date: _____ / _____ / _____

Other persons within BORROWER'S organization obtaining access to PROPRIETARY MATERIALS:

_____   _____ / _____ / _____

Print Name: _____

_____   _____ / _____ / _____

Print Name: _____

Proprietary Materials Agreement

(Keep Confidential/Non-Disclosure Agreement)

PROPRIETARY MATERIALS (items, documents, or models loaned—describe or identify fully, including number of sheets):

_____

_____

_____

_____

PROPRIETARY MATERIALS loaned by (name and address):

_____

_____

_____ ("LENDER")

PROPRIETARY MATERIALS loaned to (name and address):

_____

_____ ("BORROWER")

BORROWER acknowledges and agrees as follows:

(1) BORROWER:

   [BORROWER cross out (a) and initial (b), or vice versa, as appropriate]

   (a) has received the above Proprietary Materials from LENDER (_____)

   (b) understands that LENDER will immediately send the above PROPRIETARY MATERIALS to BORROWER upon LENDER'S receipt, from BORROWER, of a signed copy of this Agreement (_____)

(2) These PROPRIETARY MATERIALS contain valuable proprietary information of LENDER. This proprietary information constitutes a trade secret of LENDER and loss or outside disclosure of these materials or the information contained within these materials will harm LENDER economically.

(3) BORROWER acknowledges that these PROPRIETARY MATERIALS are furnished to BORROWER under the following conditions:

   (a) These PROPRIETARY MATERIALS and the information they contain shall be used by BORROWER solely to review or evaluate a proposal or information from, supply a quotation to, or provide a component or item for LENDER.

   (b) BORROWER agrees not to disclose these PROPRIETARY MATERIALS or the information they contain except to any persons within BORROWER'S organization having a good faith "need to know" same for the purpose of fulfilling the terms of this Agreement. If necessary, BORROWER may make additional copies of this Agreement and have each such person sign a copy of this Agreement and furnish such copy(ies) to LENDER.

(c) BORROWER and all persons within BORROWER'S organization shall exercise a high degree of care to safeguard these PROPRIETARY MATERIALS and the information they contain from access or disclosure to all unauthorized persons.

(d) BORROWER shall not make any copies of these PROPRIETARY MATERIALS except upon written permission of LENDER and BORROWER shall return all PROPRIETARY MATERIALS (including any copies made) to LENDER at any time upon request by LENDER.

(4) These terms shall not apply to any information which BORROWER can document becomes part of the general public knowledge without fault of BORROWER or comes into BORROWER'S possession in good faith without restriction.

BORROWER: _____
                          (Name of Organization or Individual)

BY: _____
              (Name and Title)

Date: _____ / _____ / _____

Other persons within BORROWER'S organization obtaining access to PROPRIETARY MATERIALS:

_____ _____ / _____ / _____

Print Name: _____

_____ _____ / _____ / _____

Print Name: _____

Proprietary Materials Agreement

(Keep Confidential/Non-Disclosure Agreement)

PROPRIETARY MATERIALS (items, documents, or models loaned—describe or identify fully, including number of sheets):

_____

_____

_____

_____

PROPRIETARY MATERIALS loaned by (name and address):

_____

_____

_____ ("LENDER")

PROPRIETARY MATERIALS loaned to (name and address):

_____

_____ ("BORROWER")

BORROWER acknowledges and agrees as follows:

(1) BORROWER:

[BORROWER cross out (a) and initial (b), or vice versa, as appropriate]

(a) has received the above Proprietary Materials from LENDER (_____)

(b) understands that LENDER will immediately send the above PROPRIETARY MATERIALS to BORROWER upon LENDER'S receipt, from BORROWER, of a signed copy of this Agreement (_____)

(2) These PROPRIETARY MATERIALS contain valuable proprietary information of LENDER. This proprietary information constitutes a trade secret of LENDER and loss or outside disclosure of these materials or the information contained within these materials will harm LENDER economically.

(3) BORROWER acknowledges that these PROPRIETARY MATERIALS are furnished to BORROWER under the following conditions:

(a) These PROPRIETARY MATERIALS and the information they contain shall be used by BORROWER solely to review or evaluate a proposal or information from, supply a quotation to, or provide a component or item for LENDER.

(b) BORROWER agrees not to disclose these PROPRIETARY MATERIALS or the information they contain except to any persons within BORROWER'S organization having a good faith "need to know" same for the purpose of fulfilling the terms of this Agreement. If necessary, BORROWER may make additional copies of this Agreement and have each such person sign a copy of this Agreement and furnish such copy(ies) to LENDER.

(c) BORROWER and all persons within BORROWER'S organization shall exercise a high degree of care to safeguard these PROPRIETARY MATERIALS and the information they contain from access or disclosure to all unauthorized persons.

(d) BORROWER shall not make any copies of these PROPRIETARY MATERIALS except upon written permission of LENDER and BORROWER shall return all PROPRIETARY MATERIALS (including any copies made) to LENDER at any time upon request by LENDER.

(4) These terms shall not apply to any information which BORROWER can document becomes part of the general public knowledge without fault of BORROWER or comes into BORROWER'S possession in good faith without restriction.

BORROWER: _____
                            (Name of Organization or Individual)

BY: _____
                 (Name and Title)

Date: _____ / _____ / _____

Other persons within BORROWER'S organization obtaining access to PROPRIETARY MATERIALS:

_____   _____ / _____ / _____

Print Name: _____

_____   _____ / _____ / _____

Print Name: _____

Joint Owners' Agreement

This agreement is made by and between the following parties who, by separate assignment or as joint applicants, own the following respective shares of the invention, patent application, or patent identified below:

_____ of _____ , _____%,

_____ of _____ , _____%,

_____ of _____ , _____%,

Invention Title:

Patent Application Ser. Nr.: _____ , Filed: _____

Patent Nr.:_____ , Issued: _____

Applicants: _____

_____

The above patent application data is to be filled in as soon as it becomes available if the application has not yet been filed.

The parties desire to stipulate the terms under which they will exploit this invention and patent application and therefore agree as follows:

1. **No Action Without Everyone's Consent:** None of the parties to this agreement shall license, use, make, or sell the invention or application, or take any other action, other than normal prosecution, without the written consent and cooperation of the other party or parties (hereinafter "parties") to this agreement, except as provided below. Any action so taken shall be committed to a writing signed by all of the parties, or as many parties as consent, with copies to all other parties.

2. **Decisions:** In case any decision must be made in connection with the invention or the patent application, including foreign filing, appealing from an adverse decision in the Patent and Trademark Office, or any opportunity to license, sell, make, or use the invention or application, the parties shall consult on such opportunity and a majority decision shall control. In the event the parties are equally divided, the matter shall be decided in accordance with Paragraph 5 below. After a decision is so made, all parties shall abide by the decision and shall cooperate fully by whatever means are necessary to implement and give full force to such decision. However, if an offer is involved and there is time for any parties to obtain a better or different offer, they shall be entitled to do so and the decision shall be postponed for up to one month to allow such other parties to act.

3. **Proportionate Sharing:** The parties to this agreement shall share, in the percentages indicated above, in all income from, liabilities, and expenditures agreed to be made by any decision under Part 2 above in connection with the invention or patent application. In case a decision is made to make any expenditure, as for foreign patent application filing, exploitation, etc., and a minority or other parties opposes such expenditure or is unable to contribute his or her proportionate share, then the others shall advance the minority or other parties' share of the expenditure. Such others shall be reimbursed by the minority or other parties by double the amount so advanced from the minority or other parties' proportionate share of any income received, provided such income has some reasonable connection with the expenditure. No party shall be entitled to reimbursement or credit for any labor unless agreed to in advance by all of the parties hereto.

4. **If Any Parties Desire to Manufacture, Etc.:** If any parties who do not constitute all of the parties to this agreement desire to manufacture, distribute, or sell any product or service embodying the above invention, they may do so with the written consent of the other parties under Part 1 above. The cost of the product or service shall include, in addition to normal profit, labor, commission, and/or overhead, etc., provision for a reasonable royalty which shall be paid for the term of the above patent application and any patent which may issue thereon. Such royalty shall be determined before any action is taken under this part and as if a valid patent on the invention had been licensed to an unrelated exclusive licensee (or a nonexclusive licensee if the patent is licensed to others) in an arm's length transaction. Such royalty shall be distributed to all of the parties hereto according to their proportionate shares and on a quarterly basis, accompanied by a written royalty report and sent within one month after the close of each calendar quarter.

5. **In Case of Dispute:** In case any dispute, disagreement, or need for any decision arises out of this agreement or in connection with the invention or patent application, and the parties cannot settle the matter or come to a decision in accordance with Paragraph 2, above, the parties shall first confer as much as necessary to settle the disagreement; all parties shall act and compromise to at least the degree a reasonable person would act. If the parties cannot settle their differences or come to a decision on their own, they shall submit the dispute or matter to mediation and decision by an impartial third party or professional mediator agreed to by all of the parties. If the parties cannot agree on a mediator, or cannot come to an agreement after mediation, then they shall submit the matter to binding arbitration with a mutually acceptable arbitrator or the American Arbitration Association. The arbitrator shall settle the dispute in whatever manner he or she feels will do substantial justice, recognizing the rights of all parties and commercial realities of the marketplace. The parties shall abide by the terms of the arbitrator's decision and shall cooperate fully and do any acts necessary to implement such decision. The costs of the arbitrator shall be advanced by all of the parties or in accordance with Part 3 above and the arbitrator may make any allocation of arbitration costs he or she feels is reasonable.

6. **Non-Frustration:** Neither party to this Agreement shall commit any act or take any action which frustrates or hampers the rights of the other party under this Agreement. Each party shall act in good faith and engage in fair dealing when taking any action under or related to this Agreement.

_____   _____
Signature   Date

_____   _____
Signature   Date

_____   _____
Signature   Date

Assignment of Invention and Patent Application

For value received, _____ ,

_____

of _____

_____

(hereinafter Assignor), hereby sells, assigns, transfers, and sets over unto _____

_____

of _____

and her or his successors or assigns (hereinafter Assignee) _____% of the following: (A) Assignor's right, title

and interest in and to the invention entitled "_____

_____ "

invented by Assignor; (B) the application for United States patent therefor, signed by Assignor on _____

_____ , U.S. Patent and Trademark Office Serial Number _____ ,

filed _____ ; (C) any patent or reissues of any patent that may be granted thereon;

and (D) any applications which are continuations, continuations-in-part, substitutes, or divisions of said

application. Assignor authorizes Assignee to enter the date of signature and/or Serial Number and Filing Date

in the spaces above. Assignor also authorizes and requests the Assistant Commissioner for Patents to issue any

resulting patent(s) as follows: _____% to Assignor and _____% to Assignee. (The singular shall include the

plural and vice versa herein.)

ASSIGNOR hereby further sells, assigns, transfers, and sets over unto ASSIGNEE, the above percentage of
ASSIGNOR'S entire right, title and interest in and to said invention in each and every country foreign to
the United States; and ASSIGNOR further conveys to ASSIGNEE the above percentage of all priority rights
resulting from the above-identified application for United States patent. ASSIGNOR agrees to execute all
papers, give any required testimony and perform other lawful acts, at ASSIGNEE'S expense, as ASSIGNEE may
require to enable ASSIGNEE to perfect ASSIGNEE'S interest in any resulting patent of the United States and
countries foreign thereto, and to acquire, hold, enforce, convey, and uphold the validity of said patent and
reissues and extensions thereof, and ASSIGNEE'S interest therein.

In testimony whereof ASSIGNOR has hereunto set its hand and seal on the date below.

State: _____

County: _____

Subscribed and sworn to before me _____ , _____ .

_____

Notary Public

SEAL

Universal License Agreement

1. **Parties and Summary of Terms:**

   Parties: This agreement is between:

   Licensor: _____ ,

   of _____ .

   Licensee: _____ ,

   of _____ .

   Summary: Type of License: ☐ Exclusive ☐ Nonexclusive

   Invention Title: _____ .

   Patent Application Ser. Nr.: _____ , Filing Date:

   If Exclusive License, minimum number of units to be sold to compute Minimum Annual Royalty (MAR):

   　　MARs start first quarter of _____ .

   ☐ Option Granted: Premium $_____ For term of: _____ (months)

   Patent Royalty Rate _____%   ☐ Know-How Licensed: Know-How Royalty Rate: _____%

   Total Royalty Rate (Patent Royalty Rate plus Know-How Royalty, if applicable): _____%.

   Estimated 1st year's sales (units):_____ Estimated Unit Price $ _____

   　　x Total Royalty Rate _____% = Licensing Fee $ _____

2. **Effective Date:** This agreement shall be effective as of the later of the signature dates below written and shall be referred to as the Agreement of such date.

3. **Recitals:**

   A. **LICENSOR** has developed an invention having the above title and warrants that LICENSOR has filed a patent application on such invention in the U.S. Patent and Trademark Office, which patent application is identified by the above title, Serial Number, and Filing Date. LICENSOR warrants that LICENSOR has full and exclusive right to grant this license on this invention and LICENSOR'S patent application. If the "Know-How Licensed" box above is checked, LICENSOR has also developed know-how in connection with said invention and warrants that LICENSOR owns and has the right to license said know-how.

   B. **LICENSEE** desires, if the "Option Granted" box above is checked, to exclusively investigate LICENSOR'S above invention for the term indicated. If said "Option Granted" box is not checked, or if said box is checked and LICENSEE investigates LICENSOR'S invention for the term indicated and such investigation is favorable, LICENSEE desires to make, use and sell the products embodying such invention and covered by the claims of LICENSOR'S patent application and any patent(s) issuing thereon (hereinafter "Licensed Product").

4. **If Option Granted:** If the "Option Granted" box above is checked, then (A) the patent license grant of Part 5 below shall not take effect except as defined in this part, and (B) LICENSOR hereby grants LICENSEE, for the option premium stated above, an exclusive option to investigate LICENSOR'S invention for the term indicated above, such term to commence from the date of this Agreement. LICENSOR will furnish LICENSEE with all information and know-how (if any) concerning LICENSOR'S invention in LICENSOR'S possession. LICENSEE will investigate LICENSOR'S invention for operability, costing, marketing, etc. LICENSEE shall report the results of its investigation to LICENSOR at any time before the end of the option term. If LICENSEE'S determination is favorable, it may thereupon exercise this option

and the patent license grant of Part 5 below shall become effective. If LICENSEE'S determination is unfavorable, then said option shall not be exercised and no patent license grant shall take effect, all rights hereunder shall revert to LICENSOR, LICENSEE shall deliver to LICENSOR all results of its investigations for LICENSOR'S benefit, and LICENSEE shall promptly return to LICENSOR all know-how (papers and things) received from LICENSOR or generated by LICENSEE in its investigations.

5. **Patent License If Option Exercised or If Option Not Granted:** If the "Option Granted" box above is checked and LICENSEE has investigated LICENSOR'S invention and such investigation is favorable and LICENSEE has exercised its option, or if said box is not checked, then LICENSOR hereby grants to LICENSEE, subject to the terms and conditions herein, a patent license of the type (Exclusive or Nonexclusive) checked above. Such patent license shall include the right to grant sublicenses, to make, have made, use, and sell the Licensed Product throughout the United States, its territories, and possessions. Such patent license shall be under LICENSOR'S patent application, any continuations, divisions, continuations-in-part, substitutes, reissues of any patent from any of such applications (hereinafter and hereinbefore LICENSOR'S patent application), any patent(s) issuing thereon, and if the "Know-How Licensed" box is checked above, any know-how transferred to LICENSEE.

6. **If Know-How Licensed:** If the "Know-How" box above is checked, LICENSOR shall communicate to LICENSEE all of LICENSOR'S know-how in respect of LICENSOR'S invention within one month after the date of this Agreement and shall be available to consult with LICENSEE, for up to 80 hours, with respect to the licensed invention and know-how. All travel and other expenses of LICENSOR for such consultation shall be reimbursed by LICENSEE within one month after LICENSOR submits its voucher therefor. LICENSOR makes no warranty regarding the value, suitability, or workability of such know-how. The royalty applicable for such know-how shall be paid, at the rate indicated above, for a minimum of three years from the date of this Agreement if no option is granted, or for three years from the date of exercise if an option is granted and exercised by LICENSOR, and thereafter for so long as LICENSEE makes, uses, or sells Licensed Products and has a share in the United States of at least 15% of the competitive market for Licensed Products.

7. **Royalties:**

   A. **Licensing Fee:** Unless the "Option Granted" box above is checked, LICENSEE shall pay to LICENSOR, upon execution of this Agreement, a nonrefundable Licensing Fee. This Licensing Fee shall also serve as an advance against future royalties. Such Licensing Fee shall be computed as follows: (A) Take the Total Royalty Rate in percent, as stated above. (B) Multiply by LICENSEE'S Estimate of Its First Year's Sales, in units of Licensed Product, as stated above. (C) Multiply by LICENSEE'S Estimated Unit Price of Licensed Product, in dollars, as stated above. (D) The combined product shall be the Licensing Fee, in dollars, as stated above. When LICENSEE begins actual sales of the Licensed Product, it shall certify its Actual Net Factory Sales Price of Licensed Product to LICENSOR in writing and shall either (1) simultaneously pay LICENSOR any difference due if the Actual Net Factory Sales Price of Licensed Product is more than the Estimated Unit Price, stated above, or (2) advise LICENSOR of any credit to which LICENSEE is entitled if the Actual Net Factory Sales Price of Licensed Product is less than the above Estimated Unit Price. In the latter case, LICENSEE may deduct such credit from its first royalty remittance to LICENSOR, under subpart B below. If an option is granted and exercised under Part 4 above, then LICENSEE shall pay this Licensing Fee to LICENSOR if and when LICENSEE exercises its option.

B. **Royalty:** If the "Option Granted" box above is not checked, or if said box is checked and LICENSEE has exercised its option under Part 4, LICENSEE shall also pay to LICENSOR a Total Royalty, at the rate stated above. Such royalty shall be at the Patent Royalty Rate stated in Part 1 above, plus, if the "Know-How Licensed" box above is checked, a Know-How Royalty at the Know-How Royalty Rate stated above. Said Total Royalty shall be computed on LICENSEE'S Net Factory Sales Price of Licensed Product. Such Total Royalty shall accrue when the Licensed Products are first sold or disposed of by LICENSEE, or by any sublicensee of LICENSEE. LICENSEE shall pay the Total Royalty due to LICENSOR within one month after the end of each calendar quarter, together with a written report to LICENSOR of the number of units, respective sales prices, and total sales made in such quarter, together with a full itemization of any adjustments made pursuant to subpart F below. LICENSEE'S first report and payment shall be made within one month after the end of the first calendar quarter following the execution of this Agreement. No royalties shall be paid by LICENSEE to LICENSOR until after the Licensing Fee under subpart A above has been earned, but LICENSEE shall make a quarterly report hereunder for every calendar quarter after the execution hereof, whether or not any royalty payment is due for such quarter, except that if an option is granted, LICENSEE shall not make any royalty reports until and if LICENSEE exercises its option.

C. **Minimum Annual Royalties:** If the "Exclusive" box above is checked, so that this is an exclusive license, then this subpart C and subpart D shall be applicable. But if the "Nonexclusive" box is checked above, then these subparts C and D shall be inapplicable. There shall be no minimum annual royalties due under this Agreement until the "Year Commencing," as identified in Part 1 above. For the exclusivity privilege of the patent license grant under Part 5 above, a Minimum Annual Royalty shall be due beginning with such royalty year and for each royalty year ending on the anniversary of such royalty year thereafter. Such Minimum Annual Royalty shall be equal to the Patent Royalty which would have been due if the "Minimum Number of Units [of Licensed Product] to Be Sold to Compute Minimum Annual Royalty" identified in Part 1 above were sold during such royalty year. If less than such number of units of Licensed Product are sold in any royalty year, then the Patent Royalty payable for the fourth quarter of such year shall be increased so as to cause the Patent Royalties paid for such year to equal said Minimum Annual Royalty. If an option is granted under Parts 1 and 4, then no Minimum Annual Royalties shall be due in any case until and if LICENSEE exercises its option.

D. **If Minimum Not Paid:** If this part is applicable and if sales of Licensed Product in any royalty year do not equal or exceed the minimum number of units identified in Part 1 above, LICENSEE may choose not to pay the Minimum Annual Royalty under subpart C above. In this case, LICENSEE shall so notify LICENSOR by the date on which the last royalty for such year is due, i.e., within one month after any anniversary of the date identified in Part 1 above. Thereupon the license grant under Part 4 above shall be converted to a nonexclusive grant, and LICENSOR may immediately license others under the above patent.

E. **Most Favored Licensee:** If this license is nonexclusive, or if it becomes nonexclusive under subpart D above, then (a) LICENSOR shall not grant any other license under the above patent to any other party under any terms which are more favorable than those which LICENSEE pays or enjoys under this Agreement, and (b) LICENSOR shall promptly advise LICENSEE of any such other grant and the terms thereof.

F. **When No Royalties Due:** No Patent Royalties shall be due under this Agreement after the above patent expires or if it is declared invalid by a court of competent jurisdiction from which no appeal can be taken. Also, if LICENSOR'S patent application becomes finally abandoned without any patent issuing, then the Patent Royalty under this Agreement shall be terminated as of the date of abandonment. Any Know-How Royalties under Part 6 above shall continue after any Patent Royalties terminate, provided such Know-How Royalties are otherwise due under such Part 6.

G. **Late Payments:** If any payment due under this Agreement is not timely paid, then the unpaid balance shall bear interest until paid at an annual rate of 10% until the delinquent balance is paid. Such interest shall be compounded monthly.

H. **Net Factory Sales Price:** "Net Factory Sales Price" is defined as the gross factory selling price of Licensed Product, or the U.S. importer's gross selling price if Licensed Product is made abroad, less usual trade discounts actually allowed, but not including advertising allowances or fees or commissions paid to employees or agents of LICENSEE. The Net Factory Sales Price shall not include (1) packing costs, if itemized separately, (2) import and export taxes, excise and other sales taxes, and customs duties, and (3) costs of insurance and transportation, if separately billed, from the place of manufacture if in the U.S., or from the place of importation if manufactured abroad, to the customer's premises or next point of distribution or sale. Bona fide returns may be deducted from units shipped in computing the royalty payable after such returns are made.

8. **Records:** LICENSEE and any of its sublicensees shall keep full, clear, and accurate records with respect to sales subject to royalty under this Agreement. The records shall be made in a manner such that the royalty reports made pursuant to Part 7B can be verified. LICENSOR, or its authorized agent, shall have the right to examine and audit such records upon reasonable notice during normal business hours, but not more than twice per year. In case of any dispute as to the sufficiency or accuracy of such records, LICENSOR may have any independent auditor examine and certify such records. LICENSEE shall make prompt adjustment to compensate for any errors or omissions disclosed by any such examination and certification of LICENSEE'S records. If LICENSOR does not examine LICENSEE'S records or question any royalty report within two years from the date thereof, then such report shall be considered final and LICENSOR shall have no further right to contest such report.

9. **Sublicensees:** If LICENSEE grants any sublicenses hereunder, it shall notify LICENSOR within one month from any such grant and shall provide LICENSOR with a true copy of any sublicense agreement. Any sublicensee of LICENSEE under this Agreement shall be bound by all of the terms applying to LICENSEE hereunder and LICENSEE shall be responsible for the obligations and duties of any of its sublicensees.

10. **Patent Prosecution:**

A. **Domestic:** LICENSOR shall, at LICENSOR'S own expense, prosecute its above U.S. patent application, and any continuations, divisions, continuations-in-part, substitutes, and reissues of such patent application or any patent thereon, at its own expense, until all applicable patents issue or any patent application becomes finally abandoned. LICENSOR shall also pay any maintenance fees which are due on any patent(s) which issue on said patent application. If for any reason LICENSOR intends to abandon any patent application hereunder, it shall notify LICENSEE at least two months in advance of any such abandonment so as to give LICENSEE the opportunity to take over prosecution of any such application and maintenance of any patent. If LICENSEE takes over prosecution, LICENSOR shall cooperate with LICENSEE in any manner LICENSEE requires, at LICENSEE'S expense.

B. **Foreign:** LICENSOR shall have the opportunity, but not the obligation, to file corresponding foreign patent applications to any patent application under subpart A above. If LICENSOR files any such foreign patent applications, LICENSOR may license, sell, or otherwise exploit the invention, Licensed Product, or any such foreign application in any countries foreign to the United States as it chooses, provided that LICENSOR must give LICENSEE a right of first refusal and at least one month to exercise this right before undertaking any such foreign exploitation. If LICENSOR chooses not to file any corresponding foreign applications under this part, it shall notify LICENSEE at least one month prior to the first anniversary of the above patent application so as to give LICENSEE the opportunity to file corresponding foreign patent applications if it so chooses.

C. **If Licensee Acts:** If LICENSEE takes over prosecution of any U.S. patent application under subpart A above, and LICENSEE is successful so that a patent issues, then LICENSEE shall pay LICENSOR royalties thereafter at a rate of 75% of the royalty rate and any applicable minimum under Part 7C above and LICENSEE shall be entitled to deduct prosecution and maintenance expenses from its royalty payments. If LICENSEE elects to prosecute any foreign patent applications under subpart B above, then LICENSEE shall pay LICENSOR royalties of 50% of the royalty rate under Part 7 above for any applicable foreign sales, less all foreign prosecution and maintenance expenses incurred by LICENSEE.

11. **Marking:** LICENSEE shall mark all units of Licensed Product, or its container if direct marking is not feasible, with the legend "Patent Pending" until any patent(s) issue from the above patent application. When any patent(s) issue, LICENSOR shall promptly notify LICENSEE and thereafter LICENSEE shall mark all units of Licensed Product which it sells with proper notice of patent marking under 35 U.S.C. Section 287.

12. **If Infringement Occurs:** If either party discovers that the above patent is infringed, it shall communicate the details to the other party. LICENSOR shall thereupon have the right, but not the obligation, to take whatever action it deems necessary, including the filing of lawsuits, to protect the rights of the parties to this Agreement and to terminate such infringement. LICENSEE shall cooperate with LICENSOR if LICENSOR takes any such action, but all expenses of LICENSOR shall be borne by LICENSOR. If LICENSOR recovers any damages or compensation for any action it takes hereunder, LICENSOR shall retain 100% of such damages. If LICENSOR does not wish to take any action hereunder, LICENSEE shall also have the right, but not the obligation, to take any such action, in which case LICENSOR shall cooperate with LICENSEE, but all of LICENSEE'S expenses shall be borne by LICENSEE. LICENSEE shall receive 75% of any damages or compensation it recovers for any such infringement and shall pay 25% of such damages or compensation to LICENSOR, after deducting its costs, including attorney fees.

13. **Disclaimer and Hold Harmless:**

A. **Disclaimer of Warranty:** Nothing herein shall be construed as a warranty or representation by LICENSOR as to the scope or validity of the above patent application or any patent issuing thereon.

B. **Product Liability:** LICENSEE shall hold LICENSOR harmless from any product liability actions involving Licensed Product.

14. **Term:** The term of this Agreement shall end with the expiration of the last of any patent(s) which issues on LICENSOR'S patent application, unless terminated sooner for any reason provided herein, or unless know-how is licensed, in which case the terms of Part 6 shall cover the term of this Agreement.

15. **Termination:** This Agreement may be terminated under and according to any of the following contingencies:

A. **Default:** If LICENSEE fails to make any payment on the date such payment is due under this Agreement, or if LICENSEE makes any other default under or breach of this Agreement, LICENSOR shall have the right to terminate this Agreement upon giving three months' written Notice of Intent to Terminate, specifying such failure, breach, or default to LICENSEE. If LICENSEE fails to make any payment in arrears, or otherwise fails to cure the breach or default within such three-month period, then LICENSOR may then send a written Notice of Termination to LICENSEE, whereupon this Agreement shall terminate in one month from the date of such Notice of Termination. If this Agreement is terminated hereunder, LICENSEE shall not be relieved of any of its obligations to the date of termination and LICENSOR may act to enforce LICENSEE'S obligations after any such termination.

B. **Bankruptcy, Etc.:** If LICENSEE shall go into receivership, bankruptcy, or insolvency, or make an assignment for the benefit of creditors, or go out of business, this Agreement shall be immediately terminable by LICENSOR by written notice, but without prejudice to any rights of LICENSOR hereunder.

C. **Antishelving:** If LICENSEE discontinues its sales or manufacture of Licensed Product without intent to resume, it shall so notify LICENSOR within one month of such discontinuance, whereupon LICENSOR shall have the right to terminate this Agreement upon one month's written notice, even if this Agreement has been converted to a nonexclusive grant under Part 7D above. If LICENSEE does not begin manufacture or sales of Licensed Product within one and one-half years from the date of this Agreement or the date of its option exercise if an option is granted, or, after commencing manufacture and sales of Licensed Product, discontinues its manufacture and sales of Licensed Product for one and one-half years, LICENSOR shall have the right to terminate this Agreement upon one months' written notice, unless LICENSEE can show that it in good faith intends and is actually working to resume or begin manufacture or sales, and has a reasonable basis to justify its delay. In such case LICENSEE shall advise LICENSOR in writing, before the end of such one-and-one-half-year period, of the circumstances involved and LICENSEE shall thereupon have up to an additional year to resume or begin manufacture or sales. It is the intent of the parties hereto that LICENSOR shall not be deprived of the opportunity, for an unreasonable length of time, to exclusively license its patent if LICENSEE has discontinued or has not commenced manufacture or sales of Licensed Product. In no case shall LICENSOR have the right to terminate this Agreement if and so long as LICENSEE is paying LICENSOR minimum annual royalties under Part 7C above.

16. **Notices:** All notices, payments, or statements under this Agreement shall be in writing and shall be sent by first-class certified mail, return receipt requested, postage prepaid, to the party concerned at the above address, or to any substituted address given by notice hereunder. Any such notice, payment, or statement shall be considered sent or made on the day deposited in the mails. Payments and statements may be sent by ordinary mail.

17. **Mediation and Arbitration:** If any dispute arises under this Agreement, the parties shall negotiate in good faith to settle such dispute. If the parties cannot resolve such dispute themselves, then either party may submit the dispute to mediation by a mediator approved by both parties. The parties shall both cooperate with the mediator. If the parties cannot agree to any mediator, or if either party does not wish to abide by any decision of the mediator, then they shall submit the dispute to arbitration by any mutually acceptable arbitrator. If no arbitrator is mutually acceptable, then they shall submit the matter

to arbitration under the rules of the American Arbitration Association (AAA). Under any arbitration, both parties shall cooperate with and agree to abide finally by any decision of the arbitration proceeding. If the AAA is selected, the arbitration shall take place under the auspices of the nearest branch of the AAA to the party seeking arbitration. The costs of the arbitration proceeding shall be borne according to the decision of the arbitrator, who may apportion costs equally, or in accordance with any finding of fault or lack of good faith of either party. The arbitrator's award shall be non-appealable and enforceable in any court of competent jurisdiction.

18. **Assignment:** The rights of LICENSOR under this Agreement shall be assignable or otherwise transferrable, in whole or in part, by LICENSOR and shall vest LICENSOR'S assigns or transferees with the same rights and obligations as were held by LICENSOR. This Agreement shall be assignable by LICENSEE to any entity that succeeds to the business of LICENSEE to which Licensed Products relate or to any other entity if LICENSOR'S permission is first obtained in writing.

19. **Jurisdiction and Venue:** This Agreement shall be interpreted under the laws of LICENSOR'S state, as given in Part 1 above. Any action related to this Agreement shall be brought in the county of LICENSOR'S above address; LICENSEE hereby consents to such venue.

20. **Non-Frustration:** Neither party to this Agreement shall commit any act or take any action which frustrates or hampers the rights of the other party under this Agreement. Each party shall act in good faith and engage in fair dealing when taking any action under or related to this Agreement.

21. **No Challenge:** LICENSEE has investigated the validity of LICENSOR'S patent and shall not challenge, contest, or impugn the validity of such patent.

22. **Rectification:** In case of any mistake in this Agreement, including any error, ambiguity, illegality, contradiction, or omission, this Agreement shall be interpreted as if such mistake were rectified in a manner which implements the intent of the parties as nearly as possible and effects substantial fairness, considering all pertinent circumstances.

23. **Entire Agreement:** This Agreement sets forth the entire understanding between the parties and supersedes any prior or contemporaneous oral understandings and any prior written agreements.

24. **Signatures:** The parties, having carefully read this Agreement and having consulted or have been given an opportunity to consult counsel, have indicated their agreement to all of the above terms by signing this Agreement on the respective dates below indicated. LICENSEE and LICENSOR have each received a copy of this Agreement with both LICENSEE'S and LICENSOR'S original ink signatures thereon.

Licensor: _____   Date: _____

Print Licensor's Name:_____

Licensee: _____   Date: _____

Print Licensee's Name: _____

Invention Disclosure

Sheet _____ of _____

Inventor(s): _____

Address(es): _____

Title of Invention: _____

To record Conception, describe: 1. Circumstances of conception, 2. Purposes and advantages of invention, 3. Description, 4. Sketches, 5. Operation, 6. Ramifications, 7. Possible novel features, and 8. Closest known prior art. To record Building and Testing, describe: 1. Any previous disclosure of conception, 2. Construction, 3. Ramifications, 4. Operation and Tests, and 5. Test results. Include sketches and photos, where possible. Continue on additional identical copies of this sheet if necessary; inventors and witnesses should sign all sheets

Invented by: _____ Date: _____

Invented by: _____ Date: _____

The above confidential information is witnessed and understood by:

_____ Date: _____

_____ Date: _____

Provisional Patent Application Cover Letter

In the United States Patent and Trademark Office

Mail Stop Provisional Patent Application   Mailed 200_____

Commissioner for Patents
P.O. Box 1450
Alexandria, VA 22313-1450

Sir:

Please file the enclosed Provisional Patent Application (PPA) papers listed below under 37 C.F.R. § 1.53(b)(2). Each of the undersigned understands:

A.   This PPA is not a substitute for a Regular Patent Application (RPA), cannot be converted to an RPA, cannot get into interference with an RPA of another person, cannot be amended, will not be published, cannot claim any foreign priority, and will not mature into a patent.

B.   If an RPA referring to this PPA is not filed within one year of the filing date of this PPA, this PPA will be worthless and will be destroyed.

C.   Any desired foreign Convention applications (including PCT applications) based upon this PPA must be filed within one year of the filing date of this PPA.

D.   This PPA must contain a written description of the invention, and of the manner and process of making and using it, in such full, clear, concise, and exact terms as to enable any person skilled in the art to which it pertains, or with which it is most nearly connected, to make and use the same, and shall set forth the best mode contemplated by the inventor of carrying out his invention. 35 U.S.C. § 112, ¶ 1. Otherwise this PPA will be worthless.

E.   Any RPA will be entitled to claim the benefit of this PPA only if such RPA names at least one inventor of this PPA and this PPA discloses such inventor's invention, as claimed in at least one claim of the RPA, in the matter provided in Item D above.

Tentative Applicant # 1, Name: _____   _____

Tentative Applicant # 2, Name: _____   _____

Title: _____

☐ Specification, sheets: _____   ☐ Drawing(s), sheets : _____

☐ Check for $_____   for   ☐ small entity   ☐ large entity filing fee

☐ Return Receipt Postcard Addressed to Applicant # 1.

Very respectfully,

_____   _____
Applicant # 1 Signature   Applicant # 2 Signature

_____   _____
Address (Send Correspondence Here)   Address

Express Mail Label #   (_____) ; Date of Deposit 200 _____

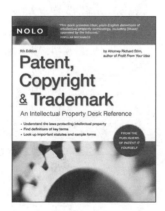

CATALOG

...more from Nolo

BUSINESS	PRICE	CODE
Business Buyout Agreements (Book w/CD)	$49.99	BSAG
The California Nonprofit Corporation Kit (Binder w/CD)	$69.99	CNP
California Workers' Comp: Take Charge When You're Injured on the Job	$34.99	WORK
The Complete Guide to Buying a Business (Book w/CD)	$24.99	BUYBU
The Complete Guide to Selling a Business (Book w/CD)	$34.99	SELBU
Consultant & Independent Contractor Agreements (Book w/CD)	$29.99	CICA
The Corporate Records Handbook (Book w/CD)	$69.99	CORMI
Create Your Own Employee Handbook (Book w/CD)	$49.99	EMHA
Dealing With Problem Employees	$44.99	PROBM
Deduct It! Lower Your Small Business Taxes	$34.99	DEDU
Effective Fundraising for Nonprofits	$24.99	EFFN
The Employer's Legal Handbook	$39.99	EMPL
The Essential Guide to Family & Medical Leave (Book w/CD)	$39.99	FMLA
The Essential Guide to Federal Employment Laws	$39.99	FEMP
The Essential Guide to Workplace Investigations (Book w/CD)	$39.99	NVST
Every Nonprofit's Guide to Publishing (Book w/CD)	$29.99	EPNO
Form a Partnership (Book w/CD)	$39.99	PART
Form Your Own Limited Liability Company (Book w/CD)	$44.99	LIAB
Home Business Tax Deductions: Keep What You Earn	$34.99	DEHB
How to Form a Nonprofit Corporation (Book w/CD)—National Edition	$49.99	NNP
How to Form a Nonprofit Corporation in California (Book w/CD)	$49.99	NON
How to Form Your Own California Corporation (Binder w/CD)	$59.99	CACI
How to Form Your Own California Corporation (Book w/CD)	$39.99	CCOR
How to Run a Thriving Business	$19.99	THRV
How to Write a Business Plan (Book w/CD)	$34.99	SBS
Incorporate Your Business (Book w/CD)	$49.99	NIBS
Investors in Your Backyard (Book w/CD)	$24.99	FINBUS
The Job Description Handbook (Book w/CD)	$29.99	JOB
Legal Guide for Starting & Running a Small Business	$34.99	RUNS
Legal Forms for Starting & Running a Small Business (Book w/CD)	$29.99	RUNSF
LLC or Corporation?	$24.99	CHENT
The Manager's Legal Handbook	$39.99	ELBA
Marketing Without Advertising	$20.00	MWAD

Prices subject to change.

BUSINESS (CONTINUED)

	PRICE	CODE
Music Law: How to Run Your Band's Business (Book w/CD)	$39.99	ML
Negotiate the Best Lease for Your Business	$24.99	LESP
Nolo's Quick LLC	$29.99	LLCQ
The Performance Appraisal Handbook (Book w/CD)	$29.99	PERF
The Progressive Discipline Handbook (Book w/CD)	$34.99	SDHB
Small Business in Paradise: Working for Yourself in a Place You Love	$19.99	SPAR
The Small Business Start-up Kit (Book w/CD)—National Edition	$29.99	SMBU
The Small Business Start-up Kit for California (Book w/CD)	$29.99	OPEN
Starting & Building a Nonprofit: A Practical Guide (Book w/CD)	$29.99	SNON
Starting & Running a Successful Newsletter or Magazine	$29.99	MAG
Tax Deductions for Professionals	$34.99	DEPO
Tax Savvy for Small Business	$36.99	SAVVY
The Work from Home Handbook	$19.99	US-HOM
Wow! I'm in Business	$19.99	WHOO
Working for Yourself: Law & Taxes for Independent Contractors, Freelancers & Consultants	$39.99	WAGE
Working With Independent Contractors (Book w/CD)	$29.99	HICI
Your Limited Liability Company: An Operating Manual (Book w/CD)	$49.99	LOP
Your Rights in the Workplace	$29.99	YRW

CONSUMER

How to Win Your Personal Injury Claim	$29.99	PICL
Nolo's Encyclopedia of Everyday Law	$29.99	EVL
Nolo's Guide to California Law	$24.99	CLAW
Your Little Legal Companion (Hardcover)	$9.95	ANNI

ESTATE PLANNING & PROBATE

8 Ways to Avoid Probate	$19.99	PRAV
The Busy Family's Guide to Estate Planning (Book w/CD)	$24.99	FAM
Estate Planning Basics	$21.99	ESPN
The Executor's Guide: Settling a Loved One's Estate or Trust	$39.99	EXEC
Get It Together: Organize Your Records So Your Family Won't Have To (Book w/CD)	$21.99	GET
How to Probate an Estate in California	$49.99	PAE
Make Your Own Living Trust (Book w/CD)	$39.99	LITR
Nolo's Simple Will Book (Book w/CD)	$36.99	SWIL
Plan Your Estate	$44.99	NEST
Quick & Legal Will Book (Book w/CD)	$19.99	QUIC
Special Needs Trusts: Protect Your Child's Financial Future (Book w/CD)	$34.99	SPNT

FAMILY MATTERS

	PRICE	CODE
Always Dad: Being a Great Father During & After a Divorce	$16.99	DIFA
Building a Parenting Agreement That Works	$24.99	CUST
The Complete IEP Guide	$34.99	IEP
Divorce & Money: How to Make the Best Financial Decisions During Divorce	$34.99	DIMO
Divorce Without Court: A Guide to Mediation & Collaborative Divorce	$29.99	DWCT
Do Your Own California Adoption: Nolo's Guide for Stepparents & Domestic Partners (Book w/CD)	$34.99	ADOP
Every Dog's Legal Guide: A Must-Have for Your Owner	$19.99	DOG
The Guardianship Book for California	$34.99	GB
A Judge's Guide to Divorce (Book w/CD)	$24.99	JDIV
A Legal Guide for Lesbian and Gay Couples (Book w/CD)	$34.99	LG
Living Together: A Legal Guide for Unmarried Couples (Book w/CD)	$34.99	LTK
Nolo's Essential Guide to Divorce	$24.99	NODV
Nolo's IEP Guide: Learning Disabilities	$29.99	IELD
Parent Savvy	$19.99	PRNT
Prenuptial Agreements: How to Write a Fair & Lasting Contract (Book w/CD)	$34.99	PNUP

GOING TO COURT

	PRICE	CODE
Becoming a Mediator	$29.99	BECM
Beat Your Ticket: Go To Court & Win!—National Edition	$21.99	BEYT
The Criminal Law Handbook: Know Your Rights, Survive the System	$39.99	KYR
Everybody's Guide to Small Claims Court—National Edition	$29.99	NSCC
Everybody's Guide to Small Claims Court in California	$29.99	CSCC
Fight Your Ticket & Win in California	$29.99	FYT
How to Change Your Name in California	$34.99	NAME
Legal Research: How to Find & Understand the Law	$39.99	LRES
Nolo's Deposition Handbook	$34.99	DEP
Represent Yourself in Court: How to Prepare & Try a Winning Case	$39.99	RYC
Win Your Lawsuit: A Judge's Guide to Representing Yourself in California Superior Court	$39.99	SLWY

HOMEOWNERS, LANDLORDS & TENANTS

	PRICE	CODE
Buying a Second Home (Book w/CD)	$24.99	SCND
The California Landlord's Law Book: Evictions (Book w/CD)	$44.99	LBEV
The California Landlord's Law Book: Rights & Responsibilities (Book w/CD)	$44.99	LBRT
California Tenants' Rights	$29.99	CTEN
Deeds for California Real Estate	$27.99	DEED
Every Landlord's Guide to Finding Great Tenants (Book w/CD)	$19.99	FIND

HOMEOWNERS, LANDLORDS & TENANTS (CONTINUED)

	PRICE	CODE
Every Landlord's Legal Guide (Book w/CD)—National Edition	$44.99	ELLI
Every Landlord's Property Protection Guide (Book w/CD)	$29.99	RISK
Every Landlord's Tax Deduction Guide	$34.99	DELL
Every Tenant's Legal Guide—National Edition	$29.99	EVTEN
For Sale by Owner in California (Book w/CD)	$29.99	FSBO
How to Buy a House in California	$34.99	BHCA
Leases & Rental Agreements (Book w/CD)	$29.99	LEAR
Neighbor Law: Fences, Trees, Boundaries & Noise	$29.99	NEI
Nolo's Essential Guide to Buying Your First Home (Book w/CD)	$24.99	HTBH
Renters' Rights: The Basics	$24.99	RENT

IMMIGRATION

	PRICE	CODE
Becoming A U.S. Citizen: A Guide to the Law, Exam & Interview	$24.99	USCIT
Fiancé & Marriage Visas	$34.99	IMAR
How to Get a Green Card	$29.99	GRN
U.S. Immigration Made Easy	$39.99	IMEZ

MONEY MATTERS

	PRICE	CODE
101 Law Forms for Personal Use (Book w/CD)	$29.99	SPOT
The Busy Family's Guide to Money	$19.99	US-MONY
Chapter 13 Bankruptcy: Repay Your Debts	$39.99	CHB
Credit Repair (Book w/CD)	$24.99	CREP
How to File for Chapter 7 Bankruptcy	$29.99	HFB
IRAs, 401(k)s & Other Retirement Plans: Taking Your Money Out	$34.99	RET
Lower Taxes in 7 Easy Steps	$16.99	LTAX
The New Bankruptcy: Will It Work for You?	$21.99	FIBA
Nolo's Guide to Social Security Disability (Book w/CD)	$29.99	QSS
Solve Your Money Troubles	$19.99	MT
Stand Up to the IRS	$29.99	SIRS
Surviving an IRS Tax Audit	$24.95	SAUD

PATENTS AND COPYRIGHTS

	PRICE	CODE
All I Need is Money: How to Finance Your Invention	$19.99	FINA
The Copyright Handbook: What Every Writer Needs to Know (Book w/CD)	$39.99	COHA
Getting Permission: How to License and Clear Copyrighted Materials (Book w/CD)	$34.99	RIPER
How to Make Patent Drawings	$29.99	DRAW
The Inventor's Notebook	$24.99	INOT

PATENTS AND COPYRIGHTS (CONTINUED)

	PRICE	CODE
Legal Guide to Web & Software Development (Book w/CD)	$44.99	SFT
Nolo's Patents for Beginners	$24.99	QPAT
Patent, Copyright & Trademark: An Intellectual Property Desk Reference	$39.99	PCTM
Patent It Yourself	$49.99	PAT
Patent Pending in 24 Hours	$34.99	PEND
Patent Savvy for Managers: Spot & Protect Valuable Innovations in Your Company	$29.99	PATM
Patenting Art & Entertainment: New Strategies for Protecting Creative Ideas	$39.99	PATAE
Profit from Your Idea (Book w/CD)	$34.99	LICE
The Public Domain	$34.99	PUBL
Trademark: Legal Care for Your Business and Product Name	$39.99	TRD
What Every Inventor Needs to Know About Business & Taxes (Book w/CD)	$21.99	ILAX

RETIREMENT & SENIORS

Get a Life: You Don't Need a Million to Retire Well	$24.99	LIFE
Long-Term Care: How to Plan & Pay for It	$19.99	ELD
Retire Happy	$19.99	US-RICH
Social Security, Medicare & Goverment Pensions	$29.99	SOA
Work Less, Live More: The Way to Semi-Retirement	$17.99	RECL
The Work Less, Live More Workbook (Book w/CD)	$19.99	RECW

SOFTWARE

Call or check our website at www.nolo.com for special discounts on Software!

Leasewriter Plus 2.0—Windows	$49.99	LWD2
LLC Maker—Windows	$69.99	LLP1
Patent Pending Now!—Windows	$89.99	PP1
PatentEase 6.0—Windows	$259.00	PEAS
Personal RecordKeeper 5.0—Windows	$39.99	RKD5
Quicken Legal Business Pro 2008—Windows	$79.99	SBQB8
Quicken WillMaker Plus 2008—Windows	$49.99	WQP8

Special Upgrade Offer

Save 35% on the latest edition of your Nolo book

Because laws and legal procedures change often, we update our books regularly. To help keep you up-to-date, we are extending this special upgrade offer. Cut out and mail the title portion of the cover of your old Nolo book and we'll give you 35% off the retail price of the New Edition of that book when you purchase directly from Nolo. This offer is to individuals only.

Order Form

Name	
Address	
City	
State, Zip	
Daytime Phone	
E-mail	

Our "No-Hassle" Guarantee

Return anything you buy directly from Nolo for any reason and we'll cheerfully refund your purchase price. No ifs, ands or buts.

☐ Check here if you do not wish to receive mailings from other companies

Item Code	Quantity	Item	Unit Price	Total Price

Method of payment

☐ Check ☐ VISA
☐ American Express
☐ MasterCard
☐ Discover Card

Subtotal	
Add your local sales tax (California only)	
Shipping: RUSH $12, Basic $6 (See below)	
"I bought 2, ship it to me FREE!" (Ground shipping only)	
TOTAL	

Account Number

Expiration Date

Signature

Shipping and Handling

Rush Delivery—Only $12

We'll ship any order to any street address in the U.S. by UPS 2nd Day Air* for only $12!

* Order by 9:30 AM Pacific Time and get your order in 2 business days. Orders placed after 9:30 AM Pacific Time will arrive in 3 business days. P.O. boxes and S.F. Bay Area use basic shipping. Alaska and Hawaii use 2nd Day Air or Priority Mail.

Basic Shipping—$6

Use for P.O. Boxes, Northern California and Ground Service.

Allow 1-2 weeks for delivery.

U.S. addresses only.

For faster service, use your credit card and our toll-free numbers

Call our customer service group Monday thru Friday 7am to 7pm PST

 Phone
1-800-728-3555

 Fax
1-800-645-0895

 Mail
Nolo
950 Parker St.
Berkeley, CA 94710

Order 24 hours a day @ www.nolo.com

Get the Latest in the Law

(1) Nolo's Legal Updater
We'll send you an email whenever a new edition of your book is published!
Sign up at **www.nolo.com/legalupdater**.

(2) Updates at Nolo.com
Check **www.nolo.com/update** to find recent changes in the law that
affect the current edition of your book.

(3) Nolo Customer Service
To make sure that this edition of the book is the most recent one, call us at
800-728-3555 and ask one of our friendly customer service representatives
(7:00 am to 6:00 pm PST, weekdays only). Or find out at **www.nolo.com**.

(4) Complete the Registration & Comment Card ...
... and we'll do the work for you! Just indicate your preferences below:

Registration & Comment Card

NAME _____ DATE _____

ADDRESS _____

CITY _____ STATE _____ ZIP _____

PHONE _____ EMAIL _____

COMMENTS _____

WAS THIS BOOK EASY TO USE?   (VERY EASY)   5   4   3   2   1   (VERY DIFFICULT)

☐ Yes, you can quote me in future Nolo promotional materials. *Please include phone number above.*

☐ Yes, send me **Nolo's Legal Updater** via email when a new edition of this book is available.

Yes, I want to sign up for the following email newsletters:

　　☐ **NoloBriefs** (monthly)
　　☐ **Nolo's Special Offer** (monthly)
　　☐ **Nolo's BizBriefs** (monthly)
　　☐ **Every Landlord's Quarterly** (four times a year)

☐ Yes, you can give my contact info to carefully selected
partners whose products may be of interest to me.

INOT5

Send to:　**Nolo** 950 Parker Street, Berkeley, CA 94710-9867, Fax: (800) 645-0895,
　　　　　or include all of the above information in an email to regcard@nolo.com
　　　　　with the subject line "INOT5."